D1234073

The United States Coast Guard

1790 To The Present

The

United States
Coast Guard
1790 to the Present

A History

REVISED EDITION

Thomas P. Ostrom

Red Anvil Press

RED ANVIL PRESS

1393 Old Homestead Drive, Second Floor
Oakland, Oregon 97462-9506.
E-MAIL: editor@elderberrypress.com
TEL/FAX: 541.459.6043
www.elderberrypress.com
Red Anvil books are available from your favorite bookstore, amazon.com, or from our 24 hour order line: 1.800.431.1579

Library of Congress Control Number: 2004109624
Publisher's Catalog-in-Publication Data
The United States Coast Guard: 1790 to the Present/Thomas P. Ostrom
ISBN 10: 1932762655
ISBN 13: 978-1-932762-65-5

1. United States Coast Guard.
2. USCG.
3. Military History.
4. U.S. History.
5. Coast Guard.
I. Title

This book was written, printed and bound in the United States of America.

CONTENTS

APPENDICES

A. USCG CHRONOLOGY

B. NAUTICAL TERMINOLOGY

C. USCG WAR CASUALTIES

D. USCG ACTIVE DUTY PERSONNEL

E. USCG COMMANDANTS

F. USCG DOCUMENTS

BIBLIOGRAPHY, REFERENCES, AND
SUGGESTED READINGS

DEDICATION

To the men and women of the USCG
who have served with honor and courage.

Thomas P. Ostrom, Rochester, Mn.

ACKNOWLEDGEMENTS

The author would like to extend his appreciation to the sources listed at the end of this book; to the USCG civilian and military personnel who contributed their time, materials, and expertise, and Coast Guard Historian Scott T. Price.

We appreciated the professionalism, guidance and support of David St. John and his staff at Elderberry Press, Fred Herzberg (Captain, USCG, Ret.), founder and director of the Foundation for Coast Guard History, and Captain Gene Davis, USCG, curator of the Coast Guard Museum, NW.

I am especially grateful to my wife Mary Lamal Ostrom who shares my Wisconsin origins and whose encouragement and support made this book possible.

INTRODUCTION

In 1961, I accompanied two Wisconsin friends from Superior to the office of the United States Coast Guard recruiter in Duluth, Minnesota. The Duluth-Superior Harbor serves commercial shipping on the western terminus of Lake Superior. The Great Lake's expanse, frightening storms, and extremes of humid continental climate challenge the U.S. Coast Guard personnel so appropriately stationed there.

Port security, aids to navigation, search and rescue, law enforcement, marine inspection and ice breaking duties are among the responsibilities of this element of the U.S. armed forces. The Coast Guard meets those challenges daily in U.S. waters and overseas.

My friends, William Frels and Harvey Hoven, and I had just graduated from college and were about to embark on exciting ventures in the USCG Reserve. We entered basic and advanced training at USCG Base, Alameda, California. After rigorous training and some ocean going experience, we returned home to continue USCG monthly meetings, summer training and education, and our civilian careers.

I subsequently taught secondary and college courses in history, geography and anthropology. Bill and Harvey went on to successful careers in banking, finance and investment. Our USCGR obligations ended in 1969, but our interest in the USCG prevailed. I continued to monitor the history and contemporary activities of the proud service.

It is from that experience that the idea for this history of the United States Coast Guard germinated. The research completed and knowledge gained made me all the more appreciative of the Coast Guard motto, "Semper Paratus." Indeed, the Coast Guard, throughout its complex history from the time of the Revenue Marine Service to the present, has confirmed its gallant motto, "Always Ready."

CHAPTER I

COAST GUARD ORIGINS

The U.S. Revenue Marine and Life Saving Services (1790-1915)

The United States Coast Guard traces its origins to 1790, but the official USCG name was designated in 1915. The Coast Guard is the product of the assimilation of several government agencies over a long period of time.

When America was a British colony, the first lighthouse was built in Boston Harbor on Little Brewster Island in 1716. The lighthouse was an aid to navigation to guide ships along the rocky Atlantic coast. In August of 1789, the first Congress federalized the lighthouse that had been built by the colonists, and funded the construction and maintenance of buoys and lighthouses. These early lighthouses were sturdy stone structures with thick walls whose lights under the care of keepers guided mariners into dangerous ports. Oil wick lamp lights were amplified by large optical lenses, reflectors and prisms.

Where lighthouses could not be placed, government lightships were stationed at strategic locations in coastal waters. The first lightship was located in Chesapeake Bay in 1820 under the supervision of the Lighthouse Service. Storms sometimes blew lightships off location and other ships sometimes sunk them. On May 16, 1934, "the Olympic, sister ship of the ill fated Titanic, struck and sank the Nantucket Shoals Lightship (No. 117) in fog and drove the vessel to the bottom with the loss of seven (of eleven) crewmen." Hundreds of these floating lighthouses guided mariners until the 1980's when the vessels were superseded by sophisticated electronic buoys

("A Historical Overview: Aids to Navigation; Lightships...," CGHO, January 1999).

Upon winning independence from the United Kingdom in the Revolutionary War (1775-1783), the former British subjects governed themselves by a states rights oriented union of former colonies stretching from the southern boundary of British Canada to Spanish Florida. The first constitution of the United States was the Articles of Confederation which was designed to maximize the autonomy of each state.

The Articles by definition failed to forge national unity. To remedy the situation, the Constitutional Convention, with representation from each of the states, met in Philadelphia in 1787 and created the federal Constitution which was ratified by the states in 1788 and went into effect in 1789.

Revolutionary War general and first U.S. president, George Washington, was determined to put the fledgling nation on a strong political and financial footing. On August 4, 1790, President Washington signed an Act of Congress "to regulate the collection of duties imposed by law on the tonnage of ships or vessels, and on goods, wares and merchandise, imported into the United States."

Ten boats "for securing the collection of revenue" were built, and officers and men were hired in this first U.S. navy to operate the vessels in coastal waters and on the high seas. During the Revolutionary War, the Continental Congress authorized a navy to battle the British fleet, but it was disbanded at the end of the war.

The first navy of the United States consisted of the ten "revenue cutters" built to enforce customs laws, save lives at sea, and apprehend smugglers and pirates. The origins of the U.S. Coast Guard began with the Revenue Cutter or Revenue Marine Service formally inaugurated by act of law in 1790.

Secretary of the Treasury Alexander Hamilton recommended the creation of the Revenue Service, and sent a detailed "Letter Of Instructions To The Commanding Officers of the Revenue Cutters" explaining their duties, powers of enforcement, and the professional traits ("prudence, moderation, and good temper") they should exhibit. Hamilton manifested those leadership qualities as a brave Revolutionary War officer and in his service as President Washington's treasury secretary, during which time he laid the financial and commercial foundations of the new Republic. Hamilton enunciated many of the political philosophies that define the basic principles of the federal republic.

Hamilton required "that a regular journal be kept in each cutter" describing "all occurrences relative to the execution of the laws" and that "the coasts, inlets, bays and rivers of the United States" be studied and described in such ways "as may be useful in the interests of navigation" ("Hamilton's Letter..," Office of Coast Guard Historian).

The Revenue Cutter (or Revenue Marine) Service of 1790 set the stage for the dual role of the future United States Coast Guard: military service with the added responsibility of serving the civil function of law enforcement and the protection of life and property.

For the first years of the U.S. Republic, the Revenue Service "was the only Navy we had...this little collection of cutters, with their swivel guns, muskets, pistols and cutlasses" (Halberstadt, p. 4).

President John Adams was determined to strengthen the military forces of the United States. The U.S. Navy had been disbanded at the end of the Revolutionary War, so when North African Algerians waged war on U.S. merchant vessels (1794), only Treasury Department revenue cutters were available for defense. Congress authorized the arming of larger ships, a plan not fully completed when the conflict ended (1796). Congress authorized a new Department of the Navy (1798), and the U.S. built more than 30 ships by 1799, in time to do battle with France on the high seas in the Undeclared Naval War of 1798-1800 (Tindall , pp. 330-31).

During the war (1799) Congress set the precedent followed ever since and authorized the placement of the Revenue Cutter Service (Revenue Marine) under the U.S. Navy in time of war. The cutters captured several French vessels in the conflict.

The Revenue Marine and the future Coast Guard fought gallantly in several conflicts and wars on the high seas, covered in subsequent chapters. In 1832, South Carolina nullified federal tariff laws, and refused to collect duties on imported goods. President Andrew Jackson ordered five cutters to Charleston Harbor "to take possession of any vessels arriving from a foreign port, and defend against any attempts to dispossess the Customs Office of her custody." The former general defiantly added, "if a single drop of blood shall be shed there in opposition to the laws of the United States I will hang the first man I can lay my hands on, upon the first tree I can reach."

Piracy plagued merchant ships well into the 1800's. Revenue Service cutters Louisiana and Alabama captured a pirate ship operating out of the New Orleans (1819) and demolished the headquarters of the sea faring bandits. Not confined to the tropical waters of maritime North America, the cutter Louisiana joined vessels of the U.S. Navy and Royal Navy of Britain and "swept the Caribbean, capturing five pirate vessels (and) intercepting contraband... the Coast Guard's most controversial commerce protection responsibility."

In the pre-Civil War period (1794-1860), revenue cutters were ordered to prevent the importation of African slaves into U.S. ports. Cutters captured slave ships and released hundreds of slaves (U.S. Coast Guard: A Historical Overview; Law Enforcement, CGHO, January 1999).

Cutters were responsible for the enforcement of President Jefferson's unpopular Embargo Act (1807) which was intended to stop the British seizure of U.S. commercial vessels during the Napoleonic Wars. The law prevented American overseas trade and cost Jefferson the support of manufacturing and shipping interests, unemployed workers, and export-sensitive farmers in the South and West. Jefferson suffered a damaged reputation "caused by the miseries of the embargo and the often cruel and disreputable attempts to enforce it." A defeated Jefferson signed a repeal of the Embargo Act in 1809 (Paul Johnson, pp. 255-57).

The diverse duties assigned to the Revenue Service are illustrated by an 1833 law which required the mariner police to enforce what are now called environmental regulations, and protect forests on public lands from illegal logging operations. This duty stemmed from an 1822 act of Congress which created a timber reserve for the U.S. Navy to be protected by cutters designed for shallow water service.

With the acquisition of Alaska from Russia (1867), the Service assumed the duty of protecting fur seals from being hunted to extinction. Revenue Service personnel camped on the Pribilof Islands. In 1885, the Revenue Service began to assist the Bureau of Fisheries in enforcement duties. In 1908, the Revenue Marine was given the power to enforce Alaskan game laws.Pollution control and clean water have long been an interest of the Coast Guard. The Revenue Cutter Service joined the Army Corps of Engineers in enforcing the Refuse Act of 1899 (USCG Historical Overview, OCGH, 1999).

In 1832, Treasury Secretary Louis McLane directed Revenue Service cutters to cruise the oceans and seas during the rigorous winter months and assist vessels in distress. The duty was legislated by Congress in 1837. The Great Lakes region was added in 1870.

Rescues of ships wrecked close to shore and the saving of life and property were important and dangerous tasks relegated to private organizations, underwriters, and state appointed "wrecking personnel." Among these organizations was the Massachusetts Humane Society (1786). By the mid-nineteenth century, eighteen life boat stations with line throwing equipment were located at strategic locations on the state coastline. In 1847, Congress appropriated money to equip "lighthouses and other exposed places where vessels are liable to be driven on shore, with boats and other suitable means of equipment." These stations were extended along the New York and New England shores, the Gulf Coast, and the Great Lakes under the supervision of Revenue Marine Corps officers.

In 1843 Captain Alexander Fraser was appointed by the Treasury Secretary to lead the new Revenue Marine Bureau. Fraser modified the administrative structure along military lines and met the challenges of the Mexican War (1846-48). In 1871, Sumner I. Kimball became the chief of the Revenue Marine Division and expanded the lifesaving service to 189 stations along the Pacific, Gulf and Atlantic coasts, and on the

Great Lakes. In 1878, Congress created the U.S. Life Saving Service and Kimball was its superintendent. The life saving stations were gradually equipped with surfboats and lifeboats and the necessary support systems and equipment.

U.S. and British warships jointly patrolled the Bering Sea in 1891. U.S. Navy gunboats were joined by Revenue cutters. Treasury Secretary William Windom appointed Captain Leonard G. Shepard to head the Revenue Marine Division in 1889.

Shepard established the Bering Sea Patrol Fleet in 1895 (Johnson, R.E., pp. 3-7, 9, 17).

The cutter Lincoln was sent to Alaskan waters in 1867 to establish coaling stations, lighthouse and custom house sites, and collect oceanographic and floral and faunal information. Subsequent cutters continued the explorations and were the base of operations for scientific expeditions.

Dangerous life saving missions were performed by cutter crews. In the late 19th century, the cutters Bear, Corwin, Jeannette and Wayanda distinguished the early Coast Guard in the icy northern waters. In the courageous tradition of the service, Public Health Surgeon Samuel J. Call, and Lieutenants Ellsworth Bertholf and David H. Jarvis were awarded Congressional gold medals for carrying out a 1500 mile rescue mission (1897-98) to the Barrow region of northern Alaska to rescue an ice-bound whaling crew, bringing with them a large reindeer herd!

Law enforcement duties in the Arctic and Subarctic regions were fraught with peril. River exploration in turbulent Alaskan waters was dangerous. Policing alcohol, ammunition, firearms and fish and game laws, and assisting the Bureau of Indian Affairs and Education Bureau were enough to keep the Service busy. The difficulties were compounded by the chaos and lawlessness that ensued during the Klondike-Yukon gold rushes (1896-99) in northwestern Canada and Alaska.

Abandoned and wrecked ships were a menace to navigation which cutters assumed responsibility for the disposition of. Derelict duty could be dangerous in rough seas and icy weather, and along rocky shorelines and surging rivers. The disabled vessels were towed into port for salvage, beached, or destroyed by explosives, gunfire and ramming, methods of which posed specific dangers to crews (Evans, chp. 9, and pp. 100-01, 111-15, 147-48).

The competency and reputation of the Revenue Service was determined by the quality of the officers and crew. Experienced seamen initially came from merchant ships, state and the Continental navies and the civilian privateer forces of the Revolutionary War. Initially, each revenue cutter was manned by officers (a master and subordinate mates), mariners (sailors) and "boys." Naval ranks (captain, lieutenant, and enlisted seamen) evolved after 1799.

Between 1799 and 1832, officer ranks were filled by political appointments and transfers from the U.S. Navy. Secretary McLane ended that practice, and directed that junior officers be promoted by competence and seniority. In 1845, legislation required that cutter officers be appointed upon demonstration of seamanship and navigation skills. During the Civil War (1863) Congress gave the president the authority to appoint the commissioned officers of the service "with the advice and consent of the Senate." Revenue Service chief Sumner Kimball, along with military and political figures, established a School of Instruction for officers to commission third lieutenants after two years of nautical instruction (Johnson, R.E., p. 14).

The origins of the present U.S. Coast Guard Academy in New London, Connecticut, began with the School of Instruction for the Revenue Marine in 1876. The cadets commenced training on the schooner Dobbin, and sailed from Fisher Island, New Bedford, Massachusetts. In 1878, the Chase replaced the Dobbin in the home port of Arundal Cove, Maryland, where shipboard training was complemented with classroom instruction in shore facilities. In 1910, the cutter Itasca trained the cadets from Fort Trumbull, a former Army post in New London, Connecticut.

The Hamilton became the service training ship in 1914, and the school name changed to the Revenue Cutter School of Instruction. The merger of the Life Saving Service and Revenue Cutter Service (1915) marks the origin of the Coast Guard and the U.S. Coast Guard Academy, which moved to its present New London site in 1932.

After World War Two, the barque Eagle, acquired as a war reparation from Germany (1947), was used to train sea-going Coast Guard cadets ("Academy History and General Information," OCGH, July, 1998).

The curriculum of the Revenue Service cadets in the first decade of the School of Instruction featured summer months cruising the Atlantic, and a pragmatic schedule of history, mathematics, geography, seamanship, navigation, French, and English (Evans, pp. 95-96, and Johnson, R.E., p. 14).

The United States Lighthouse Service has a proud tradition from its origins in 1716 to its union with the Coast Guard in 1939. Typical of the dedicated and courageous service personnel was Frank Albert Drew, Keeper of Green Island Station, from 1909 to 1929. Drew was born on the island, four miles off Marinette, Wisconsin, in Green Bay, an arm of Lake Michigan. Drew's father, Samuel, was the first keeper of Green Island Light.

Frank Drew left the island to serve as a cook on a schooner which sailed to Chicago. He worked on other boats and earned the rank of captain on a passenger and package boat at age of 25. In 1909, Drew emulated his father and joined the lighthouse service, becoming the head keeper on Green Island. Between 1912-14, Drew rescued more than 30 individuals in storms, fires and accidents on boats and ships, and the entire crew of one vessel. Drew received several lifesaving citations in his glorious career.

The United States Coast Guard Cutter Frank Drew pays proper tribute to the distinguished lighthouse keeper. The Frank Drew (WLM 557) is a 175 foot coastal buoy tender with a crew of one officer and 17 enlisted personnel. The technologically advanced aids to navigation vessel was built by Marinette Marine Corporation in Wisconsin, and commissioned on June 17, 1999. Satellite navigation and automated engineering controls enable this coastal tender to efficiently serve from its Portsmouth, Virginia port, north to Washington, D.C., and south to North Carolina, including the Potomac, York and James Rivers.

The Frank Drew crew services buoys and carries out the Coast Guard missions of maritime law enforcement, environmental protection and search and rescue ("Welcome Aboard" brochure, USCGC FRANK DREW, 1999).

The Coast Guard motto, "Semper Paratus" (Always Ready) and the slogan, "You have to go out, but you don't have to come back," aptly describe the traditions of the Revenue Marine Service and the Coast Guard. The 210 year old service is proud of its history. The early life saving "Surf Soldiers" exemplified those traditions on U.S. coasts and rivers and on the forbidding interior Great Lakes. In their day, the lifesavers were called "Soldiers of the Surf" and "Storm Warriors." Life Saving Service chief Sumner Kimball proudly called his mates "storm soldiers." The surfmen, and subsequent Coast Guard sailors and aviators, have saved thousands of lives and lost hundreds of their own in the process.

Richard K. Kolb researched the history of the costs and courage involved in the life saving duties of the Revenue Service and Coast Guard from the 19th century to the present, in war and peacetime. Memorials dedicated to Coast Guard personnel can be found throughout the nation, but Kolb believes that is not enough. "Considering the nation's mania for monument building, perhaps someday, " the journalist suggested, "the Coast Guard will receive its due in the form of an all inclusive, public memorial in the nation's capital" (Kolb, Richard K., "Surf Soldiers." VFW, August, 2000, pp. 26-30).

The last years of the Revenue Cutter and Life Saving Services were significant as the clock ticked toward the amalgamation of the two services into the United States Coast Guard in 1915. Captain Commandant Worth G. Ross requested retirement status for health reasons.

Secretary of the Treasury Franklin MacVeagh reached well down the seniority ladder and nominated Captain Ellsworth Price Bertholf to succeed Ross. It would be Bertholf, the commander of the cutter Bear and recipient of a gold medal for his part in the rescue of ice-bound Alaskan whalers, who bridged the transition from the Revenue Service to the Coast Guard from 1911-19.

Upon a delayed Senate confirmation, Bertholf immediately used his administrative talent and economic expertise to block an attempt by efficiency experts to abolish the Revenue Cutter Service and assign its functions to the U.S. Navy and the Department of Commerce and Labor, and merge the Bureau of Lighthouses into Commerce and Labor.

The Captain Commandant appeared before congressional committees and argued persuasively that the dispersal of Revenue Service functions to Commerce and Labor would require other government agencies which had coordinated services with the RS to form their own navies; that the U.S. Navy mission and training would suffer with the added responsibilities; and he presented statistics which indicated that the present system was efficient. In fact, Bertholf argued, increased costs and inefficiencies would prevail with the abolition or mergers of the Revenue and Life Saving Service with other agencies and departments.

Merchant associations, a grateful public, and supportive newspapers defended Captain Bertholf, and "the sinking of the British White Star liner Titanic with the loss of some 1500 persons focused even more attention on a service that listed saving of life and property at sea among its principal duties (but was) now threatened with dissolution (Johnson, R.E., pp. 18-21)."

To ensure the survival of his organization, Captain Commandant Bertholf prepared a memorandum for the Treasury Department which explained the necessity of the Revenue Service to assume the North Atlantic Ice Patrol to track ice bergs and warn vessels of their location to prevent the kind of collision that sank the Titanic. Bertholf explained that in 1906 Congress authorized the construction of the cutter Seneca and assigned it derelict destruction duty, so, by implication, the Revenue Cutter Service should track the floating iceberg threat. Berthholf suggested that the cutters Miami and Seneca be assigned ice patrol duty for several weeks each year because they were large enough to store the necessary provisions and withstand heavy seas.

President Woodrow Wilson's Treasury Secretary William G. McAdoo issued the orders on March 29, 1913, for the Revenue Service to commence the ice patrol. The International Conference on the Safety of Life at Sea convened in London in November of 1913, attended by 14 maritime nations. The U.S. delegation included Captain Bertholf. The final report recognized the significance of the U.S. Ice Patrol, asked that it be continued, and designated a division of expenses among the nations to support the patrol and life saving operations.

The outbreak of World War I (1914-18), called The Great War at the time, interrupted international cooperation because several of the signatories were at war with each other and ships threatened by submarine attacks chose to maintain radio silence. The Revenue Service made iceberg sightings and offered its maps and reports for publication.

Suspended during the war, the Ice Patrol was resumed in 1919. Another International Conference on the Safety of Life at Sea convened in London in 1929, where it was agreed to define the parameters of the financial contributions for the cost of the service, and the United States should continue the mission.

World War Two (1939-45) caused another interruption of the Ice Patrol, but the mission was resumed in the post-war period.

In the 125 year record of the Revenue Cutter Service, it has been estimated that at a minimum, 14 of its ships were lost at sea.

In 1913, the Treasury Department sent its proposal to merge the Revenue Service with the Life Saving Service to Congress. The Senate approved the measure in 1914, the House in 1915. President Wilson signed the bill on 28 January, 1915.

The combined service was named the Coast Guard. The name comes from the Spanish vessels known as "guarda costa" which tried to prevent illegal trade with the Crown colonies in the New World during the protectionist period of Mercantilism. The name "coast guard" was also used in 19th century Britain where coast watchers reported vessels in distress and smuggling. Members of the British "Coastguard" also served as a naval reserve force.

In the Civil War period (1865), Treasury Secretary Hugh McCulloch referred to "the duties of a coast guard" in a discourse about the Revenue Cutter Service. The enabling congressional legislation stated that the Coast Guard constituted "a part of the military forces of the United States...under the Treasury Department in time of peace (and) as part of the Navy, subject to the orders of the Secretary of the Navy, in time of war, or when the President shall so direct." Revenue Service Captain Commandant Bertholf added his description of the duties of the new military branch he now headed: "The Coast Guard occupies a peculiar position...and necessarily so from the dual character of its work, which is both civil and military. More than 120 years of practical experience has demonstrated...by means of military drills, training and discipline, that the service (is able) to maintain that state of preparedness for the prompt performance of its most important civil duties....."

Life Saving Service personnel were now in military service. District superintendents gained commissioned officer status; station keepers became warrant officers; and surfmen joined the enlisted ranks. Promotions came from within the service, based on performance and seniority. For the first time, Life Saving crews were eligible for Revenue Cutter Service retirement benefits that were enacted in 1902 and now provided to all members of the United States Coast Guard "at three quarters pay upon completion of thirty years of service" (Johnson, R.E., pp. 22-33).

The Coast Guard embarked on its many faceted mission in an era of the new "motor propelled boats" in use as pleasure and commercial vessels. Reason enough to keep life saving surfmen busy.

The United States was divided up into 13 districts under the supervision in order of authority of the Secretary of the Treasury, the Assistant Treasury Secretary, and a captain commandant who administered five divisions: operations and materiel (headed by civilians), construction repair, engineering and inspection. Each of the 13 districts was run by a district commander. Customs collectors no longer directly supervised cutters in their districts, but the Coast Guard closely cooperated with them.

A government report issued in 1915 recorded that the Coast Guard consisted of about 2,000 sailors and 2,300 lifeboat station surfmen.

The far ranging duties and dangers of Coast Guard missions are illustrated by two CG vessels, one in the North Atlantic, the other on Bering Sea Patrol and the Alaskan Gulf between 1915-17. The Ungala, commanded by Captain Francis G. Dodge, was assailed by heavy winter seas and snow and freezing fog and water vapor. In subzero temperatures, the Ungala lost her radio antennae which snapped under ice, and an estimated 150-175 tons of ice gave the cutter a starboard list of 20 degrees. A hot water hose, axes and coal shovels were wielded by crew members to even the keel and get to the security of the port of Yakutat. When in port, the cutter officers boarded and inspected fishing and other commercial vessels, and requested that they stay in port during the inclement weather. The ship surgeon treated crews and civilians in the area and shared his medical knowledge with a missionary.

The Androscoggin was a small hospital ship staffed with a Public Health Service physician-surgeon and staff which sailed from Boston to serve deep sea fishing vessels of any nationality. A flag on a schooner mast alerted the medics that attention was needed. Between 1915-16 the Androscoggin treated more than 200 fishermen and came to the aid of ships in other ways. Ice Patrol cutters usually had a surgeon on board and a sick bay with appropriate medical supplies.

In 1915, President Wilson signed the Seamen's Act into law which required that U.S. merchant and passenger ship crews be adequately trained and able to handle life boats. The Steamboat Inspection Service licensed merchant sailors but was unable to ascertain the proficiency of all of the thousands of mariners who required training and testing. The Department of Commerce asked for Coast Guard help in ports containing CG district offices. Competent Coast Guard officers and enlisted personnel, including lighthouse keepers, rose to the occasion and licensed or rejected hundreds of merchant seamen. Thus, another function was given to the Coast Guard which eventually assumed the full responsibility for the licensing process (Johnson, R.E., pp. 34-41).

Orville and Wilber Wright changed transportation, warfare and search and rescue with their mechanical skills, intuition and courage. The two bicycle mechanics and manufacturers experimented with gliders and motor powered aircraft. In 1903, they launched the first piloted, heaver than air, motor powered aircraft at Kitty Hawk, North Carolina. In 1909 the U.S. Army purchased one of their air planes. Glenn Curtis Company made a flying boat (1912), and the U.S. Navy purchased a few aircraft and started training pilots from their Pensacola, Florida base. Aircraft were used as fighter and surveillance craft in World War I (Evans, p. 188).

Coast Guard aviation began in 1915 when Lieutenants Norman B. Hall and Elmer F. Stone, stationed on board the Norfolk, Va., based Onondaga, convinced their skipper, Captain Benjamin M. Chiswell, to let them use borrowed aircraft on search missions (Johnson, R.E., p. 42).

Hall and Stone secured the assistance of a famous balloonist, Captain Baldwin, who loaned them an aircraft "in which they flew scouting missions for the Onondaga through the summer of 1915." Air and sea rescue tactics evolved from the experience.

Lieutenant Hall was sent to study aeronautical engineering at the Curtiss Airplane and Motor Company. Lieutenant Stone, with several other officers and enlisted men, was assigned to formal flight training at Pensacola.

Wintry North Atlantic gales inflicted rudder and mast destruction upon coastal sailing schooners which could not report their positions in an accurate or punctual manner without benefit of radio communication. Rescue operations by the Onondaga and sister cutters were therefore often delayed at risk to vessels and crews because of the necessarily extended search patterns. The advent of air search and rescue proved to be of inestimable value (Evans, pp. 188-89).

Coast Guard ship and air station construction were put on hold. On April 6, 1917, the United States issued a declaration of war against Germany. "PLAN ONE ACKNOWLEDGE" was the official notice to all Coast Guard units that they were now assigned to the United States Navy for a dangerous and extended mission (Johnson, R.E., p. 43)

CHAPTER II

U.S. REVENUE MARINE
(1790-1850)

The War of 1812; The Seminole Wars; and the Mexican War

The Revenue Marine Service fulfilled its naval military functions in operations with the United States Navy in several wars as mandated by law. The first military conflict was the Undeclared War With France (1798-1800), reviewed in Chapter One. Having served gallantly in that conflict, the Revenue Marine was called upon to augment the U.S. Navy in other military conflicts.

The War of 1812-14 challenged U.S. naval forces. They had to face the formidable British fleet on the high seas and inland waters in what some historians have called The Second War of Independence. The United States declared war on the United Kingdom because the British had not yet withdrawn from all U.S. territory at the end of the Revolutionary War, as required by the Treaty of Paris (1783). And British ships had used force to prevent U.S. commercial vessels from engaging in free trade during Britain's blockade of France in the Napoleonic Wars. In the course of searching U.S. merchant vessels, the British forcibly impressed some U.S. seamen into the King's Navy.

The theaters of war were along the Atlantic Coast, Great Lakes, and Lake Champlain (New York). The competence of American naval forces was quickly illustrated on September 10, 1813 on Lake Erie. United States Navy Commodore Oliver H. Perry suspended his ship building activities and engaged the British Navy. When his flagship was destroyed in the battle, Perry transferred to another ship and continued the fight. When the British surrendered, Perry sent his famous message to General William H. Harrison, his colleague in arms in the Ohio theater: "We have met the enemy, and they are ours." Securing the Lake Erie region forced the British to leave Detroit and retreat to the northeast. It also facilitated the defeat of Britain's Indian allies and the formidable Shawnee warrior, Tecumseh, and put the Northwest back in American control. U.S. forces, however, were soundly defeated in the unsuccessful invasion of British Canada (Tindall, pp. 362-67).

The U.S. Navy and Revenue Marine waged war against the British Navy as state militia and federal troops clashed with His Majesty's troops in New England, along the Atlantic Seaboard, and in Southern waters at the port of New Orleans.

The U.S. frigate Constitution (Captain Isaac Hull) defeated HMS Guerriere in Canadian waters off the coast of Nova Scotia. The U.S.S. Wasp conquered the British warship Frolic off the Virginia shore. Captain Stephen Decatur in the frigate United States brought the British vessel Macedonian into New London, Connecticut as a war prize. Despite these defeats, the British Navy achieved several victories and maintained a coastal embargo which dislocated U.S. commerce and decreased federal tariff revenues (Johnson, Thomas H., pp. 830-32).

Internal dissent threatened the war effort. The Federalist political party strongly opposed Republican President "Madison's War," as they called it. Anti-war leaders even threatened the secession of the New England states from the Union.

British troops challenged American forces after landing soldiers at Cape Cod (Massachusetts) and on the shores of Chesapeake Bay. They defeated U.S. troops at Bladensburg, Maryland. British troops swept through Washington, D.C. and burned several buildings, including the Capitol and White House, forcing President and Mrs. Madison to abandon their meal and flee to Virginia. The British Navy sailed to Baltimore and bombarded Fort McHenry, an event which stimulated Washington lawyer Francis Scott Key to write what became the U.S. national anthem, "The Star Spangled Banner" (Tindall, pp. 362-74).

Prior to the outbreak of hostilities, Congress (1809) fortuitously authorized the construction of 12 new Revenue cutters which averaged 125 tons, crews of about 20, and several light guns, a significant addition to U.S. naval forces in the War of 1812. Among the new cutters was the Eagle, built for the New Haven station to, as Treasury Secretary Gallatin described, "prevent the escape of vessels." In October 1814, Captain Frederick Lee sailed the Eagle in a mission to rescue the U.S. merchant vessel Susan from capture by the Dispatch, an 18 gun English brig. In a battle off Long Island, the outgunned Eagle was driven ashore but continued the fight from an island bluff with muskets, and guns taken from the cutter. The British ship withdrew. Captain Lee refloated the Eagle the next day, only to be surprised and captured by the enemy after waging battle.

In June 1812, Captain William Hamm on the USRC Jefferson captured a British ship and brought it into the Virginia port of Norfolk. On July 4th, the Surveyor further distinguished the Revenue Marine by capturing a British ship which had sailed from Jamaica. In 1813, the Surveyor, on Virginia's York River, was outgunned, out manned, and boarded by the crew of His Majesty's frigate Narcissus. Royal Navy Captain John Crerie was so impressed with the gallantry of his outnumbered foe in the bloody sword-wielding, musket firing, hand to hand deck battle, that he returned a captured sword to Captain Samuel Travis and stated in writing, "You have my most sincere wishes for the immediate parole and speedy exchange of yourself and brave crew."

In July 1812, the cutter Madison, under the command of Captain George Brooks, captured the 6 guns and 16 men crew of a British brig on the high seas, but was lost to the British fleet later in the year.

In 1813, Captain John Cahoone searched out a British sloop which had seized more than 20 American ships in Long Island Sound. With a crew of Navy volunteers the cutter captain maneuvered his heavily outgunned Vigilant against the privateer Dart. After a cannon duel, the crew boarded and captured the British ship.

Because of the courageous service of cutter crews, Revenue Marine casualties were awarded Navy pensions which "for almost a century remained the only provision made for the retirement of disabled cutter men" (Evans, pp. 18-22).

Revenue Service captures of British vessels not only boosted the morale of the Americans in their battle against British military forces, but deprived the enemy of vital supplies and finances. In just one instance, when the cutter Madison captured the schooner Wade, $20,000 in silver and gold was acquired by the captors. When the U.S. Revenue Cutter James C. Madison took control of the Shamrock in July 1812, it escorted a 300 ton warship carrying 16 men and 6 guns into Savannah harbor and removed that military threat from the sea.

The skill and courage of cutter crews is exemplified by the fact that they often went into battle heavily outgunned and out manned. In the clash between the USRC Eagle and H.M.S Dispatch, the cutter carried six four pound cannons against the British warship's eighteen thirty-two pound weapons (Kaplan and Hunt, pp. 5-8).

The inconclusive war drew to a mutually desirable close on December 24th, 1814, when diplomatic representatives from the United States and United Kingdom signed the Treaty of Ghent (Belgium). The "status quo antebellum" was achieved. Neither side claimed victory or conceded defeat. New lands were not acquired.

General Andrew Jackson defeated strong British forces at the battle of New Orleans (8 January, 1815), unaware the Treaty of Ghent had been signed weeks earlier. The battle did, however, influence post-war interpretations and applications, and forced the international community to recognize U.S. control of the Louisiana Purchase (1803) from France. The Battle of New Orleans proved the United States matched British military might and was a player in international diplomacy. The victory paved the way for military hero Andrew Jackson to claim the presidency in the Election of 1828 (Johnson, P., pp. 275-79).

Andrew Jackson's military exploits also sparked the Seminole Wars (1816-18; 1835-42) which can be traced to the incursion into Spanish Florida by U.S. troops in search of escaped slaves who fled into Indian territory and merged with the indigenous populations. The Seminole bravely defended their lands. A youthful General Andrew Jackson led a retaliatory expedition into Florida which stimulated Spain to cede East Florida to the United States. Military pressure forced the Seminoles across the Mississippi River. Seminole leader Osceola refused to migrate and led his followers in a long war against U.S. military forces sent into the Everglades swamps by then President Andrew Jackson. Osceola was treacherously captured at a truce conference and imprisoned in Fort Moultrie in Charleston Harbor, South Carolina, where he died (Tindall, pp. 387-89; 324-25).

The Revenue Service got involved in the Seminole wars when the customs collector at New Orleans sent the cutters Dallas and Jackson to relieve the Gulf coastal towns of of St. Marks and Tampa from Seminole warriors.

In his dispatch, Captain Webb, commanding the U.S.S. Vandalia, commended the crews of the 10 revenue cutters who participated in the Seminole Wars: "Their prompt and ready cooperation (with the U.S. Navy and U.S. Army) called forth the highest commendations. Their light draft (permitted operations which) no frigate could have accomplished in the shallows off the Florida west coast." The cutters, continued Captain Webb, "carried guns...supplies...soldiers and marines to strategic points (and) landing parties of revenue men went to the relief of beleaguered settlements" (Evans, pp. 25-26).

Cutter crews were offered homestead lands by grateful officials. Among the distinguished war vessels was the cutter Washington which landed men and guns in time to save Fort Brook, an operation chronicled by historians as "the first amphibious landing by combined forces in U.S. history" (Kaplan and Hunt, pp. 9-10). The years between 1812 and Civil War placed other duties upon the Revenue Marine which was ordered (1815) to protect merchant shipping, save lives and property, and suppress piracy and the slave trade. The cutter Active captured pirates ("privateers") in Chesapeake Bay. The Dallas performed similar operations off the Georgia coast. The Florida Keys and waters off New

Orleans were other pirate haunts. The Revenue Marine had to respond to piracy on the high seas to protect domestic and foreign trade routes.

Cutters Louisiana and Alabama were constructed in 1819 to battle the pirate fleets. The cutters were 6 feet in depth, 17 feet abeam, and had a length of 57 feet. They were assisted by other cutters which shared patrol duties in the Gulf of Mexico and off the Florida coasts. Piracy, thanks primarily to the Revenue Service, was virtually driven from U.S. waters by 1840.

In 1843, Captain Alexander Fraser was appointed by the Treasury Department to be Captain-Commandant of the Revenue Marine Bureau. Fraser was an early advocate of the iron and steam powered vessels which eventually eclipsed the graceful, wooden sailing cutters. Initial engineering and mechanical problems in the steam fleet caused conflicts between Fraser and his supervisors which for a time damaged his career. Captain Fraser's experience on both merchant vessels and Revenue cutters in peace and war gave him the credibility necessary to impose the military structure and administrative reforms which served so well in the Mexican War of 1846-48 and subsequent service missions (Kaplan and Hunt, pp. 13-18).

The mid-nineteenth century exuded the spirit of "Manifest Destiny" which motivated and compelled the United States to expand from the Atlantic to the Pacific, and south to the Gulf of Mexico, an expansion rationalized as a right and necessity, abetted by diplomatic, financial and military means. The objective was the geopolitical and strategic control of as much of North America as possible. The rationale was based on imperialistic high mindedness; a quest for national stability; and an alleged humanitarian obligation to Christianize and civilize the societies, peoples and nations which blocked U.S. expansion. The term "American expansion" is often used, but says little, because all of the cultures, Hispanic, Black, and Indian, as well as other immigrant nationalities, were "American" by virtue of the fact that the Western Hemisphere consists of North and South "America." All of it is therefore "American." Mexico was the site of ancient Indian cultures that ranged in socioeconomic complexity from simple hunting and gathering cultures to the centralized empires of the Aztecs and Mayas which produced complex architecture, calendars, and related mathematical and astronomical knowledge. The Spanish conquests of the 16th, 17th and 18th centuries came to an end in a series of rebellions which led to the independence of Mexico from colonial control in 1823. Spanish-Mexican territory extended into what is now the U.S. Southwest and California.

Mexico's northern frontier was sparsely populated and invited the migration of European Americans from the United States, indigenous Indian populations, and Spanish-speaking settlers. In 1835, Texans rebelled and declared independence from Mexico. The Mexican army invaded Texas and achieved an initial battle success at the mission-fortress of the Alamo. Subsequent military defeats forced the Mexicans to reluctantly acknowledge the sovereignty of the Republic of Texas (1836).

After failing to convince the Mexican government to sell its northern provinces, and, at the request of the Texas government, the United States annexed Texas in 1845. President James Polk sent soldiers to the Mexican/Rio Grande border in 1846. Having officially acknowledged neither the independence or annexation of Texas, Mexico declared war on the United States and sent troops into the disputed territory north of the Rio Grande. President Polk claimed that "American blood had been shed on American soil." On May 13, 1846, Congress declared war on Mexico.

Several prominent U.S. political and literary figures denounced the war against Mexico, including the new Congressman from Illinois, Abraham Lincoln. A young officer who fought in Mexico declared the war "unjust." That officer was the future Union commander, General Ulysses S. Grant, who served in Mexico with fellow officers he would later fight in the Civil War: then Captain Robert E. Lee and Colonel Jefferson Davis (Johnson, P., pp. 373-80).

The U.S. Navy and Revenue Marine, by law part of the Navy in war time, contributed to the conquest of Mexico by enforcing naval blockades and supplying, transporting and supporting Army and Marine Corps troops.

The naval theater of operations reached from New Orleans to the eastern Gulf coast of Mexico, the Campeche Gulf and along the western shore of the Yucatan Peninsula. On the Pacific coast, the naval blockade extended from the latitude of Mexico City, and northwest along the Baja California Peninsula to San Francisco. The northern Gulf region was patrolled by navy and cutter vessels which protected commercial vessels from pirates. Captain Farnifold Green of the U.S. Revenue Marine commanded the cutter Woodbury with distinction in that area in the 1830's.

In 1845-46, Captain Winslow Foster, USRM, commanded the Woodbury on patrols from the mouth of the Mississippi and along the Texas coast, laden with dispatches, doing reconnaissance for U.S. Army Commanding General Zachary Taylor, and convoying troop and supply vessels. For his exemplary service, Captain Foster received commendations from General Taylor and W.W. Bliss, Assistant Adjutant General, U.S. Army.

Captain John A. Webster, USRM, commanded a cutter squadron with orders to conduct revenue and war operations from the Rio Grande to the Mississippi, and cooperate with the Army and Navy. Webster understood the U.S. Navy, having served in the USN until he enlisted in the Revenue Marine (1819) as a captain. Webster commanded sail and steam cutters. Two of the steamers had machinery problems and had to return to home port. The three remaining steamers were more heavily armed than the lighter sailing cutters, but the latter had shallower draft which allowed for more effective operations inshore and across river sand bars.

The cutter steamers in the mission, Bibb and McLane, each carried four 22 pounders and one or two 18 pound pivot weapons. The steam cutter Legare had an 18 pounder and lighter weapons. The sailing schooner cutters Woodbury, Wolcott, Van Buren, Forward, Morris and Ewing carried from four to six 6, 9, and 12 pounders. The McLane was commanded by Captain W.A. Howard. The Forward was under Captain H.B. Nones.

Overseeing the Navy and Revenue Marine mission was Commodore M.C. Perry, USN, from his flag ship, U.S.S. Mississippi. On the Tobasco River of Mexico, a U.S. Navy vessel ran aground and suffered withering shore fire which wounded and killed several crewmen. The cutter Forward closed in and protected the naval vessel with cannon and small arms fire until the ship was able to free itself and sail on with the convoy. Commodore Perry then ordered the cutters McLane and Forward to river and blockade duty.

Captain Webster's cutter convoy carried mail, supplies, rifles, and troops; and performed scouting, convoy, blockade, towing, revenue and law enforcement duties.

In a subsequent dispatch to his superiors, Commodore Perry reported he was "gratified to bear witness to the valuable services of the Revenue Schooner Forward, in command of Captain Nones, and to the skill and gallantry of her officers and men" (Evans, pp. 60-63).

The Mexican War ended with the Treaty of Guadalupe Hidalgo (1848), signed in a village outside of Mexico City under the watchful eye of the victorious U.S. Army. Mexico gave up claim to Texas and ceded New Mexico and California to the United States in return for $15 million and a U.S. commitment to assume the financial claims of its citizens against the Mexican government. The cost to the United States: more than 16,000 military casualties (killed, wounded, or died of disease); naval and army expenditures of nearly $98 million in return for 1 million square miles of territory; and untold value in terms of future land use and mineral wealth (Tindall, pp. 557-59). Revenue Marine Bureau Captain Commandant Alexander Fraser's term ended in 1848. In an 1846 treaty with the United Kingdom, the United States acquired the Oregon Territory. A customs district was established in the Pacific Northwest and California, and revenue laws were enforced. The revenue cutter Lawrence was assigned to the district. Captain Fraser, at his own request, assumed command.

The Lawrence voyaged from the United States, along the South American coast, into the rough waters of Cape Horn, and north to San Francisco. Subsequent law enforcement duties during the Gold Rush era earned Captain Fraser further acclaim in the annals of maritime history (Kaplan and Hunt, 15-18).

The danger that confronted 19th century mariners is illustrated by the SS Central America, a side wheel sail and steamer enroute from Panama to New York. Its 592 passengers returning from the California gold fields with 20 tons of gold on board under the command of Captain William Herndon, a distinguished mariner and explorer. The vessel engaged an Atlantic hurricane for several days. On September 12, 1857, after a courageous battle by crew and passengers, the ship sank off Cape Hatteras, North Carolina, at the cost of 400 lives, including the gallant skipper who went down with his ship. Several hundred survivors were rescued by the lifeboat skills of crew members, and the timely arrival of two heavily damaged vessels. The United States Coast Guard provided assistance in the 1980's during the salvage operations of the Central America (Kinder, 19-75; 123-218; 230-58; 491-507).

CHAPTER III

THE REVENUE CUTTER SERVICE (1850-1915)

The Civil War and the Spanish American War

The Election of 1860 brought President Abraham Lincoln and the new Republican party to Washington, D.C. The election result caused South Carolina (December 20, 1860) to begin the secession process which formed the Confederate States of America (CSA). The Confederacy was a states rights oriented political association modeled after the Articles of Confederation which governed the United States after the Revolutionary War.

The first CSA capital (Montgomery, Alabama) was moved to Richmond, Virginia, closer to Washington, D.C. Jefferson Davis, West Point graduate and former U.S. army officer, was elected president of the CSA.

The Civil War was called The War Between the States by Southerners who equated secession with de facto sovereignty. President Lincoln's immediate post-secession objectives were to preserve the Union by persuasion, hold on to remaining federal lands, collect duties and deliver the mail.

The causes of the Civil War were decades in the making and germinated by the different geography and socioeconomic systems of the North and South. Historians call the regional differences "sectionalism." The agricultural South, for example, preferred low tariffs (taxes) on imports which theoretically caused lower prices from market place competition between foreign and domestic goods. Europe was a market for Southern plantation crops, especially the cotton which fed the British textile industry. Northern members of Congress generally favored high tariffs to protect the interests of industry. Southern congressmen believed high U.S. tariffs encouraged retaliatory tariffs in Europe and blocked Southern exports.

The South favored a states rights philosophy which opposed federal (Northern) control of the Southern way of life. The moral, political and economic issue of slavery caused conflict between the Southern states, whose plantation agriculture system was dependent on the "peculiar institution," and the Northern "Free Soil" states which were geographically unsuited for it.

Slavery was a causal factor in the Civil War, but not the only one. In a letter to an abolitionist, Lincoln wrote, "My paramount object in this struggle is to save the Union and it is not either to save or to destroy slavery. If I could save the Union without freeing any slaves, I would do it; and if I could save it by freeing all the slaves, I would do it" (Johnson, Paul, p. 469).

Most Southerners did not own slaves. General Robert E. Lee, the predominant CSA military commander, deplored slavery. The eminent Virginian, like most rebels, was fighting for the independence of his home state.

The war between the USA and CSA commenced on April 12, 1861, when naval vessels arrived to provision Fort Sumter in the harbor of Charleston, South Carolina. General P.G.T. Beauregard responded with a 30 hour bombardment, forcing Major Robert Anderson to surrender after using up his food and ammunition. No battle deaths occurred, but two Union soldiers were killed when a cannon used in the surrender ceremony exploded. President Lincoln reacted by asking all the Union states to contribute militia to supplement federal land and sea forces. On April 19 Lincoln ordered a blockade of southern ports.

In 1862, at the entrance to Chesapeake Bay, the ironclad vessel CSS Virginia, constructed from the abandoned USS Merrimack, encroached upon several Union vessels. The Union ironclad USS Monitor made contact with the Virginia on March 9. The battle was a dual victory, but the Virginia was scuttled when the Confederates lost the port of Norfolk (Virginia) to Union troops (Tindall, pp. 646-48; 658-59).

Naval forces were recent beneficiaries of technological innovations. Side-wheel and propeller (screw) steamers and sail vessels, with sail and steam sometimes combined, plied the waterways. U.S. ships were built by the Navy and Revenue Service, or acquired through purchase or donation of civilian vessels. The less industrialized South built very few ships, but acquired Union vessels when some U.S. and Revenue Service crews joined the Confederate cause and commandeered U.S. boats and ships. Both sides sank or captured enemy vessels. CSA intermediaries contracted for ships to be built in Britain and France.

The following designations indicated national origin and military service. CSS meant Confederate States Ship. Union vessels had several designations. USAT was U.S. Army Transport. USCS was a vessel from the U.S. Coast Survey. A United States Navy warship was designated USS (U.S. Ship). USLHS was a ship from the United States Light House Service, and USRC was a United States Revenue Cutter.

Ships were made of wood, or had iron armor plates placed over timber, making them "ironclads". Most blockade runners, Southern ships trying to get supplies past Union patrols, were usually privately owned and mission certified with government documentation (Silverstone, pp. ix-xiii).

The main theaters of naval operations were the Louisiana area and Mississippi River; the Texas-Gulf Coast; the Atlantic Coast from New England, New York, and Maryland, through Virginia, the Carolinas, Georgia and Florida; and the inland rivers and waterways along those coasts (Silverstone, pp. 226-33, 235-37, and 244-49).

The Confederate Navy lacked the Union's industrial capacity and security and had to improvise. Southern engineers designed ironclad rams for defense and ramming. Submarines were developed, but often sank, drowning their crews.

CSS Alabama, Shenandoah, and Florida preyed on U.S. merchant ships on the high seas and outside foreign ports, forcing USN and USRS ships to protect commercial vessels and search for CSA warships.

Union naval forces challenged Confederate control on the Red, Tennessee, Cumberland, Ohio and Mississippi rivers, and a few others. U.S. naval and ground forces fought for control of the Mississippi River region to split the Confederacy in half. The Union victory at Vicksburg, Mississippi (1863) forced the river wars to be fought on less strategic but still significant waterways.

The United States Revenue Service possessed only 28 ships in 1861. Rebel forces took control of six of the vessels. Four were patrolling the Pacific coast. Five Great Lakes ships were shifted to the Atlantic coast. Coast Survey and Light House ships were temporarily loaned to the USRS. The Revenue Marine's Harriet Lane, transferred to the U.S. Navy, fired the first naval round at Ft. Sumter.

The cutter Caleb Cushing was captured by Confederate forces off the coast of Maine in 1863 and destroyed when U.S. military forces closed in to recapture the steamer.

In 1863, the cutters Ashuelot, Kankakee, Kewanee, Mahoning, Patuxet, and Wayanda were constructed for the USRS. At the end of the war, the U.S. Navy transferred its surplus ships Delaware, Juniper, Jasmine, Nansemond, Wilderness and Moccasin to the Revenue Marine Service for permanent duty (Silverstone, pp. 83; 187; 199-200).

The transfer of ships between military services and from military to commercial agencies challenges historians who wish to chronicle the history of maritime vessels.

The nautical engineering ingenuity of the CSA is illustrated by its pioneering development of electrically detonated underwater mines. The Confederacy crafted crude submarines, most of which met a cruel fate. The CSS H.L. Hunley, a submarine out of Charleston harbor, was powered by 8 men who turned cranks to spin the propeller. In the dark of night (17 February 1864) the Hunley armed a spar torpedo and rammed and sank the USS Housatonic. Five Union sailors were lost, along with the Hunley crew which went down with the Union warship (Stern, Philip Van Doren, p. 8; 176-77).

Because it was the first submarine vehicle to sink an enemy warship in battle, it was of considerable historical interest when, in August, 2000, the 40 foot, cigar-shaped Hunley was raised by a barge off Sullivan's Island on the South Carolina coast (Kropf,Schuyler, Reuters, 8 August, 2000).

The Federal fleet flagship USS Minnesota was seriously damaged by a spar torpedo at Hampton Roads, Virginia on 9 March 1862 (Stern, Philip Van Doren, p. 183). A screw frigate, Minnesota had gone aground and was damaged by gunfire from the CSS Virginia. While anchored off Newport News, Virginia (9 April 1864) the USS Minnesota escaped damage when attacked by the CSS torpedo boat Squib (Silverstone, p. 28).

Confederate emissaries had limited success in procuring raiding ships from overseas sources. To evade British law which forbade selling warships to belligerents, Confederate agents purchased vessels from the United Kingdom and sailed out of British waters to outfit the ships with guns and cannon. Eighteen such vessels sailed for the CSA in the Atlantic, Indian, and Pacific oceans, damaging or sinking hundreds of enemy ships.

CSS Alabama and Florida damaged or destroyed an estimated 100 Yankee ships in their mighty seafaring careers. The British, in deference to U.S. pressure and in response to the moral persuasion of Lincoln's belated and geographically limited Emancipation Proclamation (1863), made it more difficult for the Confederacy to acquire English warships.

The CSS Shenandoah was still attacking U.S. whaling ships in the Bering Sea as late as July, 1865, when the master of a British ship informed the Confederate captain that the war had ended (Tindall, p. 678).

The Shenandoah then sailed more than 17,000 miles in the Pacific, around Africa, and north to Liverpool England, where its intrepid skipper, Lt. James I. Waddell, surrendered to British authorities. The United States consul took control of the vessel and auctioned it off (Stern, Philip Van Doren, pp. 250-53).

The U. S. revenue cutter Caleb Cushing, a heavily armed sailing ship, met its end in Portland harbor, Maine on June 27, 1863. Lt. Charles W. Read, CSN, sailed into the Yankee port on the captured ship, Archer, one of more than 14 vessels he had forced to surrender that summer. The Confederates boarded the cutter in a midnight assault. After setting the Caleb Cushing on fire, Lt. Read was immediately pursued by U.S. naval vessels and forced to surrender (Stern, Philip Van Doren, pp. 140-41).

Upon secession, five cutters of the Revenue Service were seized in port by Southern officials or turned over to the CSA by pro-Confederate revenue cutter officers. The Confederacy used the cutters as blockade runners, privateers and warships.

President Lincoln invoked the Act of 1799 which required revenue cutters to provide assistance to the United States Navy. The Revenue Service, while assisting directly in the war effort, continued their peace time functions of protecting life and property at sea, and search and rescue missions. Secretary of the Treasury Salmon P. Chase ordered Revenue Service officers and customs collectors to halt commerce to persons in armed insurrection against the Union.

The naval blockade of the Confederacy was a difficult task because the CSA controlled 3500 miles of coastline, 10 significant ports, and hundreds of bays, river mouths and inlets especially suited for Revenue cutter duty.

In 1861, the U.S. Navy had only two Southern bases: Key West Florida, and Hampton Roads, Virginia at the James River mouth, opposite the Confederate base at Norfolk. That strategic geography explained the eventual army, marine and naval attacks and conquests at Hatteras Inlet (North Carolina) and Norfolk, Virginia. Every significant harbor was controlled by Union forces by the end of the first year of war (April 1862) with the important exceptions of Wilmington (North Carolina) and Charleston (South Carolina).

Wilmington was the target for blockade runners because the port was protected by difficult shoals and challenging inlets at the Cape Fear River mouth, and the big Confederate guns of Fort Fisher. West Indies ports provided weapons and supplies to blockade runners, but the Union blockade inevitably deprived the South of the resources necessary for Confederate victory (McPherson, James M., 369-82).

One of the most illustrious sailing cutters was the 180 foot Harriet Lane.

Thirty foot abeam with a 10 foot draft, the handsome vessel carried an auxiliary sail and was propelled by side (paddle) wheels powered from a steam boiler. The sail-steamer combination allowed vessels to be able to save fuel by using wind power on long voyages.

The Harriet Lane was built in 1857, and in 1858 was assigned to the U.S. Navy for an expedition to explore the major rivers of Argentina and Paraguay, show the flag, and crush nationalist resistance.

Commodore William B. Shubrick (USN) headed the 15 vessel fleet which carried a force of nearly 300 sailors and marines and guns and ordnance. The Harriet Lane had a component of 82 sailors, 22 Marines, and 7 large guns. The show of force facilitated a treaty which provided for "perfect peace and sincere friendship" between the Latin American nations and the United States, and provided for extensive trade rights.

Commodore Shubrick's Navy Department report credited Captain John Faunce (USRS) and the Harriet Lane with being instrumental in the success of the expedition. In 1859, the cutter was back with the Revenue Service patrolling the Florida coast to enforce slave trade laws, and then went north to assume patrol duty at the port of New York City.

The Civil War caused the Harriet Lane to again be transferred to the Navy to join the ships which attempted to relieve Fort Sumter. In Charleston harbor. Captain Faunce "fired the first shot from any vessel in the long war waged for the preservation of the federal union" (Evans, pp. 73-75).

The fast, heavily armed cutter was a valuable component of the naval forces. The Harriet Lane took part in the first Union victory, the capture of Forts Hatteras and Clark in the Hatteras Inlet of North Carolina in an Army, Navy, Revenue Marine and Marine Corps amphibious mission. Assigned to the Navy, the Harriet Lane (Captain John Faunce) served as the flag ship of Admiral David Porter, USN (Kaplan and Hunt, p. 20). The famed U.S. gunboat was captured by Confederate forces in the port of Galveston (Texas) after being rammed and damaged on January 1, 1863. Confederate forces boarded the cutter, forced the crew to surrender, and found Captain Jonathan Wainwright (USRM) dead (Stern, Philip Van Doren, pp. 124-25).

After the Civil War, the Harriet Lane was found in Havana, Cuba, sold to a Boston firm, and sailed as a bark until it went down in the Caribbean sea in 1884 (Faust, p. 344).

The Revenue Marine acquired the Naugatuck from its owner, E. A. Stevens of New Jersey. Stevens designed the iron clad as a semi-submersible vessel which took in ballast to sink it to water level to make it a small target. The ship could pump out the water in 8 minutes. The cutter performed well on its war time missions and served the Revenue Marine until 1890.

A yacht before the war, the cutter Miami, with four brass cannons, cruised the Potomac River in May 1862. On board in this secret mission were Union military and civilian leaders, including General E. L. Viele (USA), Treasury Secretary Salmon P. Chase, Secretary of War Edwin M.

Stanton, and President Abraham Lincoln. The reconnaissance mission was designed to find out why Union forces were bottled up at Norfolk, Virginia. Upon reaching the beach, Lincoln walked into Confederate territory, determined a military landing was possible, and ordered a successful U.S. attack the next day (Evans, pp. 79-80).

The Lighthouse Service assisted the Revenue Marine and contributed to the ultimate federal victory. With the outbreak of war, more than 100 lighthouses were captured. Most of the lightships in the South were captured, destroyed, or sunk to serve as defensive harbor obstructions in Confederate ports. As Union forces conquered Confederate coastal regions, the Lighthouse Service reconstructed strategic stations and placed navigational aids (lightships, lights and buoys) in areas of naval activity.

An editor of the "Army and Navy Journal," November 26, 1864, described the contributions of the Revenue Marine, and predicted the eventual United States Coast Guard motto and name: "Keeping always under steam and ever ready in the event of extraordinary need, to render valuable service, the cutters can be made to form a coast guard whose value it is impossible at the present time to estimate" (Evans, pp. 84-5). By the middle of 1864 federal military forces dominated the key regions of the Confederacy; cut Texas off from the CSA by controlling the Mississippi River; established naval bases all along the Atlantic shoreline; and boxed in the major elements of the Confederate army.

General Robert E. Lee (CSA) surrendered his troops to General Ulysses S. Grant (USA) at Appomattox, Virginia on 9 April 1865 (Faragher, p. 168).

President Lincoln got little chance to celebrate the Union victory. On 14 April 1865, while attending a play at Ford Theater in Washington, D.C., Lincoln was assassinated by John Wilkes Booth who escaped the scene but was chased and gunned down by Union troops two weeks later in Virginia (Johnson, Paul, pp. 494-95).

The Confederate economy crumbled. The CSA collapsed. Union victory preserved the geographic and political unity of the United States; ended slavery (13th Amendment to the Constitution, 1865); and made the former slaves U.S. citizens (14th Amendment, 1868). The 15th Amendment (1870) gave suffrage to the newly freed, adult African-American males (Faragher, 168-69).

Reconstruction (1865-77) was imposed upon the defeated South by Union troops and federal law. The socioeconomic and political system was changed to pave the way for the admission of the former Confederate states into the Union.

The Congressional Reconstruction Acts (1867) divided the South into five military districts under the control of generals who enforced martial law. Republican politicians, well intentioned social service workers, Southern Whites (scalawags) and Northerners (carpet baggers) ran the political system. Newly freed Blacks were elected to local, state and federal offices. Political compromises crafted by the Democrat and Republican parties in Washington, D.C., gave the presidency to Rutherford B. Hayes and facilitated the withdrawal of federal troops from the South in 1877 (Faragher, pp. 769-71).

"Within a decade of its establishment, Congressional Reconstruction had been destroyed" and "new white regimes set about legislating the blacks into a lowly place in the scheme of things." America was tired of the Southern problem and moved on to economic expansion and involvement in foreign affairs (Johnson, Paul, p. 507).

The Civil War stimulated industrialization and urbanization. Mass production created the goods that expanded international trade. Ships were now steam powered and made of iron. Larger ships, cargoes and more passengers required more lighthouses, other aids to navigation, search and rescue, protection of life and property at sea and tariff enforcement. All of that was fertile ground for the expansion of the Revenue Marine Service which, by the late 1860's, was designated the U.S. Revenue Cutter Service.

Secretary of the Treasury George S. Boutwell was determined to make the Revenue Service more efficient and less costly. Those instructions were passed on to Sumner I. Kimball, the first civilian head of the Revenue Marine and the Lifesaving Service.

Kimball thought iron ships were too costly and new Revenue Marine cutters should be made of wood. The Revenue chief weeded out incompetent officers, reduced pay scales, and ended the personal use of cutters by Customs officials. A system of merit promotions was established. To train officers, Kimball established a "School of Instruction" (1876-1877), which paved the way for the future training school of Coast Guard officers, the U.S. Coast Guard Academy. The schooner Dobbin was the training (practice) cutter for for the School of Instruction.

Chief Kimball built upon previous efforts to operate a more effective Lifesaving Service. He convinced Congress to appropriate funds for the Service and placed Revenue Cutter Service officers in charge of the program. Lifesaving stations gradually expanded along the ocean and Gulf coasts and on the Great Lakes. Brave, full time professional crews of "surfmen" trained for their dangerous duties and manned the stations. Captain Douglas Ottinger built the first Lifeboat Stations on the New Jersey coastline. The lifeboat stations were also called U.S. Lifesaving Stations. The Lifesaving Service bonded with the Revenue Service in a "most important partnership in marine safety" (Kaplan and Hunt, pp. 27-28).

The Spanish-American War (1898) was the next challenge the Revenue Service faced. Spanish control of the Western Hemisphere began with the 1492 voyage of Columbus. By the mid-19th century, nationalism prevailed. Most of the former Spanish colonies had rebelled and gained sovereignty, except Cuba. American agricultural and business interests were not anxious to go to war to win Cuba its freedom, but the spirit of U.S. expansionism ("Manifest Destiny"), the desire of many U.S. citizens to see the oppressed Cubans independent, and moralistic motivations to "Christianize" Spanish Cuba and the Philippines coalesced into an interventionist spirit. Never mind that Spanish subjects were already Roman Catholic. Imperialistic urges were enhanced by balance of power considerations in light of the expansion of European naval power and the acquisition of bases and colonies. Captain Alfred Thayer Mahan (USN) added fuel to the imperialistic fires with his classic, The Influence of Sea Power on History (1890) in which he encouraged U.S. naval expansion (Tindall, p. 904).

The United States was the launching pad for several interventionist rebel movements in Cuba. President Grover Cleveland (Democrat) did his best to enforce neutrality laws. The Revenue Service and U.S. Navy intercepted gun smuggling expeditions from Gulf and Atlantic ports to Cuba (Tindall, pp. 910-14).

President William McKinley (Republican) did his best to stay neutral but encouraged the Spanish to invoke political reform and gradual Cuban sovereignty. Interventionist fervor finally influenced McKinley to send the USS Maine to Havana, Cuba, to protect U.S. citizens and economic interests. On February 15, 1898, the Maine was blown up in an explosion which killed 260 crew members. On April 20 Congress sent McKinley a resolution of war which he signed. The President ordered the blockade of Cuba, an act of war. The United States and Spain declared war on each other within the next week (Johnson, Paul, pp. 611-13).

The destruction of the U.S. battleship Maine was blamed on the Spanish and interpreted as an act of war. Subsequent explosion experts determined that an internal explosion had caused the tragedy.

With the declaration of war, Admiral George Dewey (USN) sailed his fleet to the Philippines from the Chinese-British port of Hong Kong and destroyed the Spanish flotilla in the Battle of Manila Bay (May 1). The recently updated U.S. Fleet under Rear Admiral William T. Sampson blockaded Cuba to cut off reinforcements and supplies to the 150,000 Spanish troops. When U.S. troops captured the Cuban port of Santiago, Spanish Admiral Pascual Cervera tried to escape the U.S. blockade. His entire fleet was destroyed on July 3 (Faragher, p. 876).

The United States Navy was supported by 13 revenue cutters during the Spanish American War. The USRC McCulloch served gallantly in the Battle of Manila Bay (the Philippines). The Hudson rescued a Navy torpedo boat under heavy enemy fire in the Battle of Cardenas Bay, Cuba (Chambers, p. 145).

President McKinley commended the feat of the cutter in a letter to Congress dated 27 June 1898: "In the face of galling fire from the enemy's guns, the revenue cutter Hudson, commanded by First Lieutenant Frank H. Newcomb, United States Revenue Cutter Service, rescued the disabled Winslow, her wounded commander, and crew." McKinley recommended "the thanks of Congress" and gold, silver and bronze medals to Lt. Newcomb and every crew member "who served with him at Cardenas" (Evans, pp. 171-2).

Other cutters performed meritorious service, including the McLane, which guarded the communication cable which tied the Key West (Florida) Naval Station to the peninsula; the Woodbury, which manned the blockade of Havana; the Windom (Capt. S.E. Maguire), which performed combat and life saving duties off the Cuban coast; and the Manning (Capt. F.M. Munger) which carried out a number of blockade, shore security and amphibious operations while coordinating with Army and Navy authorities (Evans, 172-75).

The Spanish-American War ended with the signing of the Treaty of Paris on 10 December, 1898. Cuba gained its independence, along with U.S. intervention rights which would be subsequently excersized. Spain ceded Puerto Rico, the Philippines and Guam to the United States. The U.S. was now an imperialist power which contradicted the anti-imperialist motives that propelled America into the Cuban insurrection.

The United States stepped onto the stage of global intervention and acquired interests which involved the nation in several Asian wars, the first of which was the bloody crushing the Philippine uprising against U.S. occupation.

McKinley was reelected in 1901. He chose as his running mate former Assistant Navy Secretary Teddy Roosevelt, the leader of the San Juan Hill Rough Riders in the recent war. On 6 September, 1901, McKinley was assassinated by the anarchist, Leon Czolgosz, propelling Theodore Roosevelt into the presidency (Johnson, Paul, pp. 613-14).

The United States Revenue Cutter Service resumed its peace time duties. The Revenue Cutter Grant inaugurated wireless telegraphy on 1 November 1903.

The wartime service of the USRCS garnered national and Congressional attention. With post-war concerns about economic efficiency, Congress enacted a bill on 20 January 1915 which combined the Life Saving Service and the Revenue Cutter Service into a new agency: the United States Coast Guard. Revenue Service Commodore Ellsworth P. Bertholf (1911-1919) became the first USCG Commandant.

CHAPTER IV

THE WORLD WAR I ERA

After performing its role in the Spanish-American War (1898), the Revenue Service resumed its marine safety and law enforcement responsibilities. In the next few years the Revenue Service was absorbed into a new agency and joined the global conflagration of World War I (1914-18), when the United States declared war on Germany in 1917.

Captain Stephen H. Evans (USCG) dedicated his definitive history, The United States Coast Guard 1790-1915 (Annapolis: United States Naval Institute, 1949) to his brother, "Arthur Bliss Evans, Jr., Lieutenant, junior grade, U.S. Coast Guard Reserve, lost in action against the enemy while serving on board U.S.S. Leopold (DE-319), North Atlantic Ocean, 9 March 1944," a reminder of the cost in lives the Coast Guard paid in both world wars.

Evans described the World War I origins of the Coast Guard. The Act to Create the Coast Guard was approved by the House (20 January 1915) and signed into law by President Woodrow Wilson (January 28). The New York Times chronicled the event in its 31 January edition: "Revenue cutters now Coast Guard. Our famous force of little ships merged with the Life-Saving Service. New law puts this highly trained body of sea police in the military establishment and in the Navy in time of war" (Evans, pp. 215-16).

Initially called the Great War, World War I was caused by European rivalries stimulated by nationalism, imperialism, militarism and alliance systems. The immediate cause was an assassination in the Balkans which sparked the defensive alliances which had been designed to deter aggression (Barzun, pp. 689-91).

The contending diplomatic factions consisted of the Central Powers (Germany, Austria-Hungary, the Turkish Ottoman Empire, and Bulgaria) versus the Allies: Britain, France, Serbia, Tsarist Russia, Greece, Japan, Rumania, Italy (which deserted the Central Powers in 1915), and the United States.

President Wilson and Congress tried to maintain American neutrality, but Germany's unrestricted submarine warfare attacks on belligerent and neutral ships on the high seas, including U.S. vessels, led to a U.S. declaration of war upon Germany on 6 April 1917 (Johnson, T.H., pp. 873-74).

German submarine warfare tactics were in response to the Allied trade blockade and pro-British U.S. trade policies. The United States responded to the "appalling slaughter of seamen and civilian passengers in the Atlantic sea-lanes" and the revelation of a proposed "German-Mexican offensive alliance against the United States under which Texas and other territories would be handed back to Mexico" (Johnson, P., pp. 643-45).

The bloody multi-continental land and sea war came to an end with the signing of the Armistice (November 11, 1918) and the Treaty of Versailles in France (1919). The Versailles Treaty dismembered Austria-Hungary, handed German and Turkish colonies over to several Allied nations in the form of "mandates," required Germany to sign a questionable "war guilt clause," and exacted huge "reparations" from the former Central Powers. "Thus, Versailles was the impulse behind Adolf Hitler's rise to power, the pretext for his aggressions, and the ultimate cause of World War Two" (Johnson, P., pp. 650-51).

The United States Senate opposed the Treaty of Versailles because of political quarrels between the Republicans and the Democratic president, fear that membership in the proposed League of Nations would require U.S. involvement in never-ending overseas conflicts, and disagreements over the territorial and economic policies imposed on Germany. Wilson refused to consider any Republican amendments to the Treaty. On 19 November 1919, the Senate voted to reject the Treaty of Versailles and withdrew from the League of Nations (Gilbert, pp. 574-76).

In July 1921, in the new administration of Republican President Warren G. Harding, Congress declared an end to World War I and later signed peace treaties with Germany, Austria and Hungary (Johnson, T.H., p. 817).

During the War, the Coast Guard policed the enormous cargoes and innumerable ships which inundated U.S. ports. Coast Guard cutters escorted Allied convoys, a dangerous activity which lost the cutter Tampa to a German submarine. Several cutters were destroyed or damaged in collisions (Chambers, p. 145).

The USCGC Tampa had served 8 months with a Navy task force escorting British ships from Gibraltar in the Mediterranean Sea to the United Kingdom in waters infested with German submarines. The gallant service of the Tampa and crew under the able command of Captain

Charles Satterlee (USCG) had earned them a special commendation from Rear Admiral Albert P. Niblack (USN), Commander of the Atlantic Fleet Patrol Force.

Six weeks before the end of World War I, on 26 September, the Tampa was sunk by German U-Boat 91 in British waters with the loss of 111 Coast Guardsmen and four U.S. Navy crew members (Johnson, R.E., p. 55).

The Coast Guard contributed 15 cruising cutters, 5,000 men and 200 officers to the U.S. Navy in World War I. Particularly successful among the Atlantic anti-submarine warfare units were the cutters Algonquin, Manning, Ossipee, Seneca, Tampa, and Yamacraw. The Coast Guard cutters and crews escorted Allied convoys, dropped depth charges on U-boats, and engaged in search and rescue missions during battle action when ships were damaged, sunk, or turned into flaming infernos in petroleum saturated waters.

The Coast Guard cutter Seneca, under the command of Captain William J. Wheeler (USCG), distinguished itself in Atlantic convoy duty defending British vessels and rescuing crews. Sir Winston Churchill, then First Lord of the Admiralty, said of the ship and crew: "Seldom in the annals of the sea has there been exhibited such cool courage and such unfailing diligence in the face of almost insurmountable difficulties" (Kaplan and Hunt, pp. 44-45).

The USCG suffered significant losses at sea, proportionately more the other U.S. armed services in World War I.

Within U.S. territorial waters and out of home ports, members of the Lighthouse Service and and the intrepid surfmen of the Life Saving Service patrolled beaches in search of spies and saboteurs, and responded to ships in distress and vessels which were torpedoed by patrolling German submarines.

On the home front, the Coast Guard carried out search and rescue and port security assignments, guarded against sabotage and espionage, and supervised explosive loading in strategic harbors. Many lives were saved at a cost of several Coastguardsmen as the USCG responded to fuel and munitions explosions on land and sea. The disastrous explosion at Black Tom Island terminal (New Jersey), across the Hudson River from New York City, was responded to by the crew of the CG cutter Hudson and Captain Alex Foss (USCG). The Black Tom explosion encouraged Congress to pass the Espionage Act of 1917 which delegated to the Coast Guard the responsibility of protecting waterfront and port areas. Every strategic harbor was placed under the control of a Captain of the Port. The USCG has been responsible since that time for what the service calls "Port Security."

Coast Guard aviation began during World War I when the service acquired a flying lifeboat and began a tradition of search and rescue and reconnaissance from the air. The Coast Guard assisted the Wright brothers in their first flight when members of the Kill Devil Life Saving Station were on hand to secure the craft in heavy winds during the famous Kitty Hawk (North Carolina) flight (1903).

The Coast Guard made history in a pioneering transatlantic flight by Lieutenant Elmer F. Stone (USCG) in 1919. Lieutenant Stone flew an NC-4 model seaplane from Rockaway, New York (8 May) to the Azore islands, and eventually landed in Plymouth, England (31 May). Fueling stops were made in Canada (Newfoundland) and the Azores (Kaplan and Hunt, pp. 45-47).

In the immediate postwar period (1919-23), the fledgling U.S. Coast Guard fought for survival as it was restored to peace time status. The Service maneuvered to maintain its autonomy against civilian and military officials in the federal bureaucracy who claimed that efficiency and budgets required the Coast Guard to be absorbed by the U.S. Navy. Coast Guard Commodore-Commandant Bertholf, his successor, Commandant-Captain William Edward Reynolds (1919-24), and Treasury Secretaries Carter Glass and David F. Houston fought off politicians and a cadre of Coast Guard officers to maintain the independent status of the Service.

President Wilson aided the cause with an executive order (28 August 1919) directing the Coast Guard to resume operation under the Treasury Department. Wilson's successor, Republican President Warren G. Harding, further cemented Coast Guard autonomy at the request of Treasury Secretary Andrew W. Mellon. Harding signed into law (January 1923) a measure which made Coast Guard and Navy officer ranks and pay more equivalent, promoted more officers to captain rank, made the Coast Guard commandant a rear admiral, and mandated more frequent and timely promotions for officers and enlisted personnel.

Plans were made to upgrade the Coast Guard fleet and from 1920 to 1923, appointments to the Academy increased from 23 to 72 (Johnson, R.E.., pp. 57-68).

Between 1919 and 1924 the Coast Guard saved more than 14,000 lives, assisted more than 81,000 persons on board vessels, dealt with 6,000 vessels either seized or reported for legal violations, and removed or destroyed more than 200 hazardous derelict vessels. The value of vessels and cargoes assisted was tabulated at $15 million in 1919, $65 million in 1920, and $25 million in 1924. Yet, the annual appropriation for the Coast Guard in each of these years averaged around $10 million (Johnson, R.E., p. 69).

The value of human life cannot be calculated, but in material terms the Coast Guard earned its keep and achieved a highly efficient cost-benefit ratio.

The Coast Guard offered its services in symbolic and prestigious ways monitoring holiday boating, rowing, yachting, and commercial and sport fishing festivities. In the 1920's, the Coast Guard sent cutters to New London (Connecticut) to superintend Harvard-Yale boating regattas on the Thames River.

Sometimes the missions were deadly serious. In 1918-19, the Coast Guard launched a health care expedition to aid epidemic victims. When a deadly influenza epidemic struck several villages on Alaska's Seward Peninsula, Coast Guardsmen responded on dog sleds packed with medicines and supplies. On 6 December 1918, Surfman L. E. Ashton and an Eskimo (Inuit) driver completed a 160 mile mission aiding seriously ill villagers along the route. Ashton reached his terminal point to find sick and deceased victims. He set up a dispensary at a post office, brought survivors to hospital care in a school house, arranged funeral services for more than 100 of the deceased, and then returned to Station No. 305 in Nome to resume his regular responsibilities.

The cutter Unalga, under the command of Captain Francis G. Dodge (USCG), braved a Bering Sea storm to reach influenza victims in Unalaska. While there, Captain Dodge received news of another epidemic in the region but concluded that the situation in Unalaska and Dutch Harbor needed the full attention of his crew and Surgeon F. H. Johnson (United States Public Health Service). Providing medicine and food to nearly 100 patients, and administering funeral services for the dead was a full time job, interrupted only when Captain Dodge and several crew members got sick, and later recovered. A hospital ship joined the battle against disease, as did the U.S. Navy gunboat Vicksburg near Bristol Bay. The situation deteriorated to the point where service personnel had to shoot starving dogs to prevent them from eating the corpses of the deceased. When the situation subsided, the Unalga dispatched the last of the food, medicine and other supplies, returned to Unalaska for coal, and continued on Bering Sea Patrol.

In late January 1920, action in the Atlantic challenged the Coast Guard cutters Gresham, Ossipee, and Acushnet 500 miles off the Massachusetts coast. When the U.S. Army transport ship Powhatan became disabled, two Navy destroyers and a Canadian steamer joined the rescue in heavy seas and a blinding snow storm. Coordinated towing and improved weather conditions allowed the Powhatan to eventually reach the Halifax lightship and safe harbor.

From 1919 to 1924, the United States Coast Guard and its colleagues in the Life Saving and Lighthouse services distinguished themselves. Lives were saved and commendations were awarded to surfmen, lighthouse keepers, and officers and crew members of cutters on the Great

Lakes, along the Eastern Seaboard, in the Gulf of Mexico, the Pacific from California to the Pacific Northwest, Alaskan waters and the Bering Sea. Grounded vessels, disabled ships sometimes more than one hundred miles off shore, sinking or burning vessels, and endangered crews received the attention of the Coast Guard. Hundreds of lives were saved. Some were lost.

Among the heroes were Lieutenant Commander Henry G. Hemingway (USCG) and the crew of the 152 foot cutter Snohomish out of Port Angeles, Washington. Enduring heavy seas and 75 mile per hour gale force winds in February 1923, the crew of the Snohomish rescued some crew members from a burning steamer off Vancouver Island, and others from lifeboats in darkness and heavy rain.

In the same year the Coast Guard was called upon by Major General Mason M. Patrick (US Army) to monitor, supply and perform search and rescue missions along the planned route of an attempted global circumnavigation. The aircraft consisted of four Douglas single engine biplanes. Army pilots commenced their flight in Alaska, then westward through the Aleutian and Kurile islands to Japan, and on from there.

Coast Guard cutters Haida and Algonquin cooperated with the U.S. Army and U.S. Navy in monitoring weather, carrying out search and rescue operations, transporting equipment and supplies, and hosting tired crews. Upon completion of the successful enterprise, the cutters returned to search and rescue and law enforcement duties and the expressed gratitude of General Patrick (Johnson, R.E., pp. 70-78).

Several World War I cutters went on to serve with distinction during Prohibition and World War Two. In the 1930's, the cutter Haida assisted ships in the Gulf of Alaska, enforced fisheries regulations, and was transferred to less turbulent waters out of the port of Juneau.

Other old cutters were transferred from cold and stormy Northern waters to sunnier Southern ports. The cutter Unalga was assigned to San Juan (Puerto Rico). By the middle of the decade, the Unalga was the oldest ocean going cruising cutter.

Some of the older, more durable cutters stayed on for difficult duty. The Ossipee had been built for ice breaking service, and the cutter Acushnet was strengthened for duty in ice clogged Northern waters.

The 1930's saw the decommissioning of several old cutters, including the Seneca, Gresham and Yamacraw (Johnson, R.E., pp. 153, 155).

The cutter Seneca achieved a distinguished record in World War I, Prohibition law enforcement (1920's), oceanographic survey, and search and rescue during the devastating Florida hurricanes of 1926 (Johnson, R.E., pp. 80, 99, and 117).

CHAPTER V

PROHIBITION AND DEPRESSION
(1920-1940)

The decades of Prohibition (1920-33) and Depression (1929-39) presented a new set of responsibilities, problems and successes for the U.S. Coast Guard. The controversial and unpopular duties of Prohibition law enforcement and budget cuts during the Great Depression presented significant challenges to the small service. As if that were not enough, the two decades ended on the eve of U.S. entry into a global war which confronted the Coast Guard with more dangerous obligations.

The Volstead Act (1919) defined Prohibition and enforced the Eighteenth Amendment which went into effect in 1920 and made it illegal to manufacture, sell, or transport intoxicating liquor. The federal government appropriated more than $10 million annually to prevent the importation and domestic production of alcohol. Hundreds of thousands of arrests and court convictions resulted from the enforcement.

Drinking alcohol became a challenge and a cause. Home breweries blossomed, "speakeasies" and "night clubs" served customers, and enterprising "bootleggers" made liquor in woodland stills. The social devastation caused by alcohol fueled this well-intentioned moral crusade whose origins can be traced to pre-Civil War temperance campaigns (Faragher, John Mack, p. 749).

The Wickersham Commission Report (1931) concluded the laws could not be enforced. The 21st Amendment (1933) repealed the 18th, but not before the damage was done (Johnson, T.H., p. 660).

The Prohibition Bureau was placed under the Treasury Department after an attempt to make it part of the Justice Department failed. The Treasury jurisdiction brought in the Coast Guard.

Prohibition caused liquor industry distribution and profits to be transferred to criminal organizations which got more powerful by reinvesting profits into prostitution, drug smuggling and gambling (Johnson, P., 680-83).

The moral fervor of Progressives and abstainers stimulated the prohibition movement, as did war-time patriotism which championed the cause of using grain for food instead of "booze."

Canada and the West Indies were sources of the illegal fluid. Canadian vessels plied the waters of the Atlantic, Pacific and Great Lakes to drop liquor off to domestic boats. Liquor laden vehicles traversed U.S. border points with surprising ease. Detroit made almost as much money from the liquor industry across the river in Ontario as it did from automobile manufacturing.

Gangsters and racketeers became folk heroes. "Scarface" Al Capone moved from New York to Chicago in 1920 and became a wealthy vice lord supplying, the mobster claimed, a "legitimate demand." "Some people called it racketeering," Capone declared. "I call it a business. They say I violate the prohibition law. Who doesn't?" Capone was eventually prosecuted and imprisoned, not for murder or other crimes he committed, but income tax evasion, a charge based on evidence gathered by diligent Treasury agents (Tindall, pp. 1036-38).

Federal law enforcement officers, called "G" (government) men, did their best to enforce prohibition laws in the face of bribery, threats and death. Their limited success made social critics conclude that laws governing morality should not be made and could not be enforced. The Prohibition era experience does suggest that some laws cannot be well administered, but most laws are designed to reward good and punish bad behavior. Civil rights laws serve as an example.

In his inaugural address, President Calvin Coolidge declared war on illegal liquor syndicates. Treasury Department enforcement of Prohibition laws brought in the Coast Guard sea police. The Coast Guard "Rum Fleet" consisted of craft ranging from small coastal and inland water patrol boats to 20 destroyers transferred from the U.S. Navy by Act of Congress (April 21, 1924). Rum-running foreign vessels stayed outside the 3 and 12 mile territorial limits monitored by Coast Guard cutters and destroyers. The cutters reported the location of the speed boats which off-loaded the liquor. The boats tried to outrun inshore patrol boats which had orders to stop and board vessels, seize evidence and confiscate contraband. Suspect foreign and domestic vessels were boarded by Coast Guard officials in U.S. ports.

U.S. Coast Guard Commandant, Rear Admiral Frederick C. Billard (1924-32) reluctantly assumed the prohibition mission and testified that the total value of cargo seizures compared favorably with the annual federal appropriations for the Service. Unfortunately, the dangers Coast Guard crews faced from chasing down contraband vessels and making seizures were ignored by some judges and law enforcement officials who dealt with law breakers leniently and released seized vessels which returned to the illicit business.

The dangers of drug enforcement were illustrated in the Florida Straits in 1927. Rum runners bought liquor in the British Bahamas with counterfeit U.S. money. Chief Boatswain's Mate Sydney Sanderlin, the skipper of patrol boat CG-249, a seven man crew, and Secret Service agent Robert K. Webster, were sent out to suppress the activity. A motorboat was stopped after warning shots were fired over the bow a few miles out of Fort Lauderdale. One hundred cases of liquor were found and the smugglers arrested. A gun battle broke out on the cutter. Chief Sanderlin and Agent Webster were killed. Using hand tools, the Coast Guard crew overwhelmed and apprehended the two smugglers, one of whom was found guilty of murder and hanged at the Fort Lauderdale Coast Guard Base.

International law sometimes canceled out Coast Guard efforts. A court found that the "hot pursuit" claim of the Coast Guard in the capture of a Canadian rum runner was invalid because two cutters were involved at different times before the vessel was finally captured in international waters. Arbitration resolved the dispute. Some observers questioned the court's logic.

Coast Guard diligence is illustrated by the USCG cutter Acushnet which towed a schooner with 2,000 cases of alcohol into Boston Harbor (16 December 1922); and the cutter Redwing and the 75 foot patrol boat CG-237 which cooperated in the joint seizure of a contraband runner (10 June 1925).

The Coast Guard benefited from the willingness of Congress to release funding for the construction of faster cutters and the acquisition of aircraft for surveillance and rescue missions. In 1934, Henry Morgenthau, President Roosevelt's Treasury Secretary, designated the Coast Guard responsible for coastal and inland border surveillance, and assisting the U.S. Border Patrol.

Treasury Department flying missions were placed under Coast Guard control. The USCG acquired 15 aircraft from the Customs Service, 6 from the U.S. Navy, and air bases in San Diego, San Antonio and Buffalo.

Among the aircraft acquired by the Coast Guard in the 1920's were two Chance Vought biplane seaplanes, with "U.S. Coast Guard" emblazoned on both sides of each fuselage (Kaplan and Hunt, pp. 49-57).

The 46 "off shore patrol boats" which went into service in 1926 and 1927 were named for Revenue Cutter Service officers and early cutters. The new boats were 100 or 125 foot diesel powered twin-screw steel vessels, each mounted with a 3-inch 23 caliber gun.

Some patrol craft were acquired by federal seizure of contraband vessels. Boats taken into the service were given CG numbers based on whether they were more or less than 40 feet in length.

Radios were used for intelligence and communication. Rum runners learned to monitor CG frequencies so new codes had to be developed. The codes were initially based on Navy communication systems until Major William F. Friedman, a U.S. Army cryptographer, and his wife Elizabeth, developed special Coast Guard ciphers.

The Coast Guard was operating 15 destroyers at the end of Prohibition (1933). By 1934, all of them were returned to the U.S. Navy. U.S. Coast Guard Headquarters reported (as of 30 June 1933) some progress in the war against Prohibition smuggling on the Great Lakes and the Atlantic, Gulf and Pacific coasts. But public demand and the creative counter measures employed by domestic and foreign traffickers made it impossible for the Coast Guard and other federal agencies to completely close down the lucrative operations (Johnson, R.E., pp. 89-93).

Coast Guard Commandant Frederick C. Billard dedicated himself to improving the morale of personnel posted at isolated stations or serving on long, monotonous and dangerous sea voyages. Libraries and correspondence courses were made available, along with athletic equipment, films, radios and phonograph record players. Correlated with these support activities was the founding of the League of Coast Guard Women which promoted "the morale, contentment, and happiness of service personnel by visiting and aiding the sick and distressed....and being 'always ready.'"

The U.S. Navy cooperated with Admiral Billard in making correspondence courses available to Coast Guard personnel. The U.S. Marine Corps extended its educational facilities to Guardsmen and established the model for the Coast Guard Institute at the Academy in New London. The Institute graded advanced rating exams for enlisted personnel and awarded certificates and correspondence school diplomas. Billard had previously served as superintendent of the Coast Guard Academy, and used his authority to influence members of Congress and Connecticut officials to improve facilities and purchase the necessary land to maintain the Academy's reputation. Treasury Secretary Mellon and department architects were instrumental in building Hamilton Hall on campus, a fitting tribute to the first U.S. Treasury Secretary and founder of the Revenue Cutter Service, Alexander Hamilton. Captain Quincy B. Newman, appointed to head the Department of Engineering at the Academy, revised the engineering courses to match leading laboratories and colleges and prepare cadets with the knowledge needed to meet the needs of the service (Johnson, R.E., pp. 108-110).

In 1928-29, Bethlehem Shipbuilding Corporation (Quincy, Massachusetts) built five Lake-class cutters, so called because they were named for U.S. lakes. Christened Champlain, Chelan, Mendota, Pontchartrain, and Tahoe, their trial runs proved the 3,000 horsepower ships could do 17 knots. The cutters were designed to mount 5-inch and 3-inch guns.

At Oakland, California, the General Engineering and Dry Dock Company constructed the Cayuga, Itasca, Saranac, Sebago, and Shoshone. In 1932 the Escanaba was launched. The Bay City, Michigan cutter had a reinforced bow and waterline plating designed to cope with Great Lakes ice. From 1933-34, five sister ships named for previous vessels followed the Escanaba: the Tahoma, Mohawk, Onondaga, Comanche, and Algonquin. To distinguish Coast Guard cutters from Navy vessels, Admiral Billard contributed the letter designation "W."

The Coast Guard gradually assumed the responsibility of accommodating weather, fisheries and other scientific observers on its patrols to facilitate the gathering of data. One appropriately educated Coast Guard officer eventually assumed the duties of scientist and oceanographer. The Coast Guard Oceanographic Unit was initially staffed by two scientists, an officer and a civilian, and several enlisted personnel. Harvard University offered graduate study in oceanography to Lt. Edward H. "Iceberg" Smith, USCG. Smith studied oceanography under Norwegian scientists, published a paper on ocean currents, and sailed on the cutters Tampa and Marion to collect iceberg and oceanographic data in the North Atlantic between Canadian Labrador and the Danish possession of Greenland. The cramped 125 foot patrol boat Marion proved to be a good oceanographic vessel. It met the challenges of fog, frigid temperatures and stormy sea (Johnson, R.E., pp. 115-122).

Lifeboat, lighthouse, and other shore stations received needed attention in the Billard years. The commandant did his best with limited resources and Depression era budget cuts to improve those facilities. Crews launched lifeboats and surfboats from shores, bays, inlets and rivers, using techniques and boats from the days of the old Life-Saving Service. By the 1920's, the wooden 34 and 36 foot lifeboats were powered by gasoline engines, but some oar-pulling boats remained in use.

In 1928 several Coast Guard representatives visited European life-saving stations and observed gasoline and diesel powered boats and methods of operation. Some European innovations were adopted, but Coast Guard procedures were generally reaffirmed.

Budget constraints stimulated administrative decentralization. More authority was given to area commanders. Exceptions were granted for the Coast Guard Academy, the International Ice Patrol, the Permanent General Court, and the cable ship Pequot, each of which reported directly to the assistant commandant (Johnson, R.E., pp. 122-25).

The Great Depression (1929-39) was caused by a complexity of interlocking domestic and foreign variables. Herbert Hoover's presidency ended because of the severe economic dislocation for which he was unfairly blamed. In his memoirs, the former president concisely assessed the blame: "The primary cause of the Great Depression was the war of 1914-1918" (Kennedy, David M., p. 9).

Domestic causes included agricultural stagnation and falling prices, consumer consumption decline, speculative abuses in the securities markets, and an antiquated banking and financial system. European causes included the impact of World War I and the Versailles Treaty provisions concerning reparations, allied war debts, and protective tariffs which stifled global trade (Kennedy, pp. 69-73).

The Depression changed American society, politics and economics, ushered in a new balance in business, labor and government relations, and expanded the role of the federal government in social welfare and economic regulations.

The Roosevelt administration and Congress created a plethora of federal agencies to regulate the economy, and tried to intimidate the U.S. Supreme Court into approving the expansion of legislative and executive power. Critics of Franklin Delano Roosevelt contend his policies put the United States on the slippery slope of socialism. Supporters insist FDR saved American capitalism and prevented a revolution and dictatorship in the face of more than 25% unemployment.

The outbreak of war in Europe (1939) bolstered the U.S. economy as labor markets expanded and the domestic and wartime needs of Europe were met by the American industrial machine. World War Two, which the U.S. belatedly entered in 1941, transformed the nation into an economic, military, and geopolitical giant (Faragher, John Mack, pp. 370-74).

The United States Coast Guard entered World War Two as the service was again temporarily merged with the U.S. Navy to embark upon another dangerous mission.

CHAPTER VI

WORLD WAR II
(1939-1945)

Some historians have argued that World War Two was the dominant event of the Twentieth Century. The multi-national, intercontinental conflict took place on land, sea and in the air. The killing that took place on and behind the front lines "was the greatest loss of military and civilian life in so short a time in recorded history" (Gilbert, p. 263).

The official dates of the war (1939-1945) are imprecise because prewar Axis aggression occurred in the Spanish Civil War where future belligerents Germany and the Soviet Union fought on opposite sides; in Europe and Africa when Germany and Italy absorbed territories in violation of the Treaty of Versailles; and in China, which Japan invaded in the 1930's. The European conflagration began when Britain declared war on Germany after Hitler's army invaded Poland on 1 September 1939 (Gilbert, pp. 263-64).

The clouds of war were visible during the 1920's. The United States hosted international disarmament conferences to cool nationalist and militarist passions ignited by the unresolved problems of World War One. The League of Nations could not prevent the aggression of the Axis Powers (Germany, Japan and Italy). Some observers thought the failure of the U.S. to join the League made it powerless.

After Great Britain and France declared war on Germany, the U.S. government proclaimed neutrality. President Franklin Delano Roosevelt covertly and overtly challenged congressional policy. FDR met secretly with British Prime Minister Winston Churchill off the Canadian (New Foundland) coast (August 1941), where they drew up war and post-war objectives (the Atlantic Charter). Congress voted to strengthen the U.S. military, initiate conscription (the Selective Service and Training Act of 1940), and extend credit, military equipment and supplies to Britain with the Lend-Lease Act of 1941 (Johnson, T.H., pp. 874-77).

Roosevelt claimed his policies were intended to protect American self-interest and keep the nation out of war, but his actions increased the likelihood of U.S. military involvement. The President ordered an expansion of the security zone for Atlantic naval patrols, acquired British naval bases in the Western Hemisphere in return for lending destroyers to the British navy, and shipped military supplies to Britain. By the summer of 1941 the U.S. was in "an undeclared and clandestine war against Hitler's navy" (Dorwart, p. 151).

Hitler's Fascist Germany and Josef Stalin's Communist Soviet Union were ideological enemies, but joined in a pragmatic alliance which allowed each nation to absorb portions of Eastern Slavic Europe unimpeded. Hitler then inexplicably invaded his Slavic partner (June of 1941), a decision which brought the U.S.S.R on the Allied side and spelled the beginning of the end of the German war machine. The Russians eventually pushed the German army all the way back to Berlin. The Soviet armies pressed Germany from the East, and the U.S. and British Commonwealth nations attacked Germany from the West and South.

The Fascist military forces of Imperial Japan expanded in East and Southeast Asia and absorbed several Pacific islands. Emperor Hirohito's army, navy and air force were initially successful because the U.S. was neutral, and European colonial powers were stretched thin from Asia to Europe and in a fight to the finish with the German Third Reich.

Roosevelt's decision to try to stop Japanese expansion by depriving the Nipponese of iron and petroleum forced the overpopulated insular nation to occupy mineral rich Southeast Asia. Believing the U.S. was the only power which could challenge them, Japanese naval and air forces carried out a daring attack on the U.S. Pacific Fleet and U.S. Army and Marine bases at Pearl Harbor (Hawaii) on 7 December 1941 (Johnson, T.H., pp. 874-77).

President Roosevelt blamed the Hawaiian commanders, Admiral Husband Kimmel (USN) and General Walter Short (USA), for not being prepared for the Japanese attack. During the war, several investigating commissions found the two commanders at fault. But critics contend that army and navy testimony was changed under pressure, essential information was withheld from the Pearl Harbor commanders, and the blame lay with bungling and deceptive Washington bureaucrats (Foner and Garraty, pp. 1175-76).

The Pearl Harbor disaster, according to one historian, was a "failure of intelligence doctrine" in which good counterespionage work, the decryption of Japanese codes, and evidence from informants was not properly classified, transmitted, or heeded. The blame for intelligence failures must be shared by the Office of Naval Intelligence which had access to important information and received warnings from a variety of concerned sources (Dorwart, p. 172, 178-82).

Admiral Kimmel and General Short were aware of the possibility of war with Japan, but like most knowledgeable U.S. civilian and military officials, expected the attack to be in the Philippines or Dutch East Indies. After the Pearl Harbor attack, Kimmel and Short were charged with "dereliction of duty," relieved of command, and forced into retirement (Spector, pp. 93-96). A subsequent hearing limited the charge to bad judgment.

The attack lasted less than two hours. Japanese aircraft (183) and submarines sank 5 U.S. battleships, damaged or destroyed more than a dozen other vessels and 150 aircraft, and killed 2500 Americans. The Japanese missed three aircraft carriers and their escorts which were away at sea, and failed to destroy fuel and repair depots (LaFeber, p. 211).

Admiral Isoroku Yamamoto, the Japanese naval strategist who reluctantly planned the Pearl Harbor mission, had spoken out against the alliance with the Axis powers, Germany and Italy. Prince Konoye, the former prime minister of Japan, echoed the predictions of Admiral Yamamoto upon finding out about the Pearl Harbor attack. Having favored a diplomatic solution to U.S.-Japanese conflicts, Konoye said, "It is a terrible thing...I know that a tragic defeat awaits us at the end" (LaFeber, pp. 210-13).

Admiral Yamamoto was shot down and killed by U.S. fighter pilots (April 18, 1943) while on a military inspection trip in the South Pacific. The U.S. aviators were guided by intelligence gained from American interceptions and deciphering of the Japanese radio transmissions which detailed Yamamoto's flight plans (Margiotta, p. 1108).

The Japanese attack obliterated the strong neutralist and isolationist feelings in the United States. The U.S. declared war on Japan on 8 December. Japan quickly conquered British, Dutch, and French territories in East Asia and the American Philippines, eventually extending her reach into the Alaskan Aleutian islands of the north Pacific.

By mid-1942, U.S. Army, Navy, and Army Air Force units began to defeat Japanese military forces on land and sea. A bomber raid from a U.S. aircraft carrier allowed the U.S. Army Air Force to bomb the home islands of Japan. Strategic island hopping around enemy troop concentrations pushed Allied forces closer to Japan. The Pacific War ended when President Truman gave orders to drop atomic bombs on Hiroshima (6 August) and Nagasaki (9 August). Japan surrendered on 14 August 1945 (Johnson, T.H., pp. 874-77).

The Battle of the Atlantic commenced before Pearl Harbor. German submarines sank U.S. commercial vessels which sailed along the Gulf and Atlantic coasts because they supplied Britain and France. U.S. naval patrols convoyed supply vessels to Europe and reported the location of German submarines to the British. Consequently, German U-boats torpedoed and sank the U.S.S. Greer (September 1941) and the U.S.S. Reuben James (November 1941), outraging an officially neutral U.S. ostensibly determined to stay out of the war (Faragher, John Mack, p. 1032).

After Pearl Harbor, the United States struck back at the military forces of Hitler and Italian dictator Benito Mussolini in the North African invasion (November 1942) commanded by General Dwight Eisenhower, USA. In July the Mediterranean island of Sicily was invaded by the Allies, providing a launching pad for subsequent attacks on the Italian peninsula. Rome fell in June of 1944 but German troops fought on.

Eisenhower commanded Allied forces in Operation Overlord (6 June-25 July 1944), the invasion of continental Europe through the French province of Normandy. The invasion commenced on "D-Day," when Allied forces, dominated by the U.S., Britain, and Canada, carried out the largest amphibious (sea to land) invasion in history. That was the beginning of the end for Germany. Allied forces gradually moved toward Germany from the West, and the Russians converged on Berlin from the East, meeting in German Saxony (April 1945). In May, Hitler committed suicide and German officials signed an unconditional surrender. The formal end of the European war came on 8 May (Johnson, T.H., pp. 876-77).

With the context of World War Two briefly established, the role of the United States Coast Guard in the global conflict can be put in perspective.

Wartime recruitment increased the number of Coast Guard personnel to 171,000, which included the Women's Reserve (SPARS) and 50,000 Coast Guard Reserve volunteers. The Coast Guard Beach Patrol watched for enemy espionage agents and saboteurs. Port Security duties were performed by about 20% of the service (Chambers, p. 145).

The wisdom of establishing the Beach Patrol carried out on foot with dogs and on horse back, was affirmed in June 1942 when Seaman Second Class John C. Cullen came in contact with suspicious persons who threatened and bribed him on a foggy Long Island beach. Coast Guardsman Cullen calmly withdrew, made his way back to his station, and contacted the Federal Bureau of Investigation. The FBI later apprehended the suspects who turned out to be German saboteurs landed by U-boat. The enemy agents were tried and executed. Petty officer Cullen was awarded the Legion of Merit (Kaplan and Hunt, pp. 70-72).

American civilian workers contributed immeasurably to eventual victory in World War Two. Meeting the needs of the domestic and European economies helped to end the Depression. Women and minorities contributed to the effort. The war-time economy helped change the socioeconomic landscape of the United States. With millions of men off to war, women moved into the vacuum and performed valiantly in demanding and sometimes dangerous civilian and military occupations. Nearly 200,000 women joined the newly established Women's Army Corps (WACS), Coast Guard (SPARS), Navy (WAVES) and Marines (Tindall, pp. 1194-95).

During the war, "the United States enrolled 11,260,000 soldiers, 4,183,466 sailors, 669,000 marines, and 241,093 coastguards. Despite this vast diversion of manpower to the armed forces, U.S. factories built 296,000 planes and 102,000 tanks, and U.S. shipyards turned out 88,000 ships and landing-craft" (Johnson, Paul, p. 780).

Courageous people from all walks of life rose to the occasion with the talent necessary to slay the Axis dragon. British and American scientists built the technology of war and created the equipment necessary for victory. Civilian and military managers provided the logistical and tactical knowledge necessary to move troops and supplies. New technologies and sophisticated espionage techniques facilitated the breaking of German and Japanese codes which contributed to Allied military victories (Johnson, Paul, p. 782).

By the end of the war the U.S. was an economic and military super-power with global influence and responsibilities. World War Two, like the Great War before it, "left small fires burning" and "the United States and Russia confronted each other for 40 years in a Cold War" as "liberated colonies split apart" and older nations assumed "the task of policing where some liberation army is raiding and massacring in order to cut up still further a nation carved out of a larger unit" (Barzun, p. 762). The Coast Guard Reserve Act of 1939 was designed to train civilians to assist the Coast Guard in monitoring a growing number of pleasure boaters in ceremonial and marine safety matters. In February 1941 Congress restructured the Coast Guard Reserve. The civilian component was named the Coast Guard Auxiliary. The Coast Guard Reserve was mandated to provide a pool of trained military personnel reserve similar to the pattern and purpose of U.S. Army, Army Air Force, Navy and Marine reserve units. A "Temporary Reservist" (TR) was an unpaid volunteer who served for a limited time, usually close to home. "Regular Reservists" could be assigned when and where needed and were paid while on duty.

During World War Two 115,000 people served in the Reserve, including 12,000 Women's Reserve "SPARS" (Chambers, p. 146). On 23 November 1942 Congress created the Women's Reserve of the Coast Guard, modeled after the newly created U.S. Navy Women's Reserves ("WAVES"). Female Coast Guard Reservists initially could not serve outside of the U.S. or in combat situations.

U.S. Coast Guard Captain Dorothy C. Stratton, a Purdue University dean, directed the wartime Coast Guard Women's Reserve and originated the nickname "SPARS" based on *Semper Paratus*, Always Ready, the Service motto. The 12,000 SPAR personnel, including 1,000 officers and civilian employees, performed clerical and other functions at the Washington, D.C. Coast Guard headquarters and other stations. Women earned most of the Coast Guard rates from yeoman to boatswain. In 1944 Congress lifted the ban on stationing women outside the continental United States. After the war women served in regular and reserve Coast Guard units. In the 1970's women began to be accepted into all of the regular U.S. armed forces and the service academies (Chambers, p. 669).

The Coast Guard Auxiliary and the Coast Guard Reserve acquired permanent status after World War Two (Chambers, p. 146). Another significant institutional change occurred in March 1942 when the Bureau of Marine Inspection and Navigation was transferred from the Department of Commerce to the U.S. Coast Guard (Chambers, p. 145).

To meet wartime safety and construction needs the Coast Guard placed temporary and reserve officers in the Marine Inspection Office and recruited merchant marine officers (Kaplan and Hunt, p. 155). Marine Inspection Office responsibilities include regular inspection of merchant vessels to ensure the proper operation and maintenance of loading, fire safety, and life saving equipment; the investigation of

merchant mariner casualties and disciplinary problems; and the issuing of merchant vessel inspection and license certificates. Coast Guard officers and enlisted personnel carry out the inspections and examine ship logs. Serious problems may subject merchant marine officers, crew members and company officials to U.S. Coast Guard hearings and fines. Punishments include license and certificate suspension or revocation (Johnson, R.E., pp. 201-202).

The Bureau of Merchant Marine Inspection monitors maritime safety. MMI specialists have made essential contributions in peace and war, but it was fortuitous that the BMMI was created during World War Two.

To prepare for wartime duty, white cutters and patrol boats were painted with camouflage, equipped with heavier armament, depth charge and sonar equipment, and assigned to convoy escort duty and submarine patrol.

Coast Guard officers and enlisted personnel manned more than 350 U.S. Navy ships, boats, troop transports and landing craft, and more than 280 Army Transportation Corps vessels. During the D-Day (Normandy, France) invasion of continental Europe, Coast Guard patrol boats rescued hundreds of battle survivors. Coast Guardsmen joined in most of the amphibious campaigns in the European and Pacific theaters of operation.

The Coast Guard patrolled Greenland waters before and during the war. The legendary Lieutenant Commander Edward H. "Iceberg" Smith commanded the Greenland Patrol which consisted of cutters and tug boats. The cutter Northland made the first wartime naval capture when it seized a German trawler in September 1941.

Converted merchant and civilian craft under Coast Guard command contributed to the war effort. In June 1944 the first helicopter landing on board a cutter took place on the cutter Cobb. The first racially integrated naval crew (1943) sailed on the cutter Sea Cloud, a converted yacht and weather ship.

The significant contributions of the Coast Guard in World War Two are illustrated by the following statistics: 28 Coast Guard manned vessels were sunk; 572 Coast Guardsmen were killed in action out of a total of 1,030 wartime fatalities; eleven enemy submarines were sunk by Coast Guard manned vessels and one by a Coast Guard airplane; and more than 4,000 battle survivors were plucked from the sea (Chambers, p. 145).

The Coast Guard was involved in a controversial and tragic incident prior to U.S. entry into the war. As the brutality of Hitler's anti-Semitic genocidal policies became clear, thousands of European Jews tried to escape from continental Europe. The Hamburg-American line passenger vessel SS St. Louis entered the harbor at Havana, Cuba (27 May 1939) with nearly 1,000 Jewish refugees. Refused entry, the captain steamed up the eastern coast of the United States within sight of Miami and other ports. The U.S. State Department ignored the pleas of negotiators to let the Jews land, and a Coast Guard cutter trailed the St. Louis with orders to return any passengers to the vessel who tried to escape. On 6 June, Captain Gustav Schroeder set an easterly course, "bearing his doomed cargo back to Europe." The captain deposited his passengers in Belgium, Holland, France and Britain, but, within two years Germany controlled Western continental Europe "exposing the Jews to Nazi reprisals" (Kennedy, pp. 417-18).

Only 240 Jewish passengers from the St. Louis were alive at the end of the war. Many of the 181 Jews who disembarked in Holland ended up in the infamous Auschwitz (Poland) concentration camp (Gilbert, pp. 248-9, 521).

After this diplomatic tragedy, the Coast Guard went on to perform valiantly in World War Two and contributed significantly to the role sea power played in the conflict.

In the Mediterranean and Atlantic, carrier-borne aircraft assisted land-based planes in the sinking of 60% of the German U-boats, diminishing the threat enemy submarines posed to communication and supply lines. Allied sea power steadily constricted Japanese control of the Pacific after 1942 in major maritime confrontations which decimated the Japanese fleet (Margiotta, pp. 26-27).

In 1940, under the authority of the Espionage Act of 1917 and the new Dangerous Cargo Act, Coast Guard regular and reserve personnel were trained to inspect and police vital harbor areas to protect ships from sabotage, prevent or respond to fires and explosions, and monitor the ships of belligerent nations. The USCG took several vessels into custody after acquiring evidence of pro-Axis activities.

In May 1941, while the U.S. was still officially neutral but monitoring convoy routes, the cutters Northland, General Greene and Modoc came within range and near collision with the German battleship Bismarck which had sunk the HMS Hood. The Bismarck was later sunk by the Royal Navy southwest of Ireland (Kaplan and Hunt, p. 60). During the naval battle between British warships and the Bismarck, the Modoc was nearly hit by the German vessel's anti-aircraft shells and narrowly missed being attacked by the HMS Prince of Wales which belatedly recognized the cutter (Willoughby, p. 97).

Commander Edward "Iceberg" Smith (USCG) had the oceanographic expertise and knowledge of the region to prepare him to lead the Greenland Patrol (1941) in command of the cutters Raritan, Comanche, Modoc, Bowdoin, Northland, Bear, and North Star. Ordered to keep the convoy routes open; escort ships; carry supplies; find and destroy Nazi ships, submarines and radio and weather stations; and perform search and rescue missions, Smith and his intrepid fleet were kept busy.

Commander Smith organized a Danish and Eskimo (Inuit) dog sled patrol which discovered a German radio shack. A landing party from the Northland under Lieutenant Leroy McCluskey (USCG) secured the radio shack and took three surprised German radio operators into custody (12 September 1941), three months before the official entry of the U.S. into World War Two.

As part of the Lend-Lease plan, President Roosevelt (10 April 1941) transferred 10 Coast Guard cutters to Britain. U.S. military forces set up bases in Greenland. Coast Guard personnel in the Greenland military operation established aids to navigation and radio beacons in often inclement weather conditions (Kaplan and Hunt, pp. 60-62).

Roosevelt's Lend-Lease donation to Britain was generous and controversial. Prior to the Japanese attack on Pearl Harbor only 3 Coast Guard cutters remained at the Pacific base when Rear Admiral Claude C. Bloch, Commandant, Fourteenth Naval District, instructed the USCG "to put vessels outside to run up and down and listen for (enemy) submarines" (Prange, Goldstein, Dillon, pp. 390, 406-07).

The Coast Guard's responsibility for maintaining aids to navigation involves complex technology. In 1940 the British were using radar to track incoming German bombers. In 1941 civilian scientists from the Massachusetts Institute of Technology and American Telephone and Telegraph Company laboratories learned about a new British radio navigation system designed to guide bombers to targets on the European continent. Admiral Russell R. Waesche, the distinguished World War II Coast Guard Commandant, assigned Commander Lawrence M. Harding, an expert on radio aids to aerial navigation, to collaborate with other federal agencies to establish an accurate triangulating system for determining ship and aircraft locations (Johnson, R.E., p. 220).

The electronic aid to navigation system was named LORAN ("Long Range Navigation") by Commander Harding. It became a valuable war and peace time navigational supplement for military and civilian ships and aircraft which crossed the high seas and traversed the continents. The Loran system complemented the high endurance cutters assigned to designated patrol regions (Ocean Stations) in the vast and unpredictable waters and weather of the Atlantic and Pacific. Ocean Station vessels radioed iceberg and weather reports, collected oceanographic data, and performed search and rescue missions for ships, boats, and aircraft in distress (Chambers, pp. 145-46).

The pulse transmitting navigational aid exceeded the radar range by 50 to 100 miles. To experiment with the system, civilian scientists used two inactive Coast Guard lifeboat stations in Delaware (Fenwick Island) and New York (Montauk, Long Island). After Pearl Harbor, U.S. Navy Research and Development Coordinator Rear Admiral Julius A. Furer became interested in this long range navigational aid system. After consultation with the Joint Chiefs of Staff and Naval Operations, U.S. Navy officials requested the assistance of the Coast Guard. So, now the newly promoted Coast Guard Captain Lawrence Harding coordinated his activities with the U.S. Navy, U.S. Army Engineers, MIT, and the Royal Canadian Navy which provided experimental sites in Nova Scotia.

In 1943 the British Admiralty became involved. Loran stations were constructed in Britain, Canada, Iceland, Danish Greenland, the Aleutian Islands of Alaska, and several Asian and Pacific island locations (Willoughby, pp. 150-68).

Coast Guard personnel have served civilian and military communication and safety needs from Loran stations around the globe from World War Two to the present. The duty stations range from pleasant to extreme, to lonely and dangerous posts in the World War Two Pacific, to unmarked territory close to enemy troops in the Vietnam War.

Before and during the U.S. involvement in World War Two, German submarine commanders torpedoed American and foreign commercial ships off the Atlantic and Gulf coasts. The toll included several U.S. Navy and Coast Guard vessels. The Coast Guard cutter Acacia was sunk by a U-boat on 15 March 1942 en route to the British West Indies.

On 9 May 1942 the cutter Icarus (Lieutenant Commander Maurice Jester, USCG) depth charged U-352 to the surface off Cape Lookout (North Carolina). Heavy gun fire from the cutter kept German sailors away from their deck gun, forcing them to abandon the vessel before it was rammed. The submarine was destroyed and 33 German survivors lived to tell the story.

The 327-foot cutters Spencer and Campbell patrolled U-boat infested North Atlantic waters equipped with high-frequency direction finders which allowed them to protect convoys by precisely locating enemy submarines. In February 1943 the Spencer peeled away from a 63 ship convoy to fire upon and depth charge a U-boat whose fate is unsure, but was believed to have been sunk.

In the following days, the excitement continued when a U-boat surfaced alongside the Campbell. Commander (later Vice Admiral and Assistant Commandant) James A. Hirshfield bore down on a collision course with blazing guns, killing the German skipper and several crew members. Upon impact with the submarine, the cutter was seriously damaged but managed to take 12 enemy sailors into custody. Commander Hirshfield's courage in battle earned him the Navy Cross (Kaplan and Hunt, pp. 65-68).

World War Two chronicles have been revised by new discoveries. In June 2001 marine archeologists affirmed the discovery of a World War Two German submarine made by British Petroleum and Shell Oil Company in the Gulf of Mexico while surveying for an oil pipeline.

C and C Technologies identified the wreck as the U-166 which was sunk by Coast Guard patrol boat PC-566 45 miles from the mouth of the Mississippi River after it torpedoed the American passenger freighter Robert E. Lee. A tugboat and two Navy vessels rescued all but 25 of the 268 passengers and crew. The belatedly affirmed cutter kill changed the historic record which had erroneously credited the U-166 sinking to an aircraft two days after the event (McConnaughey, A.P., 6/9/01).

Admiral Samuel Eliot Morison (USN) wrote an acclaimed 15 volume naval history of World War Two. The Harvard historian dedicated his work to the wartime shipmates with whom he sailed on Navy and Coast Guard vessels, including the U.S.C.G.C. Campbell. Morison chronicled the effectiveness of the "Treasury" class cutter and described the tragedy of the U.S.C.G.C. Alexander Hamilton, torpedoed ten miles from Iceland (29 January 1942) and sunk while towing a disabled U.S. Navy supply ship (Morison, p. 105).

Morison explained the importance and complexity of the transatlantic convoys, including the February 1943 fleet composed of Coast Guard cutters, British and Canadian corvettes, and a Polish destroyer, all of which performed valiantly in dangerous and heavy seas. Of the 63 merchant ships, seven were lost, and, as Morison described, two U-boats were sunk, "one by Spencer with depth charges" and "one by Campbell through ramming and gunfire after the Polish destroyer (Barza) had depth charged it" ((Morison, p. 241).

Clay Blair's masterful 2 volume history of Hitler's submarine war in the Atlantic chronicles U.S. Navy and Coast Guard action, the operations and technology of U-boats, and the fate of their commanding officers and crews. The author mentioned several Coast Guard cutters, including the Thetis (Lieutenant, j.g. Nelson C. McCormick) which sank U-157 off Key West, Florida (June 1942). Blair does not neglect the courageous Allied merchant seamen who brought food and equipment to every theater of war, sometimes at the price of high casualty rates in frigid or burning waters (Blair, Hitler's U-Boat War: The Hunters, 1939-1942, Vol. I.; Blair, Hitler's U-Boat War: The Hunted, 1942-1945; and Johnson, R.E., p. 238).

Admiral Morison (USNR) commended the work of the civilian Coastal Picket Patrol organized by the Coast Guard in 1942. This "Hooligan Navy" of motor boats and yachts, often skippered by their owners, were armed with depth charges and small weapons. Empowered to monitor U-boat locations, 550 such vessels patrolled the ocean and Gulf coasts. No "kills" were made, but these civilian sailors, Morison wrote, endured dangerous seas and were completely vulnerable to the deck guns of surfaced U-boats. After 1943, active duty Coast Guard regulars and reservists assumed the picket patrol in well armed 83 foot patrol boats.

The Civil Air Patrol performed valuable and courageous service. Civilian fliers spotted ship wrecks, raft and lifeboat survivors, and 173 German submarines. The Hooligan Navy and the CAP received no pay, but, Morison explained, their crews consisted of "people who wanted to serve.....and sacrifice" (Morison, pp. 131-32).

The noted naval historian commended the regular and reserve crew members who operated small craft which were "forced to perform functions and make long voyages for which they had not been designed" (Morison, p. 585). Admiral Morison did not neglect the U.S. Merchant Marine which, he proclaimed, "deserves high praise for its world wide operations which were indispensable to the Navy, Army and our Allies. Merchant mariners and the Naval Armed Guards on the ships showed exemplary courage in convoy duty" in the Atlantic and Pacific theaters of combat (Morison, p. 586).

The cross-channel invasion from Britain to French Normandy and continental Europe by Allied military forces (6 June-25 July 1944) was the beginning of the end for Hitler's Germany. Allied naval and ground forces put pressure on the Nazis from the West as the Soviet army pushed toward Germany from the East.

The Normandy invasion (Operation Overlord) commenced on what military planners designated as "D-Day." General Dwight D. Eisenhower (USA) was the commander of the massive naval and army assault. Beach front landing zones had names like Utah, Omaha, Juno and Sword. The U.S. Coast Guard commanded 83 foot rescue patrol boats which saved thousands of Allied lives. Coastguardsmen served as combat photographers and handled various kinds of landing craft categorized as: LCA (landing craft assault); LCC (primary control vessel); LCI (landing craft infantry); LCM (landing craft medium); LCT (landing craft tank); LST (landing ship tank); LCTR (landing craft rocket); and the LCVP (landing craft vehicle and personnel), generally known as the Higgins boat (Ambrose, pp. 585-586).

D-Day historian Stephen E. Ambrose was told by General Eisenhower that if Andrew "Higgins had not designed and built those LCVPs, we never could have landed over an open beach. The whole strategy of the war would have been different." Eisenhower said Higgins "is the man who won the war for us" (Ambrose, p. 45).

Andrew Jackson Higgins designed racing motorboats, Prohibition-era rum running boats, and the fast patrol boats which the Coast Guard used to pursue the rum runners. The Higgins boat was the landing craft used by U.S. Marines in the Guadalcanal invasion. Higgins influenced the design of the well armed PT patrol boats of Pacific war fame and several types of landing craft (Dunnigan and Nofi, The Pacific War, p. 268).

Most of the LCVP coxswains were members of the Coast Guard. Their ranks included white and African-American personnel, a rarity in this period of the segregated armed forces (Ambrose, pp. 260, 372).

The U.S. Coast Guard commanded 97 D-Day vessels and the landing craft carried on three troop transports. Coast Guard personnel served on other ships with U.S. Navy crews. Lieutenant Commander Alexander V. Steward (USCGR) commanded the 60 wooden 83-foot rescue cutters that crossed the English Channel with the troop transports as part of the Rescue Flotilla suggested by President Roosevelt.

The fast rescue boats dodged German gunners and fighter pilots, mines and underwater obstructions and saved 1,437 soldiers and a female nurse. The landing craft brought tanks and other vehicles, artillery, supplies and troops to the beaches and wounded and dead personnel back to larger naval vessels at sea.

The 492-foot attack transport USS Bayfield, under the command of Captain Lyndon Spencer (USCG), landed troops on the beach, doubled as a hospital ship, served as the flag ship of Rear Admiral Don P. Moon (USN), commander of the naval assault force, and was the headquarters of U.S. Army and U.S. Army Air Force liaison officers.

Captain Edward E. Fritzche (USCG) commanded the USS Samuel Chase which unloaded supplies, infantry troops, vehicles and three small aircraft. The 328-foot LSTs off loaded personnel, supplies, trucks and freight cars. Captain Miles H. Imlay (USCG) commanded twenty LCI(L's), large 158-foot infantry landing craft.

Commander Quentin R. Walsh (USCG) led a 16 person U.S. Navy commando reconnaissance team into the French port of Cherbourg. The unit killed snipers, freed more than 50 captured U.S. paratroopers, and took several hundred German prisoners (Chandler and Collins, pp. 159-61).

Illustrative of the courage of U.S. armed forces personnel was the crew of patrol cutter CG-16 (Lieutenant j.g. R.V. McPhail) which rescued the crew of a sinking, burning LCT under fire and carrying ammunition. Volunteers went on board during the conflagration and rescued all the wounded. Fifteen CG-16 crew members and Lieutenant McPhail received the Navy and Marine Corps medal for bravery (Willoughby, pp. 250-51).

The naval component of Operation Overlord was called Operation Neptune. A British naval officer paid tribute to Lieutenant j.g. George Clarke of, as Royal Navy Commander Kenneth Edwards put it, "the United States Coast Guard Service." Clarke "drove his cutter," Edwards explained, "through the flames and rescued the survivors of a British landing craft carrying high-octane petrol to the beach." The Lieutenant was decorated for his valor by the British Admiralty (Edwards, p. 158). Lieutenant Clarke (USCG) modestly described the mission in his report: "Survivors rescued, five. Corpses, none. Comments, none" (Willoughby, pp. 251-52).

Intelligence played a significant role in the defeat of Japanese Imperial naval, air and ground forces. Wireless telegraph and radio communications were used by all the belligerent governments and armed services. Efficiency in communication and privacy were facilitated by the coded messages military units transmitted. But countermeasures developed by cryptologists (code breakers) allowed the coded messages to be intercepted and used to strategic advantage. The U.S. Army and Navy began to use cryptanalysis just before World War I, and specially trained personnel became quite proficient in the 1920's.

The U.S. military and diplomatic services were decoding Japanese messages before the attack on Pearl Harbor. Unfortunately, the plethora of messages transmitted by Japan overwhelmed the analysts. U.S. officials correctly concluded the Japanese planned to attack American and European territory in the Pacific, but did not know precisely where.

After Pearl Harbor, the Federal Bureau of Investigation and the U.S. Army and Navy successfully intercepted Japanese communications. A U.S. Coast Guard intelligence unit assisted the Navy (Spector, pp. 445-46; 454).Coast Guard forces served under the U.S. Navy in the Pacific. Coast Guard crews served on Navy vessels and independently on ships and landing craft during assaults on Japanese-held islands. As in the European theater, Coastguardsmen ran a variety of landing craft, ships and gunboats variously equipped with armor, mortar and rockets (Morison, p. xxvi). Coast Guard officers and enlisted personnel operated anti-aircraft guns, rifles and machine guns which took a toll on Japanese troops, bombers and fighter aircraft.

The military services are a microcosm of society at large. Unfortunately, racism existed in the segregated armed forces. Black personnel served in the military as labor troops, stewards and mess personnel. Nonetheless, many African-Americans distinguished themselves in battle and suffered significant casualty rates.

The Coast Guard had a history of recruiting African-Americans. Two white rum runners killed a black Coastguardsman during Prohibition and were executed for their crime. Naval shipboard personnel had to man battle stations during general quarters drills, so in World War Two African-American Coastguardsmen could be seen at their stations aiming and firing 20mm antiaircraft guns in the Pacific (Dunnigan and Nofi, The Pacific War, pp. 101-02).

Japanese-Americans served honorably in the European and Pacific theaters while, sadly and ironically, their parents and relatives were confined to "relocation centers" in response to racism, national security and safety concerns, and fear of sabotage and espionage. A contrite society spent decades after the war settling Japanese-American compensation claims in the court system.

Women served in the armed forces at home and overseas. Nurses risked their lives to treat wounded soldiers in combat zones. Some female service personnel were killed or became prisoners of war in the Pacific theater. Whether performing medical, clerical or active military duties, women served with courage and honor.

Uniformed female Coast Guard personnel, called SPARS from the Coast Guard motto "Sempar Paratus" (Always Ready), numbered 12,000 in World War Two. They performed clerical and office management duties and served as radar operators and carpenters. Some served at sea. The Coast Guard honored their service in the name of the cutter Spars. Women served in the Army Nurse Corps, Women's Army Auxiliary Corps, Women Air Service Pilots, and the Marine Corps Reserves. Women joined the U.S. Navy in the Navy Nurse Corps and the WAVES (Dunnigan and Nofi, Pacific War, pp. 653-54).

Armed forces personnel suffered high casualties in the Pacific War due to fanatical enemy resistance and the logistical and tactical challenges of amphibious assaults on enemy-held islands. The U.S. Navy suffered a killed to wounded ratio of 49.5% out of an approximate 75,000 casualties. The Coast Guard suffered 575 killed out of 1,000 casualties, a 57% ratio. U.S. Marines suffered the heaviest losses in the Pacific because they were usually given the most difficult attack assignments (Dunnigan and Nofi, Pacific War, p. 142).

Pacific theater geography consisted of steamy, tropical jungles and coral reef barriers to isolated and heavily defended enemy-held islands. Vast and often stormy seas in the South Pacific balanced the arctic cold and storms of the North Pacific and Bering Sea. U.S. forces confronted Japanese aircraft, warships and troops in the inhospitable Aleutian Island chain which stretched southwest of the Alaskan mainland.

With dates indicating the beginning of Allied offensive military operations, the Aleutian campaign involved the islands of Kiska (August 1943) and Attu (May 1943), and the Japanese bombing of Dutch Harbor (June 1942). Other Pacific campaigns listed in geographic and military annals include the more southerly tropical and subtropical islands of Guadalcanal (August 1942), New Guinea (August 1942), Tarawa (November 1943), Guam (July 1944), Kwajalein (January 1944), Saipan (June 1944), Iwo Jima (February 1945), Okinawa (April 1945), and the Philippines (October 1944-April 1945). The Southwest Pacific Theater of Operations (1942-1945) encompassed the waters off northern and eastern Australia, south and east of New Guinea, the Coral and Bismarck seas, and the Solomon Islands (Dunnigan and Nofi, The Pacific War, pp. x-xii).

Wake Island, 2000 miles west of Hawaii, had a small U.S. Navy-Marine garrison which protected a Pan American Airlines base and civilian construction workers. The initial Japanese assault was defeated by gallant civilians and military personnel, but enemy military forces eventually prevailed (December 1941). Japanese land and sea forces attacked the Aleutians (June 1942) in an attempt to divert U.S. forces from an unsuccessful attack on Midway in the same month (Dunnigan and Nofi, The Pacific War, pp. 418-21; 645-46).

Small Army and Navy garrisons in the Aleutians did not reflect the strategic importance of the snow and fog bound island chain. Japanese forces struck the Aleutian port of Dutch Harbor in June of 1942. The Coast Guard's presence in Alaska and surrounding waters dated back to the law enforcement, search and rescue, and supply and medical services provided by the Revenue Marine Service. Coast Guard cutters and aircraft transported supplies and military personnel from the other armed services and supported military operations against the Japanese while maintaining aids to navigation.

The Alaskan Defense Command was led by Major General Simon B. Buckner (USA) who coordinated the Aleutian campaign with Royal Canadian military forces. Rear Admiral Robert A. Theobald (USN), Commander North Pacific Force, had a few destroyers, submarines and Coast Guard cutters under his control. In May 1942 Captain Ralph C. Parker (USNR), Commander of the Alaskan Sector, had two old destroyers, three Coast Guard cutters, and 10 Catalina reconnaissance planes at his disposal.

No cutters were sunk in the Aleutian campaign but several landing craft were destroyed. Coast Guard cutters supported Navy and Army sea, land and air attacks against the Japanese. The cutter Onondaga (Lt. Cmdr. Steward P. Mehlman) called general quarters and drove off several attacking Japanese fighter planes over Dutch Harbor (3 June 1942). U.S. Navy, Marine and Canadian forces tracked and engaged Japanese forces. Coast Guard search and rescue operations saved the lives of civilian and military personnel in the Aleutian operations.

The Coast Guard cutter McLane (Lt. Ralph Burns, USCG) and Coast Guard manned U.S. Navy craft searched for and depth charged a Japanese submarine. Captain Paul K. Perry (USCG) commanded the USS Arthur Middleton, one of the transports used in landing operations. Later, a Coast Guard landing craft (Lt. Cmdr. R.R. Smith, USCG) rescued U.S. Navy personnel from a destroyer grounded in gale force winds. The Coast Guard crew was added to the list of the hundreds of Coastguardsmen who earned medals for valor from the U.S. Army, Marines, Army Air Force, Coast Guard, and foreign nations and military services (Willoughby, pp. 181-91; 311-32).

The Aleutian campaign lasted for nine months after the battle of Midway. Naval bombardments were of little significance, but U.S. submarines took a significant toll on Japanese merchant shipping. Rear Admiral Charles H. McMorris (USN) fought a four hour battle against a superior Japanese force around the Komandorski Islands at eight to ten mile ranges. One of the U.S. ships suffered serious damage. Luckily, as the Japanese fleet was closing in, Vice Admiral Hosogaya inexplicably terminated hostilities and withdrew (Morison, pp. 266-70).

In May 1943, the U.S. Army 7th Infantry Division landed on Attu and defeated a suicide charge by 1,000 Japanese troops. In the end, U.S. military forces learned more about tactics and strategy in sea and air campaigns against the Japanese and freed the north Pacific of further enemy threats (Morison, pp. 271-72).

By August 1943, after a one month bombing campaign, the U.S. Armed Forces had coordinated 35,000 troops and a sea armada of nearly 100 ships to drive the Japanese military from the Aleutians, only to find that the last of the enemy forces had been evacuated in a dense fog by the Japanese Navy. The Aleutian campaign was proportionately one of the bloodiest and costly campaigns of the war (Spector, pp. 181-82).

American losses in the Aleutian campaign were about one-fourth of the 4,000 Japanese fatalities. Japan lost 9 transports, 5 submarines, 3 destroyers, and 200 aircraft. U.S. aviation engineers benefited from the capture of an intact Japanese Zero fighter plane.

In the extreme Aleutian weather conditions, the U.S. lost 500 aircraft plus 100 in battle, one submarine and three destroyers. Ten thousand Japanese troops were tied up in the Aleutians for 14 months, along with 300,000 American troops stationed in the islands and on mainland Alaska, plus hundreds of soldiers in the engineering units building the strategic Canadian-Alaskan (ALCAN) Highway.

U.S. military operations in the Aleutian campaign were coordinated with the Royal Canadian Army, Navy and Air Force. Twelve U.S. cruisers and destroyers and three U.S. battleships were confined to the Aleutians during the campaign and not available for the South Pacific (Dunnigan and Nofi, The Pacific War, pp. 38-41).

The 327 foot Coast Guard cutter Taney performed distinguished service in the Pacific. At Pearl Harbor the cutter crew drove away Japanese fighter aircraft and depth charged an enemy submarine. During the Battle of Okinawa (1945) the Taney shot down five Japanese combat aircraft. In the Korean War (1950-1953) the Taney provided meteorological and communications support while on Pacific Ocean station duty. In the Vietnam War (1969) the cutter patrolled the South China Sea along the South Vietnamese coast, monitoring enemy activities and assisting South Vietnamese and U.S. forces with gun fire support (Kaplan and Hunt, p. 163).

The cutters Cyane, Haida, Onondaga, Atalanta, and Aurora guarded convoys in the Gulf of Alaska and the Aleutians. The Coast Guard manned huge U.S. Navy transportation ships in the Pacific. One of them, the USS Wakefield, was hit by Japanese bombers while refueling in the British port of Singapore (30 January 1942). Five crew members were killed and nine were wounded. Despite the attack, the transport disembarked the troops and evacuated 500 women and children to Bombay (India) where the vessel was repaired.

The Coast Guard manned USS Hunter Liggett carrying U.S. Marines participated in the Guadalcanal invasion (7 August 1942) along with 22 other transports, eighteen of which had Coast Guard personnel mixed with U.S. Navy crews. Coast Guard gunners on the Liggett shot down several Japanese aircraft and picked up U.S. and Australian survivors when their cruisers were sunk in battle (Johnson, E.R., pp. 240-42).

Coast Guard and Navy landing craft crews suffered high casualty rates from air attacks and shore fire. Coast Guard petty officer Douglas A. Munro was in the landing party Liggett skipper Lt. Cmdr. Dwight H. Dexter (USCG) took ashore to set up a base site on Guadalcanal. On 27 September 1942 Munro volunteered to lead several landing craft in a rescue mission when Marines came under withering Japanese gun fire. Munro fired at the enemy with light weapons and positioned his craft to shield the Marines while other boats completed the evacuation. Killed in action, Munro posthumously received the Medal of Honor for gallantry in combat (Johnson, E.R., pp. 242-43).

Petty Officer Munro had previously rescued the two crew members of a downed U.S. Navy dive bomber before the fatal mission which rescued 500 U.S. Marines. Munro's portrait was hung in the enlisted barracks of Munro Hall at the U.S. Coast Guard Academy (New London, Connecticut). The World War Two hero is the namesake of the Coast Guard cutter Munro (WHEC-724) which was constructed at the Avondale Shipyards in New Orleans (Kaplan and Hunt, pp. 283-86).

Coast Guard crews manned thirty 83-foot rescue boats in the Philippines and 24 in other Pacific islands. The dangers naval crews faced while running transportation and supply vessels is illustrated by the fate of the Coast Guard manned U.S. Navy LST Serpens. While loading depth charges off Guadalcanal (29 January 1945) an explosion occurred killed 197 Coastguardsmen and 57 Army crewmen. A Coast Guard manned gasoline tanker avoided a similar fate when its crew escaped the capsized vessel after it grounded in a storm off Iwo Jima (6 June 1945).

The ships of the Army Transportation Corps were manned by Coast Guard crews and included tankers, repair ships, tug boats, and freight supply (FS) vessels. The Coast Guard manned 200 such vessels. As the end of 1944, 7,000 Coast Guard officers and enlisted personnel ran Army ships. Captain Frank T. Kenner (USCG) headed the Coast Guard-Army unit which administered the force.

The 180-foot FS cargo vessels were called Pacific "island hoppers." Drawing 9 feet of draft, they ferried personnel, mail and supplies, often returning with the bodies of combat personnel which were buried in temporary New Guinea graves. A few vessels sank in typhoons or ran up on reefs in poorly charted waters. Several came under attack from enemy warships and submarines. FS 255 lost four crew members in a torpedo attack (Johnson, R.E., pp. 246, 252-254).

So ended the tumultuous 1930s and '40s and the Coast Guard at war. Before World War Two erupted relations between the U.S. and

Japan were contentious. Some analysts thought the Japanese shot down famed pilot Amelia Earhart (1937) because she allegedly flew over a secret Japanese Pacific base. Evidence has not confirmed that conspiracy theory. The USCG cutter Itasca was in the vicinity of Earhart's Howland island destination providing a radio beacon for the scheduled flight path. Transmission failures from Earhart's plane caused radio contact to be lost.

The aircraft carrier Lexington joined USCGC Itasca in an unsuccessful search for Earhart and navigator Fred J. Noonan. Researchers concluded radio navigation errors caused Earhart to veer off course, run out of fuel, and crash into the sea (CGHO Document Created January 1998).

In 1944 the Coast Guard responded to a Navy Department directive and authorized the enlistment of African-American females. Yeoman Second Class Olivia J. Hooker, the first black woman to become a SPAR, recalled "there were six nurses of my heritage who were ensigns" (CGHO Document Updated: January 1999).

The SPARS were disbanded after the war, but female enlistments in the Coast Guard grew to 2,800 by 1992, constituting 7% of the total number of USCG personnel ("Pioneers...," Associated Press, Post Bulletin, 11/92).

Before the end of the war (1945) the USN and USCG secretly trained 12,000 Russian officers and men to operate vessels scheduled for transfer to the Soviet Union under the Lend-Lease program. The training mission was to prepare the Soviet Navy for the expected invasion of the Japanese homeland. Training took place in the Aleutian islands. The Japanese surrender (August 1945) ended Project Hula (Russell, R.A., "Project Hula," 1997).

The fate of the USS Biscayne directly influenced post-war Coast Guard training. Commissioned in the U.S. Navy (1942), the Biscayne served in the Pacific, European and African theaters. Decommissioned at the end of the war, the Biscayne was transferred to the Coast Guard and recommissioned as the Dexter (1946) to serve as a North Atlantic weather patrol vessel. In 1958 the Dexter (WAVP-385) was assigned as a training ship to the Reserve Training Center, Government Island, Alameda, California (Ostrom, personal papers, Periodicals).

In his official reports, combined in "U.S. Navy at War: 1941-1945," Admiral Ernest J. King (USN) chronicled the contributions of the U.S. Coast Guard in the Atlantic, Mediterranean and Pacific Theaters (King, pp. 27-28; 74-76; 159-60; 222-24; 232; 292-93). Commander of the U.S. Fleet and Chief of Naval Operations, Admiral King wrote: "During the period of this report, the Navy...the Fleet, the shore establishments, the Marine Corps, the Coast Guard, the WAVES, the Seabees, have all nobly done their parts. Each has earned an individual 'well done,' but hereafter all are included in the term, 'The Navy'" (King, p. 3).

The contributions and costs to the Coast Guard are well illustrated by the CGC Escanaba which suffered one of the highest losses in a single engagement in the war. Four months after rescuing 133 survivors from the sinking of a transport ship, the 165 foot Escanaba was escorting a convoy from Greenland to Newfoundland. On 13 June 1943 the cutter was torpedoed and sank in less than five minutes (Kaplan and Hunt, p. 288). Lieutenant Commander Carl U. Peterson and 100 members of the crew drowned. Two enlisted men were rescued by other ships in the convoy (Johnson, R.E., p. 226).

Admiral Chester W. Nimitz (USN) succeeded Admiral King as the post-war Chief of Naval Operations. Nimitz paid tribute to the thousands of Coast Guard personnel, Regular and Reserve, who served in World War Two. Nimitz held wartime United States Coast Guard Commandant Admiral Russell R. Waesch "in the highest esteem. It was my privilege to have many of his combatant units under my command during the War." The Coast Guard performed duties at home and overseas, Nimitz concluded, with "dependability," and served "in the highest traditions of their Service (proving) themselves worthy of their Service motto, Semper Paratus...Always Ready" (Willoughby, p. xi).

CHAPTER VII

THE COLD WAR
(1945-1960)

The postwar Coast Guard rebounded from its World War II mission and reverted to the peacetime duties of law enforcement, maritime safety, search and rescue and the new challenges of the Cold War.

The war ended with the Soviet Union in despotic control of its East European satellites behind the Iron Curtain. Mainland China emerged from a bloody civil war as the Communist dictatorship of the People's Republic of China (1949). Anti-Communist forces fled to the island of Taiwan and established the Republic of (Nationalist) China.

In 1956 guerrilla forces under Fidel Castro began a military campaign against Cuban dictator Fulgencio Batista. Castro's forces overthrew the Batista government in 1959 and executed many of his supporters. In 1960 Castro confiscated U.S. property. The U.S. retaliated by putting an export embargo on Cuba. In 1961 the U.S. categorized Cuba as a Soviet satellite and terminated diplomatic relations. Castro imposed a Marxist-Leninist dictatorship and joined the Communist Bloc (Urdang, pp. 366, 370, 372, 374).

The Cold War brought conflict and controversial boundaries to the Korean peninsula and Vietnam. Communist North Korea supported by China, the Soviet Union and Eastern Europe, faced off against Western backed South Korea. The Korean peninsula was divided by international agreement at the 38th parallel. The Korean War (1950-53) began with the North Korean invasion of South Korea. The response of the United States and several United Nations allies was called a "police action." The war ended with the Korean peninsula still divided at the 38th parallel. U.S. troops acquired the ongoing responsibility of policing the boundary with their South Korean allies. The Cold War turned hot in Southeast Asia when France tried to regain control of Indochina after the Japanese were expelled at the end of World War Two (McLean, pp. 79-80, 269, 516).

French control of Indochina came to an end on 7 May 1954 when

Vietnamese Communist (Vietminh) forces under the command of Vo Nguyen Giap overwhelmed the Franco-Vietnamese garrison at Dien Bien Phu. Equipped with Soviet and Chinese weapons, the Vietminh prevented supplies and reinforcements from reaching French troops. France, Britain, the Soviet Union and the People's Republic of China signed the Geneva Accords (1954) with the Vietminh (21 July) which recognized the independence of the Indochinese nations of Laos and Cambodia. Ho Chi Minh returned to Hanoi and control of North Vietnam after eight years in exile. Nearly half a million North Vietnamese fled to South Vietnam on U.S. Navy ships to escape the oppressive Communist regime. Emperor Bao Dai assumed power in South Vietnam. Ngo Dinh Diem's election victory over the Emperor placed the Diem family of Saigon in charge of Vietnam (Daniel, pp. 752-753, 755-756, 758-759).

The 1956 elections scheduled to unify Vietnam under one government were never held. Some historians blame South Vietnamese president Diem for blocking the election because he thought Ho Chi Minh would win. Other historians contend U.S. President Eisenhower opposed the scheduled process because elections in the Communist dictatorship would not be democratic.

Historians refer to the political, economic and geostrategic struggles between the non-Communist and Communist nations as the Cold War because the ideological confrontations generally avoided real war. The Cold War did become hot in Korea and Vietnam. Marxist and non-Marxist military confrontations occurred in postwar civil wars in Latin America, Africa, the Middle East and Southeast Asia (McLean, pp. 79-81, 517).

The U.S. Coast Guard got involved in Cold War politics at home and overseas.

At the end of World War II, Commandant and Vice Admiral Russell R. Waesche led the Coast Guard in its transition from war and subordination to the U.S. Navy to peace, personnel demobilization, and autonomous status. By the end of his career, Waesche achieved the rank of Admiral. In congressional testimony Waesche presented reports and studies which argued against the placement of the Coast Guard under permanent Navy control even though the union was advocated by military officers in both services and several members of Congress. Admiral Waesche's successor, Admiral Joseph Francis Farley, continued the transition phase in his tour of duty as commandant (1946-50).

The postwar demobilization of Coast Guard Reserve members proceeded too rapidly. A critical shortage of enlisted personnel resulted which threatened the Coast Guard mission. Recruiting quotas had to be expanded to supplement the ranks. Former Coast Guard and Navy enlisted personnel and Reserve officers were invited to enlist or reenlist at their previous ranks. Several Coast Guard vessels were acquired from the U.S. Navy and Army to accommodate the personnel needed for search and rescue, ocean station, weather, oceanographic exploration, ice patrol, aids to navigation and merchant marine inspection duties. The USCG received significant publicity in the postwar period from media stories about Coast Guard responses to disabled civilian and military vessels, downed aircraft at sea, and the saving of scores of lives, sometimes at the cost of heroic Service personnel (Johnson, R.E., pp. 257-79).

Cadet training was enhanced by the acquisition (1947) of the Horst Wessel, a three-masted diesel powered bark which had served as a German naval training ship. The ship is now better known as the Coast Guard training cutter Eagle (Johnson, R.E., p. 265).

The expanded Coast Guard mission necessitated the acquisition of more aircraft for stations in the U.S. and overseas. Helicopters, seaplanes, and land based aircraft were added to the fleet. Large craft included the Boeing PB-1G and the Grumman Albatross. Rubber rafts which inflated upon hitting the water replaced aircraft lifeboats. Sturdy icebreakers were acquired, modified or built from scratch. Coast Guard ships and boats were now painted white, except for buoy tenders and tug boats which performed rugged missions better suited to black hulls (Johnson, R.E., pp. 265, 274-76).

The Red Scare period of anti-Communism in the 1950's prompted the Treasury Department to order Coast Guard officials to investigate and take licenses from merchant seamen accused and found guilty of subversive or disloyal activities. Labor unions and other interest groups challenged Coast Guard actions in federal court (Chambers, p. 146).

One historian leveled a devastating critique of Coast Guard policies toward alleged security risks. Professor Ellen Schrecker labeled the anti-Communist era of the1950's as a repressive period in which the FBI and congressional committees ruined careers and lives. Schrecker dismissed the national security threat Communist sympathizers, U.S. Communist Party members, and Soviet agents posed, but conceded the investigators were generally correct in their accusations! Such was the ambivalence reflected in the contest between Cold Warriors and civil libertarians. Schrecker was critical of alleged USCG excesses in voiding the licenses of more than 3,000 longshoremen and merchant seamen suspected of radical sympathies. The Coast Guard enforced security regulations and laws designed to protect vessels, cargoes and ports from sabotage, espionage, labor strikes and work slow downs (Schrecker, pp. 266-70; 272, 278, 287-88).

The Coast Guard was especially diligent about policing the ports from which military and supply ships sailed to Korean ports during the Korean War. Alleged security risks subjected to federal hearings had the right of appeal. During this critical period, the Coast Guard screened around 500,000 merchant seamen and denied clearance to 3,700. A third of these decisions were reversed in the appeals process (Johnson, R.E., 282).

The United States was in the forefront of monitoring the Soviet Union and China to respond more quickly to regional threats. Dangerous surveillance flights were conducted to accomplish that objective. The toll was costly. Security considerations kept most of those missions and casualties secret. Subsequent declassified documents and interviews with mission survivors reveal a courageous and harrowing pattern of Cold War intrigues. In April 2001 a U.S. Navy reconnaissance aircraft was forced down on Hainan Island by Chinese fighter planes. Negotiations between the administration of President George W. Bush and officials of the People's Republic of China led to the release of the downed crew and the return of the aircraft.

Cold War surveillance missions were dangerous. In January 1953 the Chinese shot down a Navy Neptune patrol bomber and fired on a U.S. destroyer which attempted to rescue the survivors in the Formosa Strait. A U.S. Coast Guard PBM Mariner landed on the water to rescue 11 of the 13 crewmen but crashed and burned on takeoff. U.S. and British air and surface vessels, including a second Coast Guard amphibious plane, converged to rescue several Navy and Coast Guard survivors. Ten of the twenty-one downed U.S. military personnel were eventually rescued, but 10 were MIA (missing in action) and assumed captured or dead (Tart and Keefe, pp. lxx-lxxii).

Thousands of refugees fled from Castro's Cuba. The Coast Guard had the responsibility of enforcing complex and sometimes contradictory federal immigration laws and either denied entry to West Indies emigrants or took them to the U.S. The Coast Guard saved the lives of hundreds of capsized emigrants in the process.

Several controversial and confrontational situations attracted media attention.

Coast Guard icebreakers kept ice-clogged winter sea lanes in the Great Lakes open as early and as long as possible so domestic and foreign cargo vessels could sail from ocean to inland ports. Maritime and navigational history was made in 1957 when three Coast Guard cutters (Bramble, Storis and Spar) sliced their way through frozen Arctic ice from the Canadian west coast (Bellot Strait) to Baffin Bay on the east coast. Coast Guard cutters have navigated to both the northern and southern polar regions (Chambers, p. 146).

Commandant Merlin O'Neill (1950-54), Coast Guard Academy graduate (1921) and commander of the attack transport Leonard Wood (1942-43), was awarded the Legion of Merit. O'Neill served for 12 years at Headquarters and was the first director of the Coast Guard Reserve before being appointed commandant by President Truman.

The Coast Guard was not transferred to the U.S. Navy with the outbreak of the Korean conflict because war was not declared. To avoid the complexities of international alliances and a widened, possibly nuclear war, the United States and the United Nations called the military response to the North Korean invasion of South Korea a "police action." A Coast Guard detachment under the command of Captain George E. McCabe was sent to South Korea before the war to train that nation's coast guard which became the Navy of the Republic of Korea. It was the preference of the U.S. Navy to have the Coast Guard carry out port security, ocean station, and search and rescue duties in the Pacific during the undeclared war.

Organized Reserve Training Units were trained to carry out port security duties in the largest U.S. seaports. By the end of June 1951 the Coast Guard Reserve numbered 8300 personnel, half of whom were enlisted. Petty officers were trained at Coast Guard, Navy and Army schools in port security, law enforcement and explosives loading. Coast Guard recruits (enlisted and officer) were intensively trained at USCG bases in Groton (CT), Cape May (NJ) and Alameda (CA). The officer corps was supplemented with veteran petty and warrant officers and the granting of commissions to college and merchant marine academy graduates.

To meet the need for more Coast Guard vessels, Coast Guard Yard constructed 40, 83, and 95 foot steel hulled, diesel-propelled patrol boats and sea-going cutters (Johnson, R.E., pp. 280-84). Coast Guard Yard at Curtis Bay, Maryland, has a distinguished history dating back to the Spanish-American War when what was then the Revenue Cutter Service needed a base for vessel construction and repair. Lt. John C. Moore, a Revenue Service officer from Baltimore and several colleagues persuaded Captain Charles F. Shoemaker, Chief of the U.S. Revenue Cutter Service, to establish a central facility at Arundel Cove which had a good channel and harbor.

Lt. Moore brought the Revenue cutter Colfax, given to the Revenue Service by the U.S. Navy, into the new facility. The crew became the first Yard employees, a force which grew to over 1,000 skilled workers. Besides vessels, they constructed buoys and other navigation aids. In 1915 the Revenue Service became the U.S. Coast Guard and the facility was named Coast Guard Yard (Brooklyn-Curtis Bay Historical Committee, pp. 1-3).

The Cold War increased the need for Coast Guard port security duty and gave the Service a new mission in 1952. The State Department gave the Coast Guard the responsibility of relaying Voice of America broadcasts to Soviet controlled Eastern Europe. The Coast Guard acquired a 339 foot cargo ship, transformed it into a radio station, renamed the vessel the Courier, and anchored off the Greek island of Rhodes. The ship included a crew of 10 officers, 80 enlisted personnel, and three U.S. Information Agency radio engineers. In 1964 a shore radio station replaced the Courier (Johnson, R.E., pp. 285-86).

Vice Admiral Alfred Carroll Richmond served as Coast Guard Commandant from 1954-62. A legal specialist, Richmond was senior Coast Guard officer on the staff of the commander of U.S. Naval Forces in Europe during World War II, had eight years of sea duty, and came to Coast Guard Headquarters in 1945 with the responsibility of presenting annual budget requests to Congress. Commandant Richmond's first major task was to head off the attempt by the budget conscious Eisenhower administration to merge the Merchant Marine (King's Point, New York) and Coast Guard (New London, Connecticut) academies.

The Coast Guard report to Congress opposing the consolidation stressed the difficulty of blending a civilian commercial maritime mission with law enforcement and military missions, and alluded to the political opposition forthcoming from the New York and Connecticut congressional delegations. The U.S. Coast Guard Academy remained a separate institution. The Coast Guard position prevailed, but may not have had Congress inquired into the Service's officer procurement strategies.

Since 1949 about half of the Coast Guard's merchant marine specialists came from the merchant service. Furthermore, since 1951 the Coast Guard selected university and college graduates for the newly established Officer Candidate School. OCS gradually contributed more officers to the Service than the Academy did. Nonetheless, officers destined to the highest ranks were generally Academy graduates (Johnson, R.E., pp. 295-97).

Along with its traditional duties, the decade of the 1950s illustrated the U.S. Coast Guard's ability to protect lives and property on land as well as at sea. Disastrous floods plagued every region of the nation. Coast Guard aircraft, small boats and large cutters were sent into besieged river valleys and coastal flood plains. Tens of thousands of residents had to leave their homes and hundreds of people died in the flood waters. In joint operations with the other armed services and civilian law enforcement agencies, thousands of lives were saved along with several hundred head of cattle (Johnson, R.E., pp. 304-05).

The Bering Sea Patrol and International Ice Patrol continued. Kodiak and Seattle based cutters Storis, Winona, Klamath and Wachusett provided medical, legal and dental services to the northwest Alaskan coast and brought supplies to military and other government installations.

Four month patrols averaged around 10,000 miles as the cutter crews protected seal herds from poachers and acquired meteorological and oceanographic data. Distant Early Warning (DEW) radar facilities and military bases in northern Canada were assisted by the Royal Canadian Navy, U.S. Navy icebreakers and Coast Guard cutters Eastwind and Northwind. Supplies were brought to the military and civilian stations by the Military Sea Transportation Service (Johnson, R.E., pp. 305-07).

The MSTS was formed after World War II from the union of the Naval Transportation Service and the Army Transport Service. MSTS was renamed the Military Sealift Command (MSC) and placed under the Department of Defense (1970) to serve all the U.S. armed forces (Chambers, p. 700).

The Kennedy administration brought more funding and attention to the Coast Guard. President John F. Kennedy, a World War Two Navy officer, was interested in maritime issues, as were Treasury Secretary C. Douglas Dillon and Assistant Secretary James A. Reed, a veteran torpedo boat officer. New life boats, patrol boats and cutters were built. A plan for aviation development was initiated and shore station facilities were scheduled for upgrading.

By 1965, the Coast Guard had 56 helicopters in a total of 156 aircraft and a surface fleet augmented by several former U.S. Navy tug boats and buoy tenders built for river service. Additional 82 and 95 foot patrol craft were planned for rescue, salvage and inshore patrol work. Several 44 and 52 foot steel hulled motor lifeboats were developed with twin screws, dual rudders, diesel engines, power assisted steering, and elevated steering stations for better vision at the helm. Fire fighting equipment, radar, sonar and radio direction finders added to the safety and utility of the versatile craft. Double bottoms and special framing allowed the cutters to operate in moderate ice. A salvage pump on board facilitated better assistance to damaged sea craft. The motor lifeboats maintained their traditional self-bailing and self-righting capacities.

The increased popularity of recreational boating and the proportional acceleration of safety problems, accidents and fatalities on inland and coastal waters stimulated the passing of the Federal Boating Act of 1958. The Act required motor boat registration. States joined in the responsibility of policing recreational boating. Coast Guard active duty and Auxiliary personnel became increasingly visible as they carried out safety education and enforcement responsibilities. Popular recreation areas were patrolled by mobile boarding teams which inspected boats, enforced safety regulations, conducted boating safety classes and policed public boating events and water shows.

Promoted to four-star rank in 1960, Admiral Richmond completed his eight year tour as commandant. Rear Admiral Edwin J. Roland succeeded Richmond and served admirably from 1962 to 1966 (Johnson, R.E., pp. 312-15; 318-19).

CHAPTER VIII

VIETNAM
(1960-1975)

The Coast Guard was confronted by Cold War issues and the Vietnam conflict while at the same time responding to domestic responsibilities and political changes in the United States.

With limited budgets and personnel, the USCG has been quite creative in the utilization and modification of the technology used to carry out its responsibilities. Toward the end of the Cold War the Coast Guard signed a contract to acquire three balloons (aerostats) that could be attached to ships and tethered more than 2,000 feet in height. Coordinated with shipboard radar, small seagoing craft and airplanes could be detected by the device at a distance of over 50 miles, enhancing the Service's ability to detect drug smugglers and sea craft (Dunnigan and Nofi, 1990, p. 183). Creative technologies and complex missions are not new to the USCG. Few officers have been more creative in administering the multi-tasked guardians of inland and coastal waters than the eclectic E. J. Roland.

Admiral Edwin John Roland, Coast Guard Commandant from 1962-66, was an accomplished athlete in his cadet years at the Academy and coached baseball, football and basketball as an instructor. During World War II he commanded Destroyer Escort Division 45. After the war Roland attended the National War College, commanded several Coast Guard districts, and served as assistant Coast Guard commandant. Roland prepared the Coast Guard well for its law enforcement , search and rescue and maritime safety responsibilities and its involvement in Vietnam (R.E. Johnson, pp. 320-21).

Admiral Roland sought to involve the Coast Guard in the Vietnam War to preserve its military credibility and avoid the limited support role the Service had during the Korean War (R.E. Johnson, p. 331).

By 1962 the North Pacific Ocean and the Bering Sea were increasingly visited by Russian and Japanese whaling and fishing vessels, necessitating the stationing and patrol of up to six large ocean going cutters to police the region.

In the early 1960's the Coast Guard acquired several HO4Ss, bringing its rotary-wing strength to 37, and four Sikorsky gas turbine powered S-62 helicopters which became HH-52A amphibians constructed with boat hulls to facilitated water landings. The Air Force Sikorsky helicopter was adapted for Navy and Coast Guard missions. The two engined aircraft was called the HH-3F Pelican. By 1969 the Coast Guard operated thirty-nine of these sturdy and versatile helicopters.

Long range ice patrol and search and rescue missions were ably carried out by giant 4 engined C-130 Hercules airplanes which had a nautical range of 3,000 miles.

The Coast Guard operated sixteen 210-foot WMEC medium endurance cutters by the late 1960's, and acquired several sleek new 378 foot WHEC high endurance cutters from Avondale Shipyards in Louisiana. The WHECs had aluminum superstructures, side by side stacks, gas turbines, diesel engines and a helicopter deck. The cutter was capable of 29 knots and armed with sonar, antisubmarine torpedoes, 40 millimeter mounts and a 5-inch .38 caliber gun.

In 1965 Coast Guard Yard constructed seagoing, twin screw, diesel powered 157-foot buoy tenders with a 6 foot draft. A low hull strengthened for ice breaking maximized visibility for close work. Bow-thruster propellers increased maneuverability in windy and confined waterways. By 1965 the Treasury and Defense Departments agreed to delegate naval ice breaking duties solely to the U.S. Coast Guard. The U.S. Navy transferred its five icebreakers to the USCG; the 221 foot minesweeper Tanager to the Coast Guard Officer Candidate School in Yorktown, Virginia; and the 184-foot escort Lamar for Reserve training on the West coast (R.E. Johnson, pp. 323-31).

The origins of the Cold War in Europe and Asia and the foundations of the Vietnam conflict were surveyed in Chapter 7. The Vietnam conflict and the contributions of the Coast Guard will now be considered more fully. A brief chronological synthesis of the Vietnam War may serve as a helpful reference before the Coast Guard mission in Vietnam is discussed.

French control of Indochina ended when French forces were defeated by Vietnamese Communist (Vietminh) troops at the Battle of Dienbienphu (13 March-May 7, 1954). President Eisenhower, like Truman before him, sent military aid to the French. After Dienbienphu, the U.S. decided against direct military intervention because Britain declined to support allied action.

International agreements reached at the Geneva Conference (1954) affirmed the boundaries of Vietnam, Laos and Cambodia. The temporary boundary at the 17th parallel was to be resolved by elections in 1956 to achieve the unification of Vietnam. South Vietnamese Prime Minister (later President) Diem and the U.S. blocked the elections fearing that North Vietnam's Communist dictator Ho Chi Minh might corrupt the election process in his region or legitimately win the election because of his status as a popular Vietnamese nationalist who fought French and Japanese imperialists.

The Southeast Asia Treaty Organization (SEATO) was formed (8 September, 1954) by the U.S., Britain, Thailand, Pakistan, Australia, New Zealand and the Philippines. The SEATO allies interpreted the defensive role of the international organization differently as the Vietnam War progressed.

Eisenhower sent a special envoy to Saigon with $100 million in aid and an affirmation of support for the Diem regime. By the end of 1955, U.S. military advisors were training South Vietnamese troops and participating in military missions. The North Vietnamese government accepted military aid and support from the Soviet Union and China.

By 1957 North and South Vietnamese communists were operating in the Mekong Delta of South Vietnam and assassinating village leaders. By 1959 the North Vietnamese were infiltrating troops and supplies by sea and along the Ho Chi Minh Trail. U.S. military advisors were taking casualties. Hanoi called its southern supporters the National Liberation Front. Saigon called the guerrillas the Viet Cong.

In 1961 President Kennedy sent Vice President Lyndon Johnson to Saigon to promise the Diem regime additional support. By 1962 the U.S. Military Assistance Command Vietnam (MACV) was formed for South Vietnam and American advisors numbered 12,000.

In a 1963 military coup d'etat Diem was overthrown and assassinated. The Kennedy administration encouraged the coup, but President Kennedy was shocked to find out that Diem had been murdered after his capture. Three weeks later (22 November) John F. Kennedy was assassinated in Dallas, Texas. Vice President Lyndon Johnson ascended to the presidency and continued the war effort.

In early August of 1964 North Vietnamese patrol boats attacked two U.S. destroyers in the Tonkin Gulf. The controversial incident allowed President Johnson to escalate the war with Congressional approval. Johnson begin bombing North Vietnam in retaliation for the aggression against the U.S. Navy which had been ostensibly patrolling in neutral waters. Although U.S. military advisors had gone on offensive missions with South Vietnamese forces in the past, most historians trace the presence of U.S. combat troops in Vietnam to 8 March 1965 when two U.S. Marine battalions landed to defend the U.S. Air Base at the strategic port of Da Nang.

By the end of 1967 the U.S. had 500,000 troops in Vietnam. On 31 January 1968, North Vietnamese and Viet Cong forces launched the Tet Offensive throughout South Vietnam. The enemy suffered such high casualties against U.S. and South Vietnamese troops that some Communist cadres thought it might be the end of the war. Nonetheless, Tet was perceived as a psychological defeat for the U.S. President Johnson declined to run for a second term. His successor, Richard M. Nixon, escalated the war in the north and struck at Communist troops in Cambodia to force North Vietnam to the peace table.

While escalating and at the same time gradually withdrawing U.S. troops ("Vietnamization") Nixon's tactics forced North Vietnam and South Vietnam to sign the Paris Treaty (27 January 1973). Prisoners of war (POWs) on all sides were exchanged and U.S. combat came to an end.

President Nixon came under heavy fire for his Cambodian incursion. Nixon's claim that enemy forces in Cambodia necessitated defensive action did not persuade Congress which passed legislation which limited the president's war making power and ended all further military support to South Vietnam.

Nixon resigned from office (9 August 1974) to avoid impeachment for alleged domestic political crimes collectively referred to as "Watergate."

Some U.S. military forces remained in South Vietnam until 1975, when North Vietnamese military forces reunified Vietnam with the capture of Saigon (30 April) two years after the Paris peace agreement. Nixon's successor, President Gerald Ford, pardoned Nixon (8 September 1974) for his Watergate offenses and on 23 April Ford said the war was over for the United States. In 1976 President Jimmy Carter pardoned most of the Vietnam war draft dodgers (Karnow, pp. 691-701).

Tensions remained between the U.S. and Vietnam until 1994 when President Clinton lifted the trade embargo against Hanoi. In 1995 Clinton extended diplomatic relations to Vietnam. In 1997 the Senate confirmed former Vietnam POW Douglas "Pete" Peterson U.S. ambassador to Hanoi. In June a new U.S. trade consulate was opened in Saigon, now called Ho Chi Minh City (Tucker, pp. 429-30).

President Lyndon B. Johnson deployed Coast Guard cutters to Vietnam (29 April 1965) to help the U.S. Navy intercept supplies and weapons being sent to Viet Cong forces by sea. Coast Guard Squadron One initiated the challenge with 17 patrol boats (82-foot WPBs) and 250 personnel. Each cutter carried nine enlisted men, two officers, one 81mm. mortar and five .50 caliber machine guns. The squadron arrived in the Gulf of Thailand in July to patrol the Gulf Coast of Vietnam and the Cambodian border. One Coast Guard division based at Da Nang patrolled the Demilitarized Zone (DMZ) south of the 17th parallel. Another division of nine cutters arrived in Vietnam (1966 February) to patrol the Mekong Delta region (Tucker, p. 420).

Twenty-six U.S. Coast Guard WPB 82-foot cutters were deployed to Vietnam. The fast patrol boats searched for enemy vessels (Marolda, p. 146). In the Mekong Delta, Navy and Coast Guard patrol boats, riverine assault craft, U.S. Navy SEAL commandos, U.S. Army units, and South Vietnamese ground troops (ARVN), harassed and raided enemy forces. In 1969 the U.S. Navy constructed a mobile pontoon base (Operation Sea Float) in the middle of the Cua Lon River in the region of Ca Mau. It was assumed that this base of operations in a Viet Cong sanctuary would increase civilian support for the South Vietnamese government.

Commander Paul A. Yost, later Coast Guard commandant, led a military unit from Sea Float, a difficult and dangerous assignment because of powerful river currents, distance from logistical support centers, and strong Viet Cong resistance. Nonetheless, Sea Float's presence in this isolated region of the Mekong Delta deprived the Viet Cong of security and destroyed numerous enemy supply operations on the waterway. Sea Float units offered medical assistance to civilian Vietnamese, put military forces into a region previously dominated by the enemy, destroyed tons of enemy food, ammunition and weapons, killed 3,000 and captured 300 Communists at a cost to American and South Vietnamese forces of 1,451 wounded and 186 killed (Marolda, pp. 276-78).

The 82-foot cutters were steel hulled. The crew on the bridge controlled the engine room. The WPBs had air conditioning to comfort crews in the tropical heat. Power steering enhanced maneuverability. A draft of 5.8 feet and a 17.2 foot beam allowed the patrol boats access to shallow inland waters. Two diesel engines, one to four mounted .50 caliber machine guns and a maximum speed of 22.9 knots added a margin of safety for the 8 to 10 member crews. Fifteen WHEC (high endurance) ocean going cutters supplemented the Market Time fleet and contributed significantly to the U.S. Navy mission. The WHECs carried heavy fire power and sophisticated radar. With a length of 327 feet, 41 foot beam and 15 foot draft, the WHECs carried one five-inch gun, two 81 mm. mortars, six .50 caliber machine guns and two torpedo launchers. Two 6,200 horsepower Westinghouse engines, two boilers and two shafts powered the vessel and its complement of 13 officers and 131 enlisted men at speeds of up to to 19.8 knots. Among the ocean cutters that carried out Vietnam missions were WHECs 32 and 31, the Campbell and Bibb, respectively (Gregory, pp. 23-24).

Experts in small boat handling, Coast Guardsmen brought special skills to the Indochina war. The 81 mm. mortar used on patrol boats was designed to create illumination rounds for peace time search and rescue work. The manually fired mortar weapon proved so effective in war that Special Forces units mounted them on flat bed trucks to use on their hazardous missions.

In Operation Market Time the Coast Guard participated in more than 6,000 fire support missions and boarded an estimated 250,000 water craft (Dunnigan and Nofi, 1999, pp. 152-53).

Cutter crews searched junks and sampans and stopped arms and ammunition smugglers. WPBs patrolled heavy schedules in all kinds of tropical weather. Marine and Special Forces amphibious operations were supported by the Coast Guard patrol boats with transportation, illumination and fire support using guns and mortars (Tucker, p. 420).

Squadron Three consisted of five 311-foot WHECs which patrolled in Operation Market Time missions designed by the Navy to intercept supply lines to North Vietnamese and Viet Cong units. More than 8,000 Coastguardsmen and 50 cutters destroyed 2,000 vessels in the "Brown Water War" and suffered 60 casualties (Chambers, p. 146).

Cutters destroyed supply ships, provided gunfire support in naval missions, supported patrol boats and assisted in civilian and military medical activities. Coast Guard WHECs replaced Navy destroyers at sea on the Market Time missions after June 1969. Thirty Coast Guard cutters and 4500 officers and men were deployed in Squadron Three between 1967 and 1972 (Tucker, p. 421).

In 1966 the U.S. Military Assistance Command (USMAC) requested the Coast Guard to supervise Explosive Loading Detachments (ELDs) to increase safety in explosive loading operations in ports where untrained Vietnamese workers posed a serious threat. Two Coast Guard ELDs arrived in Vietnam in 1966 and were assigned to the U.S. Army lst Logistical Command. During the Vietnam War no explosive accidents or enemy action occurred in any Coast Guard ELD supervised port (Tucker, p. 421).

In 1966 General William Westmoreland (U.S. Army), commander of U.S. combat forces in Vietnam, requested the participation of a Coast Guard Port Security and Waterways Detail (PS & WD) to assist and train Army boat crews and inspect port facilities. A Coast Guard marine inspector was assigned to the Navy's Military Sea Transportation Service (MSTS) to police the hundreds of merchant ships supporting U.S. operations (Tucker, p. 421).

A Coast Guard Aids to Navigation Detail stationed in Saigon manned and supervised buoy tenders, maintained buoys, and established navigation aids along the Vietnamese coast and in key ports to assist U.S. military operations (Tucker, p. 421).

At the request of the U.S. Department of Defense (14 December

1965) the Coast Guard began the construction and maintenance of an electronic navigation system which guided military aircraft to and from their targets. By August of 1966 the LORAN-C chain was operational. A transmitting station 42 miles south of the DMZ monitored the Ho Chi Minh Trail. After the withdrawal of U.S. forces from Vietnam (1973) civilian technicians operated the LORAN stations (Tucker, p. 421).

In 1968 Coast Guard helicopter pilots joined the U.S Air Force Rescue and Recovery Squadron at Da Nang. Coast Guard pilots flew HH-53C and HH-3E helicopters on search and rescue missions, rescued downed U.S. pilots in North and South Vietnam, and earned military honors for their dangerous operations, often under fire (Tucker, p. 421).

These Coast Guard missions were not carried out without casualties. Fifty-three Coastguardsmen were wounded, seven were killed in action, and one was listed as MIA, missing in action (Dunnigan and Nofi, 1999, p . 153).

The U.S. Navy utilized Coast Guard skills to the maximum throughout the war. The two services were symbiotic in their contributions and reciprocal skills. Upon the formation of Naval Task Force 115 (30 July 1965), Coast Guard personnel joined coastal surveillance units at An Thoi, Vung Tau, Qui Nhon, Nha Trang and Da Nang.

U.S. support of the South Vietnamese government (GSV) continued as U.S. troops were gradually being withdrawn under President Nixon's "Vietnamization" plan. Between 1969 and 1970 the 26 patrol boats were transferred to Coast Guard trained South Vietnamese crews (Summers, 1999, p. 125). In 1971-72 four large cutters were transferred to South Vietnam (Leepson, p. 71).

Admiral Elmo Zumwalt (USN) was appointed Commander of U.S. Navy Forces in Vietnam in 1968 and directed the Coastal Surveillance Force, the Riverine Assault Force, River Patrol Force, and Coast Guard activities while coordinating U.S. and South Vietnamese naval operations (Summers, p. 365).

Among Zumwalt's specific responsibilities were command of the "Brown Water Navy" river patrol boats along the Vietnamese coast and in the Mekong Delta. Operation SEA LORD intercepted Cambodian supply lines to the Viet Cong. Zumwalt initiated the spraying of the vegetation defoliant Agent Orange into the Mekong Delta, a policy which may have had the tragic irony of exposing his son, Swift Boat commander Elmo R. Zumwalt III, to the herbicide. The young Navy officer died of cancer in 1988 (Leepson, pp. 451-52).

The logistical challenge of getting Coast Guard cutters to Vietnam was significant. Coast Guard Squadron 1, composed of three divisions, was commissioned at Alameda, California on 26 May 1965 under Commander James A. Hodgman (USCG). The original seventeen Coast Guard vessels were loaded on the decks of Military Sea Transport Service Ships (MSTS) in the ports of Norfolk, New Orleans, Long Beach, San Francisco, Seattle and Galveston. The crews were trained in weapons use, survival operations and communications. The crews and cutters joined up again at the U.S. Naval Base in Subic Bay, Philippines, and made the 1,000 mile sea journey to Vietnam, refueling from large Navy vessels in seas that manifested 35 knot winds and waves of 15 feet or more .

Upon reaching Vietnam the Coast Guard patrols commenced. On its first night patrol, USCGC Point Orient (WPB-82319) encountered shore-side enemy machine gun and mortar fire, forcing the Coast Guard to replace the white paint of traditional cutters with less visible combat ship colors (Cutler, pp. 84-85).

The smallest of the Market Time sea craft was the 13-foot fiberglass Boston Whaler, known to U.S. recreational and commercial boaters as the "skimmer." Larger Coast Guard patrol boats (WPBs) launched the skimmers from their decks to maneuver around and board small Vietnamese sampans and junks, allowing the WPBs to stand by and respond to hostile or evasive responses. The Boston Whalers were transformed into gray colored war vessels outfitted with flak protective devices, a portable radio, signal flares and a crew carrying small arms. U.S. Navy aircraft on patrol searched the coastal waters of Vietnam and radioed the location of suspicious boats to Navy PCFs (fast patrol craft) and Coast Guard WPBs (Cutler, pp. 91-93).

Operating out of the port of Cat Lo (March 1966) Coast Guard Division 13 captured 7 Viet Cong and killed 27, and acquired or destroyed several tons of military supplies, weapons and ammunition. Especially significant were the contributions of the crew of the USCGC Point White and Lieutenant Eugene J. Hickey, whose exploits include ramming a 25 foot motorized enemy junk while being fired upon, and capturing a notorious Viet Cong leader (Cutler, p. 112).

One of the many tragedies of war is "friendly fire," the accidental causation of casualties (wounds or death) from allied or friendly military forces. Such a tragedy took place early in the morning of 11 August 1966 when the USCGC Point Welcome was attacked just off the Demilitarized Zone (DMZ) boundary between North and South Vietnam. A U.S. Air Force B-57 bomber and two F-4C fighter planes bombed and strafed the cutter in a one hour contest of futile signals, radio calls and evasive actions. Coastguardsmen were forced into the water to swim to shore under initial friendly fire from South Vietnamese land forces. The final casualty toll: eleven crew members were wounded and two were killed (Cutler, pp. 112-114).

Point Welcome skipper Lt. (jg) David C. Brostrom, the son of a U.S.

Navy commander, was killed in action, as was Engineman 2nd Class Jerry Phillips. Although badly wounded, Chief Boatswain Mate Richard H. Patterson utilized his seamanship skills and courage under fire to mobilize the crew and avoid even more serious damage and casualties. Patterson was ultimately awarded the Bronze Star with Combat "V" for his performance in combat action (Scotti, pp. 104-11).

Coast Guard patrol boats put troops ashore in enemy territory and extracted them after battle. During an extraction of South Vietnamese troops (22 January 1969) the USCGC Point Banks, two Navy boats, and an Air Force C-47 gunship fired on Viet Cong positions. Gunners Mate 2nd Class Willis J. Goff and Engineman 2nd Class Larry D. Villarreal guided a small skimmer boat into the night and on to shore. Using their own machine guns to counter Viet Cong fire the Coastguardsmen rescued five South Vietnamese and got back safely to the Point Banks. Their heroism earned Villarreal and Goff U.S. Navy Silver Stars (Scotti, p. 177).

Alex Larzelere graduated from the Coast Guard Academy, the National War College, the Naval War College, commanded five cutters, was a military aid to the president (1971-73), and earned an advanced degree from George Washington University in international affairs. Captain Larzelere, a lieutenant in Vietnam, commanded two 82-foot patrol boats (Point Banks and Point Comfort) and wrote a history of the Coast Guard in the Vietnam War (1965-1975).

Larzelere's book, The Coast Guard at War (Naval Institute Press, 1997) chronicled the missions and military action in Vietnam on land and sea. Government documents, interviews, primary and secondary sources, the author's personal experiences, and more than 70 tape recorded interviews provide the basis for this exemplary history.

Captain Larzelere quotes General Howell M. Estes, Jr., (USAF Commander) on Coast Guard performance: "I am aware of the distinguished record achieved by Coast Guard pilots flying in combat with our Jolly Greens (helicopters). They are indelibly inscribed in the permanent records of the stirring and moving drama of combat and air crew recovery in Southeast Asia" (Larzelere, p. 137).

Lt. Cdr. Lonnie L. Mixon and Lt. Lance A. Eagan distinguished themselves as Coast Guard helicopter pilots. Eagan received the Silver Star Medal and his crew partner, pararescue expert Airman First Class Joel Talley earned the Air Force Cross for the rescue under enemy fire of a downed and injured Air Force pilot. Lt. Jack C. Rittichier, a USCG pilot attached to Da Nang Air Base, was shot down and killed in a rescue attempt behind enemy lines. At the time of his death, Lt. Rittichier had been recommended for two Air Medals, an Air Force Cross, and three Distinguished Flying Crosses for harrowing combat rescues (Larzelere, pp. 137-144).

Captain Joseph L. Crowe, a Coast Guard lieutenant commander in Vietnam, told Larzelere that in addition to rescues over land, "Coast Guard aviators handled missions at sea when pilots of other armed services were not trained in overwater navigation, and not familiar with the intricacies of hoisting from a rolling ship" (Larzelere, p. 147).

General Wallace Greene, Jr., USMC Commandant, said in August of 1967, "I want to make sure that the Coast Guard people in Vietnam know that I am hearing about them often and I am pleased with what I hear" (Larzelere, p. 24).

The fast Army, Navy and Coast Guard river patrol boats and the large destroyer size vessels saw their share of action ever since 1967 when Secretary of the Navy Paul H. Nitze "requested that the Treasury Department assist the Department of the Navy by assigning five high-endurance (WHEC Coast Guard) cutters to augment Market Time forces" (Larzelere, p. 121).

The USCGC Rush (WHEC 723), a 378-foot cutter under the command of Captain Robert W. Durfey, joined Navy and Coast Guard patrol boats and Navy radar picket escort ships (DERs) to engage and destroy armed, steel hulled trawlers bringing ammunition and supplies to enemy forces. Shoot outs and shrapnel dispersing explosions made the encounters dangerous. Engaged in similar combat activity was the 255-foot USCGC Androscoggin (WHEC 68) under the command of Cdr. William H. Stewart. His crew participated in action packed joint missions with Coast Guard 82-foot patrol craft (WPBs), Navy Swift boats (PCFs) and helicopter gunships. Bullet holes across the port bow of the Androscoggin gave clear evidence of the volatility of the encounters.

On 29 February 1968 Commander Herbert J. Lynch of the 255-foot Winona (WHEC 65) engaged in a gun battle with a North Vietnamese ammunition trawler which resulted in a close-quarters explosion which splattered steel fragments and human parts from the enemy vessel all over the deck of the cutter.

More than 77,000 five inch shells were fired by Squadron Three WHECs in naval support missions in Vietnam. The ocean going cutters provided logistical support, berthing, food, supplies and repairs for Navy PCFs and Coast Guard WPBs (Larzelere, pp. 121, 124-26, 128-33).

Captain Robert Durfey later reflected on his combat tour as skipper of the cutter Rush: "We got called on to do all manner of things. And we were never unable to respond to a request or order for a mission." Durfey concluded that the Coast Guard motto, "Semper Paratus" (Always Ready), was aptly proven in Vietnam (Larzelere, p. 136). The Coast Guard served in Vietnam with the other U.S. armed services and the South Vietnamese military for ten years (1965-75). U.S. combat came to an end with the Paris Treaty in 1973, but the last isolated Coast Guard LORAN navigation station was not deactivated until April 1975.

Paul C. Scotti joined the Coast Guard after four years of Air Force duty. As a Gunners Mate Second Class, Scotti saw combat action on 82-foot patrol boats in Vietnam (1967-68). Then Scotti served as a Coast Guard journalist and was promoted to chief warrant officer and public information officer, retiring with the rank of CWO4. Scotti has written a masterly history entitled Coast Guard Action in Vietnam (Hellgate Press, 2000). Dedicated to Coast Guard combat veterans and their families, the author chronicled the service's Vietnam contributions in port security, law enforcement, search and rescue, and aids to navigation, with emphasis on riverine and coastal patrol and combat.

Admiral Paul A. Yost, Jr., commanded Navy and Coast Guard units in Vietnam (1969-70) and served as Coast Guard Commandant (1986-90). Scotti interviewed the combat veteran after Yost's retirement.

"I think we should have been in Vietnam," the admiral concluded. "We gave the Vietnamese an opportunity to save their country." Due to graft and corruption, Yost explained, and South Vietnamese disinclination to "risk their lives and equipment for their country" and the fact that "the officer corps often didn't lead (and) was not professional.... they lost the war" (Scotti, pp. 200-01).

Despite that candid assessment, Admiral Yost was positive about his service experience and proud of the role the U.S. Armed Forces played in general and the Coast Guard in particular.

The lesson for the Coast Guard from the Vietnam experience is clear to Admiral Yost: "We should be aware of our military mission...The Coast Guard is a capable war-making service in a specialty area (with) the expertise and experience to run patrol boats" (Larzelere, p. 68).

CHAPTER IX

POST-VIETNAM
(1967-1991)

The U.S. Coast Guard was destined for significant change, the background of which evolved during the Vietnam War when President Johnson enunciated his desire to create a cabinet level department to administer transportation.

Admiral Edwin Roland stated his opposition to the amalgamation of the Coast Guard into such a department. Admiral Willard J. Smith, Roland's successor as USCG commandant (1966-70), reiterated that position and was supported by Secretary of the Treasury Henry H. Fowler.

The Johnson administration informed the Coast Guard that it would be stripped of several of its functions if it remained under Treasury Department jurisdiction. Admiral Roland acquiesced after being assured the USCG would retain its military status under the proposed department. The Department of Defense and the U.S. Navy testified to the significance of the Coast Guard in U.S. military history and in Vietnam. When the Coast Guard was assured of the preservation of its military status under the Department of Transportation (DOT), Admiral Roland initiated the transition process which Admiral Smith completed.

Admiral Smith, a U.S. Coast Guard Academy graduate (1933) and the first aviator to head the Service, worked diligently to maintain Coast Guard jurisdiction in a variety of maritime responsibilities which came to include bridge regulation over navigable waters, the administration of anchorage areas, supervision of the Great Lakes Pilotage Administration, and the enforcement of oil pollution laws. The jurisdictional demarcation was important to establish because the U.S. Army Corps of Engineers also performed DOT functions.

On 1 April 1967 the Coast Guard joined the Transportation Department, ending 177 years in the Treasury Department. The official U.S.

Coast Guard dates back to 1915. Its Revenue Service antecedent began in 1790 (Johnson, R.E., pp. 340-43).

The transfer of the USCG to the DOT heralded the termination of the ocean station cutter patrol, the initiation of a 12 mile off-shore fishery boundary, drug enforcement, the interdiction of West Indies refugees, and (after 1977) the policing of the 200 mile economic resource zone. These expanded duties ensured that the Service would remain challenged after its Vietnam mission.

Large deep water buoys which automatically transmit weather data made ocean station cutters obsolete. Similar buoys up to 40 tons equipped with fog signals, radio beacons, and lights ended the era of lightship cutters (Johnson, R.E., p. 344).

Cutter weaponry and external painting were modified. Vietnam-era deck guns and grenade launchers were replaced on all except the largest ocean going vessels. Other cutters sufficed with .50-caliber machine guns and small arms stored below deck.

In 1967, Coast Guard headquarters in Washington, D.C. decreed that a distinctive Coast Guard emblem on a field of blue and orange stripes be placed on the hulls of all USCG air, inland water, and sea craft.

Admiral Chester R. Bender served as Coast Guard commandant from 1970-74. Bender initiated changes in the traditional Coast Guard uniforms. Enlisted personnel who had worn traditional dress "sailor suits" acquired a more professional look in the new style which resembled chief petty officer uniforms. Officers adjusted, not without complaints, to a Coast Guard "blue" uniform distinguishable from U.S. Navy uniforms.

By 1973 qualified women became eligible for officer candidate school and the Coast Guard Academy. In 1977 women were allowed to serve on large cutters. In 1978 gender restrictions on service assignments were abolished. Lieutenant (jg) Beverly Kelly assumed command of the 95-foot Cape Newagen in the port of Honolulu (April 1979), the first female captain of a warship in United States history. Lieutenant Susan I. Moritz in command of the cutter Cape Current made a significant marijuana seizure off the Miami coast (July 1979). Linda Johansen, Coast Guard Academy Cadet First Class, was the first female to lead the cadet corps at an armed forces academy, and was among the first female graduates to receive Academy commissions in the class of 1980.

As of 1982, 130 (3%) of the officers in the Coast Guard were women, and 1700 (5%) of the enlisted personnel were female. Ten percent of the Academy cadets were female. Three female Coast Guard officers were aviators (Johnson, R.E., pp. 345-46).

Admiral Bender was credited with achievements in vessel traffic control and environmental protection as U.S. oil imports increased. The Coast Guard responded effectively to several oil spills and was represented on the Council on Environmental Quality.

Coast Guard investigators became responsible for finding the origin of oil spills and holding alleged polluters accountable for clean up costs. Coast Guard personnel learned to spot pollution from the air, match samples, and remove and disperse oil spills using the latest technology. Admiral Bender concluded that more oil was spilled at sea from tanker cleaning than from accidental spills.

The significance of anti-pollution regulations and Coast Guard enforcement was exhibited in 1973 when the International Conference on Marine Pollution met in London. Admiral Bender attended the meeting accompanied by other Coast Guard officers. Regulations were formulated which prohibited ships from discharging oil within 50 miles of shore. Vessels within national waters could be detained and held responsible for oil spills and failure to adhere to ship construction standards. In 1977 the Coast Guard was authorized to force polluting vessels out of U.S. waters and enforce a pollution control zone of 200 miles. The exploitation of Alaskan oil fields and the shipping of petroleum from Alaskan terminals to Puget Sound in Washington state caused the Coast Guard to establish marine safety and traffic systems and provide navigation assistance with LORAN-C stations along the commercial route (Johnson, R.E., pp. 346-49).

The Lockheed Shipbuilding and Construction Company (Seattle, Washington) built the icebreaker Polar Star (WAGB 10), commissioned in 1976. The 399-foot cutter was powered with gas turbines and 60,000 shaft horsepower to cope with high latitude ice. A sister vessel, the cutter Polar Sea, took to the waves in the late 1970s. The Coast Guard Support Center in Seattle solved initial engine and propeller problems to enable the extensively automated Polar class vessels to cope with extreme Arctic and Antarctic conditions.

From 1979 to 1986 the Tacoma (Washington) Boatbuilding Company planned the construction of nine 140-foot icebreaker tug boats, among them the Katmai Bay, Bristol Bay, and Thunder Bay. From 1977 into the 1980s Tacoma Boatbuilding Co. constructed several 270-foot medium endurance (WMEC) cutters which included a helicopter deck and 76-millimeter gun. The 270-footers were named after the Bear, Northland, Harriet Lane and Tampa, famed cutters in Coast Guard history. These and other cutters were increasingly used in drug enforcement and immigration interdiction in the South Atlantic and Gulf regions (Johnson, R.E., pp. 350-55). In 1973 the U.S. signed a cease fire agreement in Paris which ended the American involvement in the Vietnam War. President Richard M. Nixon was not shielded by the diplomatic achievement. The U.S. Senate investigation of "Watergate," the collective term for a series of domestic illegalities committed by the administration, unraveled the presidency and ultimately forced Nixon's resignation in 1974. Nixon was succeeded by Vice President Gerald Ford whose unconditional pardon of the former president contributed to Jimmy Carter's victory in the 1976 presidential election (Urdang, pp. 402, 404, 408).

In 1980 the Carter administration was challenged by Cuban dictator Fidel Castro's granting several thousand of his disgruntled citizens safe passage out of the country. Thousands of Cubans descended upon Key West Florida, taking advantage of automatic U.S. acceptance of refugees from the Communist nation (Urdang, pp. 416-17).

Coast Guard Commandant Admiral John B. Hayes (1978-82), proposed that cutters be stationed off the Cuban city of Mariel to process the immigrants. Because the Cuban government rejected that proposal, a haphazard boat lift threatened the lives of the refugees at sea. The Coast Guard drug enforcement mission had to be temporarily suspended. President Carter ordered U.S. Navy vessels to supplement the overwhelmed Coast Guard and authorized the commandant to call up 900 reservists. For the next several years the Coast Guard not only had to contend with Cuban refugees, but hundreds of Haitian refugees who did not have automatic asylum status in the United States, many of whose lives were saved by the USCG on treacherous seas (Johnson, R.E., pp. 355-58).

Commandant James S. Gracey (1982-86) expanded the Coast Guard cutter and air fleets, achieved success in Caribbean drug patrol interdictions and supported the U.S. military operations during the 1983 invasion of Grenada ("Commandants," Office of Coast Guard Historian, compiled: March 2000).

Not all Coast Guard publicity was positive. On 23 November 1970, during the Cold War when U.S.-Soviet tensions were high, a radio operator from the Soviet satellite of Lithuania attempted to defect to the United States. The Soviet fishing vessel Sovietskaya Litva was moored in New England waters in proximity to the Coast Guard cutter Vigilant.

Defector Simas Kudirka declared his intentions to U.S. officials who were on board the Soviet vessel to discuss fisheries issues. Officers on the Vigilant were unsuccessful in reaching the Boston (First District Headquarters) district commander who was on sick leave. The district chief of staff contacted U.S. Coast Guard Headquarters in Washington, D.C., which sought advice from the weekend foreign service staff at the Department of State. The State Department advised the Vigilant to do nothing unless Kudirka got on board the cutter.

The ailing district commander, now informed of the incident, told the acting district commander to deny the asylum request because the fisheries discussions might break off and U.S. officials on board the Soviet vessel endangered.

The defector made it to the cutter, but orders came from district headquarters to return Kudirka to the Soviet ship. Kudirka refused to comply, so the cutter commander inexplicably allowed Soviet sailors to board the cutter (U.S. territory), subdue the determined fisherman, and return him to the Litva in a Coast Guard small boat.

When President Nixon learned that a defector had been returned by the Coast Guard to Soviet authority in U.S. territorial waters one mile off the Massachusetts coast, he was outraged, as were anti-Soviet demonstrators in several American cities.

Subsequent Congressional, State Department, and Coast Guard hearings resulted in reprimands, loss of command, and early retirements (Johnson, R.E., pp. 363-64).

U.S. diplomatic pressure contributed to the release of Simas Kudirka after four years in a Soviet labor camp. Kudirka settled in the United States. His courageous quest was chronicled in a television movie. After almost 30 years in the United States, it was reported that Kudirka returned to Lithuania ("Baltic Times," published on Global Lithuanian Net, 9/23/01).

On 10 November 1975 at around 7:15 PM, the bulk cargo vessel SS Edmund Fitzgerald fully loaded with taconite pellets sunk in eastern Lake Superior during one of the most violent winter storms in Great Lakes history. Enroute from the port of Superior (Wisconsin) to Detroit (Michigan) the ship plunged to the bottom with the loss of 29 officers and crew members. Subsequent U.S. Coast Guard and National Transportation Safety Board investigations and the final report (4 May 1978) attributed the sinking to high (35 feet or more) waves, deficient weather tight bulkheads in the cargo hold, reduced freeboard as authorized by amendments to the Great Lakes Load Regulations, and massive flooding in the cargo holds caused by the collapse or loss of at least one hatch cover (NTSB Edmund Fitzgerald Accident Report, USCG Hdqtrs, Washington, D.C.)

Captain Dudley J. Paquette was on Lake Superior on the SS Wilfred Sykes trailing behind the Edmund Fitzgerald during the "storm of the century." The skipper was a weather expert and later conceded he underestimated the severity of the storm. Dudley had much to say about the weather and the mistakes made by Captain Ernest McSorley of the Fitzgerald. Paquette took issue with some of the conclusions of the United States Coast Guard Marine Board and the Commandant in their concurring opinion that loss of buoyancy, massive flooding, and the wall of water that the vessel confronted were the only causes of the marine disaster.

Paquette concluded from in-harbor observations and Coast Guard photographs that the hatch clamps were not completely fastened. Captain Paquette acknowledged the problems caused by high seas and winds, but dismissed the alleged possibility that the Fitzgerald struck shoals which caused structural damage.

Captain Paquette heralded the courage of Captain Jimmie Hobaugh (USCG) and the crew of the cutter Woodrush which sailed out of the port of Duluth (Minnesota) during the storm and pounded through high seas for 22 hours to reach the wreck site. Captain Hobaugh favored the shoal theory. Paquette concluded that structural weaknesses from repairs to the Fitzgerald and poor boat handling led to the disaster, and contended that Coast Guard marine inspectors overlooked problems in the construction and repair history of the Fitzgerald.

The Sykes skipper gathered some of his conclusions from radio conversations participated in and overheard between the Fitzgerald and other vessels on its final voyage (Bishop, pp. ix-xii; 1-14; 84-90; 94-97).

Captain Hobaugh (USCGC Woodrush) did not completely dismiss Paquette's stress fracture theory, but favored his own conclusion that flooded cargo holds "caused the bow to dive into the lake and not recover" (Bishop, p. 109).

Commandant Paul A. Yost, Jr. (1986-90) completed the decade of the 1980s as the Coast Guard celebrated its bicentennial (1790-1990), dating back to the U.S. Revenue Cutter Service. In 1990 the Coast Guard celebrated 75 years under its present name when President Woodrow Wilson signed the "Act to Create the Coast Guard" in 1915 (Johnson, R.E., p. 368).

In his long career Admiral Yost in several district command positions, assumed budgetary and legal responsibilities for the Coast Guard, and was a delegate to an organization which formulated international seafaring regulations. Yost earned two advanced academic degrees, did graduate work in engineering, international affairs and business administration, and graduated from the Naval War College in Newport, Rhode Island.

Commandant Yost provided effective leadership in his laisson work with federal and international law enforcement agencies and in marine law enforcement and drug interdiction. With his Vietnam experience, Yost enhanced the naval and military capabilities of the Coast Guard, including placing missile launchers on High Endurance Cutters. Under Yost, the USCG assisted U.S. Navy forces in monitoring vessels in the Persian Gulf during the Iran-Iraq War (1980s), and facilitated better cooperation between the US and the USSR in SAR (Search and Rescue) and with Soviet Border Guard (KGB) units.

Admiral Yost was a fitting commandant with whom to end the decade. The Admiral had served with distinction in Vietnam. Admiral Yost's military awards included the Silver Star, the Legion of Merit with combat "V" with a gold star, two Distinguished Service Medals, the Meritorious Service Medal, the Combat Action Ribbon, the Korean Service Medal, the Navy Meritorious Unit Commendation and the Presidential Unit Citation ("Commandants," Office of Coast Guard Historian, compiled: March 2000).

After retirement Admiral Yost continued to speak out for the USCG. Writing in "Proceedings," published by the U.S. Naval Institute (September 2001), Yost criticized the inadequate funding allotted to the Coast Guard, attributing the shortfall to the fact that the Coast Guard is funded through the "Transportation" section of the budget, while the other military services affiliated with the Defense Department are funded more generously out of the "National Security" section.

The retired Commandant warned that airplanes, shore facilities, ships, boats, and command and control capacities are aging, "and if we don't get the funding, we are going to have a Third World Coast Guard" (Yost, Adm. Paul A. "Toss the Coast Guard a Life Ring." Proceedings, September 2001, p. 18).

A contemporary newspaper article supported Admiral Yost's concerns, claiming budget restrictions forced Coast Guard personnel to work 84-hour weeks and patrol in boats not routinely inspected. The Transportation Department inspector general reaffirmed the problem in his alleged assertion that "the readiness of Coast Guard operations continues to deteriorate" (Milwaukee Journal Sentinel, October 1, 2001).

The bravery and hazards associated with Coast Guard search and rescue (SAR) operations is well documented in the treacherous waters, rain and snow, sleet, fog and storms so characteristic of the north Pacific-Alaskan coast (Walker, pp. 48-50).

In 1981, the 26 foot gill net salmon boat Marlene skippered by Skip Holden was ravaged by 25 foot waves and 70-100 mile per hour winds in an evening storm in Prince William Sound.

Kodiak Coast Guard Station responded with a C-130 SAR plane patrolling at 18,000 feet overhead to guide a sturdy H-3 "Pelican" Sikorsky to the stormy scene. The helicopter crew prepared to drop a cradle (body) strap to the floundering vessel. Flood and strobe lights beaming, the H-3 was driven into the mountainous waves with the loss of the four man crew. Captain Holden made a valiant but fruitless effort to rescue his rescuers. A subsequent USCG helicopter crew braved the storm to rescue Holden who later publicly proclaimed his admiration for Coast Guard personnel and his sorrow about the fate of Helicopter 1471.

An immediate search for the downed crew was mounted by USCG

and USAF aircraft from bases in Anchorage, Sitka, Kodiak and Juneau. Within days, the body of one Coastguardsman and the inverted helicopter were recovered on two different islands in Prince William Sound (Walker, pp. 3-26).

The Coast Guard admonition allegedly dating back to the Revenue Marine and the Life Saving Service says it all: "You have to go out, but you don't necessarily have to come back" (Walker, pp. 29-30).

The people of Sitka, Alaska, invariably cheer the USCG contingent in the annual Fourth of July parade because "most everyone knows someone whose life has been spared when the Coast Guard intervened" (Walker, p. 47).

The crew of the fishing vessel La Conte was the beneficiary of the Coast Guard tradition during a violent January storm in 1998. One hundred mile per hour winds and record 90 foot seas sank the vessel and left five crewmen adrift without a life raft in freezing waters. Fortuitous radio communication with the Coast Guard base at Sitka before the fishing vessel submerged activated an H-60 Jayhawk Helicopter which flew the 150 mile journey to the source of the May Day call. Three different Coast Guard helicopter crews attempted the treacherous rescue, each nearly crashing into the sea as treacherous winds and limited fuel capacities necessitated alternate returns to the base.

Three of the five fisherman were eventually saved, including a retired Coast Guard warrant officer, in one of the most hazardous and skillful rescues in maritime history (Walker, pp. 132-33, 144-45, 220-43).

In 1998 the USCG presented helicopter crew members Capt. Ted La Feuvre, Lt. Cmdr. Steven Torpey, and Petty Officers Lee Honnald, Fred Kalt and Mike Fish, the Distinguished Flying Cross. In subsequent months the crew members journeyed to national ceremonies in Washington, D.C. to receive awards from the Naval Helicopter Association, the Association of Naval Aviators, and the Smithsonian Institution's Aviation and Space Technology Laureate Award (Walker, p. 255).

The Search and Rescue legacy established by the USCG has attracted helicopter pilots from the Army, Navy, Marines and Air Force to it ranks who have enriched the Coast Guard with their professional training and contributions.

The 1980s has been described as a period of the resurgence of political conservatism, as exemplified by the Republican presidency of Ronald Reagan (1981-1989). Reagan vowed to reduce the federal budget, cut taxes and end the Cold War. "Reaganomics" achieved success on several fronts for several years, punctuated by increased defense spending and the 1982 recession.

The popular two term president covertly and overtly aided anti-Communist forces in Central America and on the Caribbean island of

Grenada. Progress was made in tempering the Cold War when Reagan and Soviet leader Mikhail Gorbachev made progress on disarmament and the reduction or banning of intermediate range nuclear missiles. Both charismatic leaders took significant steps to ease U.S.-Soviet tensions. Gorbachev's economic and political reforms also had the unintended consequence of bringing down the Soviet Communist system and causing the withdrawal of Soviet troops from Eastern Europe. The failed 10 year war in Afghanistan contributed to the unraveling of the Soviet Union.

In 1983 President Reagan sent American troops into the Lebanese civil war as part of an international peace keeping mission. When more than 200 marines were killed when a suicide bomber drove a truck into a U.S. Marine Corps barracks, Reagan withdrew the remaining U.S. forces (Kennedy, D. M., pp. 611-620).

Reagan's vice president, George Herbert Walker Bush, continued the Republican regime (1989-93). In 1989, Bush sent airborne troops into Panama to capture General Manuel Noriega, a totalitarian drug lord. Then Bush sent troops back into the Middle East in Operation Desert Storm and Desert Shield. U.S. ground and naval forces went into the Persian Gulf War (1991) to expel the brutal Iraqi dictator Saddam Hussein from oil-rich Kuwait and prevent him from acquiring Saudi Arabian territory. The February war consisted of a Bush inspired United Nations coalition of Arab and non-Arab Muslim nations, and European, U.S., Canadian and Australian military forces. Twenty-eight nations joined the anti-Iraqi coalition. U.S. forces included soldiers, sailors and pilots, regular, national guard and reserve troops, men and women. U.S. General Norman Schwarzkopf led the alliance, and Defense Secretary Dick Cheney and Joint Chiefs Chairman Colin Powell, an intelligent, articulate African-American officer, achieved their limited objectives when Saddam Hussein's troops withdrew from Kuwait. Hussein plagued the U.N. for years after by defying United Nations sanctions, suffering periodic military strikes and trade sanctions in the process (Kennedy, D. M., pp. 620-24).

In his post-war autobiography General Schwarzkopf paid tribute to the military forces of the international Persian Gulf coalition, and the success achieved by "all of the soldiers, sailors, airmen, Marines, Coast Guard, National Guard and reserves who took part in Operation Desert Shield and Desert Storm" (Schwarzkopf, p. 575).

In the Persian Gulf War, USCG utility craft crewed by regular and reserve personnel patrolled Gulf harbors to prevent water borne attacks on U.S. Navy vessels. Coast Guard and Navy personnel performed joint harbor security and defense operations and boarded foreign naval and merchant vessels to suppress enemy supply sources. The Coast Guard performed its usual law enforcement, port security, explosives loading, and search and rescue operations (Holland, Rear Adm. W. J., USN, pp. 173, 192-193). The Coast Guard role in the Persian Gulf War of 1991 is explored more fully in Chapter 10.

Prior to the Gulf War, the environmental responsibilities of the USCG made it responsible for the enforcement of Environmental Protection Agency regulations which identified toxic waste dumps as a major hazard. The EPA listed more than 400 toxic sites in the U.S. as clean-up priorities (Urdang, p. 421). The role the Coast Guard would play in responding to the 2001 terrorist attacks upon the United States were suggested by warning signs in the Middle East. In 1983, 200 U.S. Marines died when a suicide bomber drove an explosives laden truck into the Marine compound in Beirut. Several months earlier the U.S. Embassy in that nation was destroyed in similar fashion. The immigration enforcement mission of the Coast Guard was challenged that same year when more than 1 million illegal Hispanic aliens crossed the U.S. southern border fleeing Central American civil wars and Mexican poverty. In 1984, the U.S. Supreme Court ordered the rules for political asylum restricted to proof of "clear probability" of persecution or threats to aliens for political reasons in the nations from which they escaped (Urdang, pp. 422, 424).

The historic Coast Guard iceberg patrols were put into focus in 1985 when divers located the hull of the luxury passenger ship Titanic. The luxury liner sank in the North Atlantic after hitting an iceberg. In 1986 the 100th anniversary of the Statue of Liberty was the cause of a fire works display and the visitation of an international armada of warships and sailing vessels. Among them, the USCGC Eagle and a fleet of Coast Guard craft assigned to police the extravaganza (Urdang, p. 429).

President Reagan signed immigration legislation in 1986 which gave legal status to immigrants who came to the U.S. prior to 1982, and at the same time strengthened the penalties for hiring illegal (undocumented) aliens (Urdang, p. 430). Critics of the legislation warned that the granting of legal status to illegal aliens would encourage the migration of more undocumented Hispanics.

In 1986 the federal government entered the battle to clean up toxic wastes by mandating cleanup procedures and penalties with a $9 billion appropriation. In 1988 a fuel tank collapsed pouring 1 million gallons of oil into the Monongahela River near Pittsburgh. The necessity of monitoring the production and transportation of petroleum was demonstrated even more graphically in 1989 when the Exxon Valdez ran aground. The Gulf of Alaska spill was the largest in U.S. history. Besides the toll in marine and terrestrial wild life, the federal government, Exxon Oil Company, and the state of Alaska spent billions of dollars cleaning up the ecosystem. Millions of dollars were lost to the fishing industry (Urdang, pp. 431, 435, 436).

Not all goes well for the Coast Guard on every mission. Dangerous duties on hazardous water can result in damaged or sunken vessels, as was the case of a World War Two vintage Coast Guard buoy tender. On 4 December 1989, at 2:10 a.m., Lake Superior claimed the 180-foot USCGC Mesquite. The buoy tender went aground off Michigan's Keweenaw Point in the turbulent, icy waters of Lake Superior while servicing a navigational aid, and eventually sank.

A subsequent Coast Guard investigation revealed the misuse of navigational technology and errors in judgment. Officers and crew received both disciplinary actions and honors related to causal factors and reaction.

Treacherous waters and dangerous duties are part of Coast Guard life. That so few accidents happen in those conditions is a tribute to the leadership and seafaring skills of the service. When errors do occur, personnel are held accountable in foul or fair weather, whether the crews have been overworked or understaffed, whatever the seafaring conditions, which, in the case of the Mesquite, were significant (Stonehouse, pp. 1-97).

Noted maritime historian Frederick Stonehouse wrote the story of the Mesquite and has chronicled the Coast Guard in several other books. Stonehouse commends the thinly spread, understaffed and under-budgeted service for its exemplary record. The author applied an old military saying to Coast Guard ingenuity: "They have done so much with so little for so long, they can now do anything with nothing" (Stonehouse, p. iii).

Defenders of the officers and crew of the Mesquite believe that limited resources and long hours contributed to the grounding and sinking of the vessel.

The 1980-91 period constituted a challenging period for the United States and the Coast Guard, whose duties were and are inevitably influenced and expanded by domestic and international events.

CHAPTER X

THE 1990's

The 1990s decade was a challenging period for America. In Chapter 9, several events were considered: the U.S. response to the Iraqi invasion of Kuwait; President George H. Bush's creation of an international coalition to meet the Iraqi threat; and U.S. Persian Gulf allied commander General "Stormin' Norman" Schwarzkopf's tribute to the military forces under his command, including the U.S. Coast Guard.

The "Hundred Hour War" was divided into two stages: Operation Desert Shield and Operation Desert Storm. United Nations forces included male and female warriors who destroyed Iraqi dictator Saddam Hussein's troops in a relatively brief period, but geostrategic considerations made the allied forces leave Saddam in power. Hussein continued his oppressive rule, defied United Nations inspectors, and suffered the humiliation of United Nations air patrols and occasional missile strikes on his nation for more than a decade (Kennedy, 2000, pp. 622-24; 629).

At the end of the decade, NATO military forces entered the Balkan civil war between Christians and Muslims in Serbia and Bosnia (the former Yugoslavia). Western forces protected Muslims as they did in the Persian Gulf (Kennedy, 2000, pp. 628, 631), a fact many militant Muslims chose to ignore when they waged war on the West.

When Iraqi forces invaded Kuwait (2 August 1990), U.S. warships of the Middle East Force were already in the Persian Gulf as they had been throughout the Cold War. By 7 August , Navy aircraft carriers and battleships, and U.S. Army and Air Force units were deploying to the region. The Air Force Military Airlift Command carried U.S. soldiers, airmen, Marines, and members of the Coast Guard to the region. Most U.S. Navy sailors embarked to the combat theater on their own ships. The U.S. Navy Military Sealift Command transported the supplies and equipment needed by the American military to carry out the war, including artillery, ammunition, fuel, armored military vehicles and tanks. Unarmed Military Sealift Command merchant ships were guarded by NATO naval vessels en route to the theater of operations. Warships from several NATO nations (the United Kingdom, Norway, Italy, Greece, Spain, France, and the Netherlands) contributed to the war effort (Holland, pp. 191-93).

The preparation and execution of the Persian Gulf War (1990-91), the protection of Saudi Arabia, and the liberation of Kuwait involved U.S. and allied ground, naval, and air forces. U.S. naval forces (surface ships, craft and submarines) launched air strikes and cruise missile attacks upon Iraqi targets. The U.S. Navy, Coast Guard and allied forces conducted strategic operations which fooled Saddam Hussein into splitting his land forces to thwart an anticipated amphibious attack into Kuwait which was never launched. Naval forces shielded Saudi Arabian harbors from Iraqi aggression, and cleared or neutralized enemy mines placed in the Persian Gulf adjacent to Kuwait.

Vice Admiral Henry H. Mauz, Jr., (USN) was appointed Commander, U.S. Naval Forces, Central Command. Mauz selected Rear Admiral Robert Sutton to command the U.S. Naval Logistics Support Force. Sutton's Vietnam combat experience had familiarized him with the importance of protecting ports and coastal regions from sea borne threats, and the significant role the U.S. Coast Guard played in port security in Vietnam. Admiral Sutton established three Port Security-Harbor Defense (PSHD) groups composed of Navy and Coast Guard Regular and Reserve members. The U.S. Coast Guard deployed Port Security Units (PSUs) made up of male and female personnel who operated on land and patrolled harbors in armed Sea Raider utility craft to protect coalition vessels (Marolda and Schneller, p. 72).

Vice Admiral Mauz was replaced by Vice Admiral Stanley R. Arthur (USN), who further prepared U.S. naval forces for the Gulf War (Holland, p. 195).

Navy and Coast Guard teams operated with an efficiency fostered in Vietnamese operations between 1965 and 1972 when they and South Vietnamese naval units patrolled riverine and coastal areas of Vietnam and the South China Sea, stopping the enemy from infiltrating supplies and military equipment. Aircraft, patrol vessels and large warships coordinated intelligence, radar and communications to deter enemy blockade runners. That successful experience was applied to allied operations in the Persian Gulf (Marolda and Schneller, p. 85).

Coalition patrols boarded merchant vessels to inspect for contraband. Rigid hull inflatable boats (RHIBs) were used instead of motor whaleboats because of their superior speed and maneuverability. Inspection teams were composed of one Coast Guard and one Navy officer, and up to eight USN and USCG enlisted personnel. Coast Guard personnel from experienced LEDET (law enforcement detachment) teams operated in the Persian Gulf and Red Sea. Coast Guard experience in Caribbean drug enforcement operations honed their skills with small arms, boarding tactics, ship documents and maritime law, and helped to secure the allied blockade. Uncooperative and hostile Iraqi ship crews found Navy and Coast Guard personnel able and willing to use proper force and steer enemy vessels into friendly ports where cargoes could be confiscated (Marolda and Schneller, pp. 89-91).

Boarding was dangerous duty. Enemy crews were sometimes hostile and cargoes of ordnance and chemicals could be volatile. Iraqi ship captains and crews sometimes ignored radio instructions and warning shots, made decks slippery with water, falsely marked their vessels and mislabeled documents and cargoes.

Warships stood by ready to fire on defiant vessels. Special allied commando teams, including U.S. Marines and Navy Seals, frequently accompanied Navy and Coast Guard boarding parties, sometimes dropping onto cargo decks from helicopters. The successful embargo deprived Saddam Hussein and his military forces of oil export income and equipment and supplies Iraq needed to fully maintain its military forces (Marolda and Schneller, pp. 92-96).

Supportive Arab states in the coalition deployed patrol craft in Gulf waters and supplemented other United Nations forces. Coast Guard Reservists from Cleveland, Ohio (CG Port Security Unit 302) joined Navy units in port security and explosive ordnance disposal and loading operations. Electronic surveillance teams alerted naval units to suspicious vessels. Navy and Coast Guard small boats powered by outboard motors and armed with machine guns switched on communications and radar equipment and raced to the scene, often accompanied by political representatives from coalition Arab states (Marolda and Schneller, pp. 123-24).

Dutch, Belgian, French, British, Australian, Canadian and Japanese military and naval forces added their power and experience to Persian Gulf operations. Combat and search and rescue duty kept coalition crews prepared and busy. One three ship flotilla included guided missile craft, anti-aircraft guns, Navy SEAL and Coast Guard Law Enforcement Detachments, two Navy and two Army helicopters, and personnel from a U.S. Army Aviation Regiment. Coalition flotillas found it necessary to use shell fire, missiles and rockets on oil rig platforms which sheltered armed Iraqi military personnel. These enemy forces were trained to fire on vessels and sabotage oil facilities with shoulder launched missiles. Iraqi teams possessed assorted weapons, diving gear and explosives (Marolda and Schneller, pp. 212-17).

Iraqi dictator Saddam Hussein responded to coalition attacks by ordering his military to unleash eco-terrorism. Iraqi sabotage teams pumped oil from a Kuwaiti storage facility directly into the Persian Gulf, emptied five loaded Iraqi oil tankers and set fire to several oil refineries. Allied expertise coped with the spills more quickly and skillfully than Saddam had anticipated. President Bush sent U.S. Army, Navy, Coast Guard, Environmental Protection Agency, and National Oceanic and Atmospheric Administration pollution experts to the Persian Gulf to respond to the pollution disasters. Air and Navy patrols tracked spills and clean-up experts and firefighters minimized the ecological and economic damage (Marolda and Schneller, pp. 226-27).

Five hundred thousand male and female Armed Forces personnel served in the Gulf War. Supplying the huge force with the necessary food and equipment was a tactical and logistical challenge superbly carried out by civilian and military experts. After the war, multi-service logistical planners supervised the transporting on land, sea and air of military supplies, equipment and personnel from the Persian Gulf Theater back to overseas and U.S. bases. Service personnel received warm welcomes and the accolades of a grateful nation (Marolda and Schneller, pp. 330-34).

Successful military and logistical operations during the Gulf War have been attributed to the combat readiness U.S. military forces acquired from superior training, experience in Korea and Vietnam, and in military operations conducted during the Cold War in the Middle East, Central America and the Caribbean. Navy and Coast Guard forces had learned from their cooperative ventures and joint missions with allied land, sea and air services. Naval special warfare, explosive ordnance handling, harbor defense and salvage operations were missions the armed services conducted in the decades since World War Two (Marolda and Schneller, pp. 356-57).

The history of inter-service cooperation paid off in the Gulf War, where "Navy harbor defense, special warfare, explosive ordnance disposal units, and Coast Guard port security units formed the final maritime line of defense in the key ports..." (Marolda and Schneller, p. 361). Coalition naval forces achieved success in Desert Shield-Desert Storm by controlling the seas that bordered the Arabian Peninsula. Air and ground forces terminated the ability of the Iraqi military to expand its aggression (Marolda and Schneller, p. 362).

U.S. military forces found themselves more deeply involved in a war in the Muslim/Slavic/Christian Balkans in 1999 when Serbia cracked down on Muslim separatists in Kosovo in 1999. Thirteen NATO nations intervened in the controversial civil war, but U.S. Air Force and Navy aircraft carried the brunt of the burden (Holland, p. 247).

U.S. and other NATO forces had been in the Balkans since the early 1990s trying to bring peace and stability to the ethnically fragmented region (Kampschror, pp. 1-2).

The Coast Guard cutter Bear was reported to have disembarked from Portsmouth, Virginia to the Adriatic Sea in the Kosovo combat zone to interdict vessels breaking the embargo and bringing supplies and military equipment to Serbian (Yugoslav) military forces. The Coast Guard was chosen for the initially unpublicized mission at a time when its mission constituted "a significant escalation of the US-NATO war effort" (Novak, Conservative Chronicle, 26 May 1999).

Coast Guard responsibilities can generate controversy. On 4 April 1997, Kapitan Man, a Russian commercial vessel suspected of tracking and spying on a U.S. Navy nuclear submarine, was trailed and photographed by a joint Royal Canadian Navy and U.S. Navy crew in a Canadian helicopter over U.S. waters in the Puget Sound area. A Russian crew member fired a lazer at the helicopter, seriously damaging the eyes and affecting the careers of a U.S. Navy intelligence officer and the Canadian pilot.

Sensitive geopolitical considerations allegedly caused the Clinton Administration and the State Department to cover up the incident, pressure a U.S. Navy and Coast Guard boarding party to superficially search the Russian vessel, and let the merchant ship sail from Tacoma free of sanctions.

The Department of Defense favored detaining the Kapitan Man, but the State Department intervened and allegedly warned the Russian Embassy in Washington of the impending Coast Guard/Navy boarding party search. The alerted Russian crew concealed or destroyed the laser weapon. White House and State Department pressure forced the Pentagon to give up jurisdiction in the case. Leaked classified documents revealed the Pentagon's conclusion that the lazer incident was deliberate. The Russian ship was allowed to sail out of U.S. waters before medical tests on the Canadian and U.S. Navy officers were complete (Gertz, pp. 7-30; 219-25).

Lieutenant Jack Daly, the USN intelligence officer wounded in the incident and pressured not to speak to the press, later testified that he had been "betrayed and sacrificed by our government for a political agenda, one that assumed our once most feared Cold War foe has, overnight, become a friend we can trust" (Gertz, p. 25).

A personal inquiry to the Thirteenth Coast Guard District (Seattle, Washington) about the Kapitan Man produced a letter from Commander Michael J. Lodge, acting legal officer, by direction of the District Commander. Responding to the author's Freedom of Information

Act (FOIA) request, Lodge said "no such report or synthesis" alleging political interference "exists." Commander Lodge referred the author to FOIA district coordinator and assistant legal officer Lieutenant Melanie Bell for more information.

Lieutenant Bell, a lawyer with expertise in admiralty law, reviewed the 1997 Kapitan Man file and suggested the Pentagon and the State Department might possess information not available in Coast Guard records. The legal officer then forwarded "any and all documents relating to the 1997 Kapitan Man incident" as per a more precisely worded second request. Those documents revealed a professional Coast Guard search procedure. The official U.S. Coast Guard reports contained no references to political pressure or Russian obstructionism, although some documents were withheld (see Appendix).

Coast Guard response to international disaster was exemplified in November of 1998, when 10,000 people were killed in hurricanes which devastated the Central American nations of Nicaragua and Honduras. The European Union and the United States responded with more than $10 million in international aid. The U.S. Coast Guard joined a British military vessel to carry out search and rescue operations in coastal and river regions (Gilbert, Vol. Three, p. 883).

Not all of the Coast Guard's dangerous drug interdiction work is done without public challenge. Clinton Administration drug enforcement official General Barry McCaffrey (U.S. Army, Retired) was criticized for escalating the military role in drug enforcement. The Coast Guard (1999) began placing sharpshooters in USCG helicopters with orders to fire on drug smuggling vessels, primarily to disable the engines of craft carrying contraband in Caribbean waters. Machine guns were used to fire warning shots across the bows of suspected boats to force the crews to stop and allow boarding parties to investigate. One Coast Guard sharpshooter explained, "We're still humanitarian," because the choppers carried life rafts to drop to survivors if a suspect vessel sank after a confrontation (Bovard, p. 99).

President Clinton extended U.S. territorial waters from 12 to 24 nautical miles to give federal authorities more area in which to enforce immigration, customs and environmental laws. The extended sovereignty expanded U.S. Coast Guard jurisdiction and allowed Coast Guard personnel to stop and board vessels involved in drug running, pollution, illegal treasure salvage and alien smuggling. Vice President Al Gore applauded the new sovereignty extension, explaining, "We are putting would be smugglers and polluters on notice that we will do everything in our power to protect our waters and shores." The Clinton administration issued the policy document, "Turning to the Seas," which included 50 recommendations for a new ocean water strategy to support envi-

USCG Barque, Eagle, USCG Academy
(Coast Guard Historian's Office)

USRC BEAR (Coast Guard Historian)

CG port security boat (Career Guide, USCG, 2001)

Buoy tender and buoy. (U.S. Aids to Navigation, USCG, 1/2001)

Rigid Hull Inflatable Boat (RHI) (USCG)

41-foot Utility Boat (UTB)

38-ft. Deployable Pursuit Boat (DPB) (U.S. Coast Guard)

44-ft. Motor Life Boat (MLB) (U.S. Coast Guard)

Terror in New York, Coast Guard Patrol (Coast Guard, cover, Nov. 2001)

123-ft. Patrol Boat Island Class (WPB) (U.S. Coast Guard)

175-ft. Coastal Buoy Tender Keeper Class
(WLM) (U.S. Coast Guard)

378-ft. High Endurance Cutter (WHEC) (U.S. Coast Guard)

420-ft. Icebreaker (WAGB) (U.S. Coast Guard)

HH-65A Dolphin Short Range Recovery Helicopter
(U.S. Coast Guard)

HC-Hercules Long Range Surveillance Aircraft

Adm. Russell R. Waesche, Commandant 1936-1945
(Coast Guard Historian)

Adm. Paul A. Yost, Commandant 1986-1990
(Coast Guard Historian)

Adm. James M. Loy, Commandant 1998-2002
(Coast Guard Historian)

Adm. Thomas H. Collins, Commandant 2002-_____
(Coast Guard Historian)

Modern lighthouse. (U.S. Aids to Navigation, USCG, Jan. 2001)

ronmental, resource and military policies. The Coast Guard was given expanded authority to arbitrarily board ocean going vessels suspected of criminal activity (Insight, October 4-11,1999, p. 35). On the Great Lakes, the Coast Guard has long been known for battling winter weather to break up lake ice for the passage of cargo ships. In early Spring 1994, the 50 year old cutter Mackinaw was cutting pathways thorough the ice of the Soo Locks at Sault St. Marie, Michigan and the St. Mary's River. The Great Lakes had been frozen over the most extensively since the severe 1978 freeze.

The locks are the navigation connection between Lakes Huron and Superior and allow the passage of iron ore from Minnesota to the steel mills of the lower Great Lakes. In early Spring the ice can be 5 feet thick. Industrial plants welcome the Coast Guard ice breakers because by then their accumulated supplies of raw materials (limestone, iron ore, petroleum) are significantly diminished. The Great Lakes Carriers Association monitors the Soo Locks and the impact of cargo shipped through them. The locks are generally closed to traffic from 15 January to 25 March. The reopening of the locks opens the annual Great Lakes shipping season.

In 1994 the Coast Guard had to use nine ice breaking vessels in the bad areas of Lake Superior (White Fish Bay) and the Lake Huron-Michigan connection at the Mackinac Strait. The cutters guided most of the cargo carriers through the passages. Canadian icebreakers assisted in the operations. One Coast Guard cutter cut through 30 miles of ice in five days. Several giant ore carriers were caught in the ice or had to be guided to port.

The 1994 freeze resulted in extra funding for the 290-foot USCGC Mackinaw which had been scheduled for retirement. The famed cutter was reported to have a $4.5 million annual cost (Swanson, Chicago Tribune, 27 March, Sec. 7, p. 3).

Seven years later the USCGC Dolphin had to hack its way through polar weather and ice in the St. Clair River at the mouth of Lake Erie near Detroit, Michigan. A Coast Guard helicopter forwarded information to assist the cutter in tactical maneuvering. The previous week, USCGC Mackinaw and the 140-foot cutter Neah Bay penetrated the icy waters to help several freighters navigate in waters frozen from an early Midwestern cold snap. Assisted by USCGC Bristol Bay and the Canadian Coast Guard, the cutters kept the ice and the regional economy moving.

A Coast Guard helicopter mapped the ice and kept watch over ice fishermen who had driven trucks across the ice, a half mile from shore. Coast Guard veterans speculated that heavy snow and ice would melt into Spring floods which would challenge the life saving service again

(Cecil, Associated Press, Post Bulletin, 6 January 2001, p. 3A).

In the Fall of 1997, the Coast Guard chased, stopped and boarded a Chinese fishing vessel which was violating a drift-net fishing ban north of Hawaii. The master of the ship was illegally fishing with a 40-mile long net and ignored Coast Guard demands to stop. A Coast Guard cutter in Southeast Asian waters intercepted the Chinese vessel and boarded it 80 miles off the Chinese coast. The vessel was escorted to the U.S. territory of Guam where its cargo was auctioned. Deportation and the loss of fishing licenses are possible punishments levied upon drift-net violators (U.S. News and World Report, 11 August, 1997, pp.15-16).

The U.S.-Russian maritime line divides the Bering Sea between Alaska, the Aleutian Islands and Russia. The line is equivalent to the distance between Miami and Boston. The Coast Guard's responsibility in that region is to preserve marine life threatened by foreign fishing trawlers which fish the Bering Sea and sometimes traverse the boundary. Coast Guard aircraft patrol the line and USCG cutters police the bountiful, cold, forbidding waters, sometimes firing warning shots at wayward fishing vessels.

The USCGC Storis patrolled the coveted fishery, and was on duty in May 1999, as the crew monitored a radar screen to target interlopers. Fishing vessels from several Asian nations, Poland and Norway plied the waters on the Russian side of the maritime line having paid the former Soviet republic for licenses and fishing privileges. Four Coast Guard cutters supported by helicopters, huge C-130 aircraft and overworked crews, monitored the trawlers in often extreme weather and treacherous seas. High winds and waves which climbed to heights of 10 to 50 feet keep the sailors vigilant during duty tours which required weeks at sea. Wind chills in excess of 10 degrees below zero added to the rigors of the mission.

The cutter Polar Sea once chased a Chinese trawler, which fled U.S. waters after cutting away its nets. The cutter followed the Chinese vessel into foggy and rainy Russian waters and encountered a patrol boat. The Russian military vessel opened fire on the Chinese boat and the cutter headed prudently back into American water.

On patrol in May 1999, the cutter Sherman relieved the Storis and weathered three polar storms in as many weeks.

Sea birds, crab, marine mammals and hundreds of fish species, including salmon, swim these waters. The Coast Guard patrols these waters to perform search and rescue missions and enforce maritime laws so the resources of the sea can be preserved.

"Being a fish cop on the Bering Sea" is difficult, dangerous and rewarding duty (Lewan, Associated Press, Post Bulletin, 8 May, p. 9A).

In August 1999, the U.S. Coast Guard cutter Hamilton confronted a Russian trawler fishing in American waters, gave chase, and boarded the vessel 170 miles West of Alaska in Russian territory. Almost 40 tons of fish were found in the Russian holds. Quickly and menacingly surrounded by a dozen Russian ships, the Coast Guard crew turned the Russian fishing vessel over to Russian border police and sailed back into U.S. waters. Coast Guard reports of the incident were forwarded to the U.S. State Department. The Russian government was later reported to have levied heavy fines upon the violators (Reuters News Service, 7 August 1999).

CHAPTER XI

THE WAR ON TERRORISM

The 2000 presidential race between Republican candidate George W. Bush, the son of former president George Herbert Walker Bush, and Democratic candidate Al Gore, William Jefferson Clinton's vice president, was closely contested. Gore won the popular vote by 500,000 votes and Bush won the electoral vote in a close Florida victory.

The candidates' legal teams became ensnared in vote recounts, ballot design, quarrels over which votes should be tabulated, retabulated or discarded, and contentious hearings in the Florida Supreme Court and U.S. Supreme Court. The state court solutions seemed to favor Gore. The federal court challenged the actions of the Florida Court, and in a split decision, decided the recount process violated voter rights and due process. George W. Bush emerged the victor.

Bush's opponents contended the Republican dominated U.S. Supreme Court gave the election to Bush. Bush's supporters believed the federal court prevented a partisan Florida court from handing the election to Gore. Nonetheless, when Bush took office, disgruntled critics concluded the new president exhibited intellectual shortcomings which rendered him unfit for the job.

Negative perceptions of G.W. Bush diminished after September 11, 2001("9-11"), when terrorist attacks upon the World Trade Center in New York City and the Pentagon devastated America, and provided the new president with the opportunity to provide steady, inspired domestic, diplomatic and military leadership. New York Mayor Rudy Guilliani rose to the occasion out of the rubble of New York City, and inspired the nation with exemplary leadership.

The attacks killed thousands of New York residents and hundreds of brave police officers, firefighters, and other rescue workers who had rushed to the volatile scene. Similar self sacrifice was exhibited by military and civilian personnel at the Pentagon, where casualties numbered in the hundreds, and in the Pennsylvania country side where brave airline passengers attacked the terrorists who commandeered their aircraft, and forced the plane into the ground, sparing the nation's capital. Those heroic passengers had been alerted by cell phones and radios of the suicide flight of the other two fuel-filled passenger aircraft which had been deliberately flown into the Twin Towers of the World Trade Center by Islamic Middle Eastern fanatics. America was changed forever.

The 11 September attacks on the U.S killed nearly 4,000 Americans. The plot was traced to Saudi Arabian exile Osama bin Laden and his fellow Muslim extremist practitioners of "Jihad" (holy war) against the U.S. Bin Laden's al-Qaeda terrorist network was associated with the 1998 bombings of two U.S. embassies in Africa which killed 200 people; and the October 2000 attack on the USS Cole (USN) which left 17 U.S. sailors dead in Yemen (Bergen, p. 25).

Bin Laden's terrorists included suicidal followers, some of whom had trained as jet pilots in America. Those who flew passenger jets into the Pentagon and World Trade Center were "in a martyrdom operation that, in their view, would instantly take them to Paradise. They saw themselves as martyrs in the name of Allah and their attacks as acts of worship" (Bergen, p. 27).

The attacks united the nation and galvanized the training and expansion of military forces to protect the U.S. and wage war in al-Qaeda and Taliban sanctuaries in Afghanistan and elsewhere in the Middle East. Thousands of U.S. military Reserve and Regular forces were called upon to do their duty. The Afghan Taliban were eventually defeated in battle.

The USCG received increased funding for "Homeland Security," increased patrols in U.S. waters, and went on overseas escort missions with the U.S. Navy. More than two thousand Coast Guard Reservists were called to active duty to supplement Regular personnel. As the war in Afghanistan continued, Coast Guard men and women added to the security forces at the U.S. Navy base in Guantanamo (Cuba) where hundreds of dangerous al-Qaeda and Taliban prisoners were detained.

The Coast Guard cooperated in the war against terrorism with other U.S. Government anti-terrorist agencies. The Department of Transportation assumed more responsibility in domestic airport security enhancement, and utilized Coast Guard skills and experience in the war on terror. The USCG joined the other armed services, federal agencies like U.S. Customs, Immigration and Naturalization Service, FBI), the Central Intelligence Agency, National Security Council, and the Department of State (The American Spectator, Nov.-Dec. 2001, p. 55).

The "Terror From the Sky" on "9-11" mobilized the nation. President Bush responded: "I've ordered that the full resources of the federal government go to help the victims and their families and to conduct a full-scale investigation to hunt down and find these folks who committed this act. Terrorism against our nation will not stand" (Schwartz, AP/Post Bulletin, p. 1A).

The Federal Aviation Administration was ordered to shut down the national aviation system and ground all aircraft on 9/11 and for days after. U.S. borders were sealed. Military bases were put on full alert. Federal buildings, the United Nations, and skyscrapers throughout the nation were evacuated. Within hours after the attack, the Twin Towers of the New York City Trade Center collapsed into rubble, entrapping and killing hundreds of victims, bringing to mind the previous attack (February 1993) which injured more than a thousand people and killed six. Few predicted it was a warning of things to come.

Some observers called the "9-11" horror "the second Pearl Harbor." Secretary of Defense Donald Rumsfeld and the White House planned the military responses which decimated the Middle East terrorist network (Ron Fournier, AP/Post Bulletin, 11 September 2001, p. 3A).

On 14 September the Pentagon announced the activation of military reserves. Several thousand reservists from the Air Force (10,000), Marine Corps (7,500), Navy (3,000) and Coast Guard (2,000) were called to active duty (Schafer, AP, September, 2001).

The Coast Guard Captain of the Port of New York and the Port Authority of New York/New Jersey announced (13 September) a joint decision to reopen New York Harbor to commercial ships. Coast Guard units increased their port security presence. Vessels entering the port were boarded at sea and escorted into the harbor. Twelve cutters and small boats from several Atlantic stations converged on New York harbor under the command of USCGC Tahoma. Hundreds of Coast Guard women and men assisted local, state and federal officials in rescue and security duties. A C-130 cargo plane brought donated blood supplies to New York from the Coast Guard Air Station in Sacramento, California.

Coast Guard Law Enforcement Detachments (LEDETs) from northern and southern bases augmented USCG teams on board cutters and small boats in the New York and Baltimore harbors. Port Security Units (PSUs) from Florida and Virginia supplemented the Tactical Law Enforcement Teams (TACLETs). Coast Guard helicopters and ground vehicles assisted emergency response agencies in the transportation of injured persons and logistical and medical personnel, supplies and equipment. Coast Guard chaplains supported New York firefighters, police officers and military personnel with counseling and support during the dangerous and stressful humanitarian operations.

Coast Guard medium endurance cutters and buoy tenders were

positioned off major Eastern seaboard and Gulf of Mexico ports to assist in maintaining security. The vessels included the larger 210, 225 and 270 foot cutters. USCG officials reaffirmed, despite this critical deployment of vessels, that migrant and narcotic interdiction missions would continue in the Caribbean and off the Florida coast (Coast Guard News, September 16, 2001). Acting under Pentagon orders, the Coast Guard activated 1,200 reservists qualified to run armed, fast patrol boats to police the harbors of Los Angeles and New York (Dao and Myers, The New York Times, p.17).

The Coast Guard set up the most extensive port security operations since World War II. Security perimeters were established along the nation's coasts, waterways and ports. Passenger cruise ships were initially prevented from entering New York Harbor (Pear and Miller, The New York Times, p. B1).

Coast Guard duties expanded in both usual and unexpected areas. In early October, Coast Guard aircraft spent more than three days searching for a crop spraying plane the U.S. State Department had used in the drug war in Columbia. Interest in the missing aircraft was stimulated by allegations that suspected Middle East terrorists wanted to learn to fly U.S. crop dusting planes to carry out biological attacks on the United States.

A Coast Guard petty officer told the press the single-engine plane had taken off from an island near the Bahamas en route to Patrick Air Force Base near Cape Canaveral, Florida. Two Coast Guard aircraft and a cutter searched for the missing plane. A U.S. Air Force plane was scheduled to join in the hunt. State Department officials asserted they did not believe "any criminal intent was involved in the disappearance" (Drudge Report, 4 October, 2001).

Within a month of 9-11, the Coast Guard was well into its port security enhancement responsibilities. In Baltimore, the USCG required an entry notice of 96 hours for any cargo vessels entering that port. Armed Coast Guard boats patrolled Boston Harbor in waters adjacent to Logan International Airport, the terminal of origin for two of the four hijacked aircraft used in the terrorist attacks. Airport security was strengthened, but required long passenger lines and waits for departure to allow more rigorous passenger and baggage searches.

In Houston, the plethora of petrochemical plants and underground petroleum and natural gas pipelines which offered volatile terrorist targets required increased law enforcement and private security vigilance. The U.S. Coast Guard used its personnel, helicopters and boats to monitor the more than 100 petrochemical plants located in the Houston Port area (Janofsky, The New York Times, October 8, 2001).

To coordinate the many federal departments and agencies with security responsibilities, President Bush created the Homeland Security Office and appointed Vietnam Bronze Star winner and Pennsylvania Governor Tom Ridge to head it. One national newspaper editor lauded the president's objectives, but questioned whether, without complete budgetary control, the Homeland Security chief could coordinate the mission. Some members of Congress wanted to combine the Federal Emergency Management Agency, Customs, Border Patrol and Coast Guard into a new Homeland Security Agency, but all of these agencies had significant responsibilities in other areas (USA Today, October 9, 2001, p. 14A).

The September 11, 2001 attacks put increased pressure on the Immigration and Naturalization Service (INS) to round up the estimated 300,000 illegal aliens still in the U.S. after being designated for deportation by federal judges. INS officials explained that statutory reforms and increased agency funding would be required to carry out those objectives.

Related concerns were raised in October by the Congressional Immigration Reform Caucus which offered several suggestions: 1) the creation of a unified border security agency combining responsibilities shared by U.S. Customs, the State Department and the U.S. Coast Guard; 2) the establishment of an interagency database of background checks on applicants for visas; 3) data bases on international visitors and foreign students; 4) increased personnel for border and immigration enforcement agencies; 5) abolition of the diversity visa program which favored immigrants from several nations on the U.S. State Department terrorist list; and 6) implementation of a moratorium on immigration (D'Agostino,

Human Events, p. 5). The controversial items stimulated a great deal of discussion, but political realities mitigated against their immediate implementation.

By November 2001, the Coast Guard had tightened security measures in the 361 U.S. public seaports to monitor and prevent attempts by potential terrorists to sink a vessel in strategic sea lanes, knock out suspension bridges, ignite volatile cargo vessels, or launch explosive weapons from sea. Another horrible scenario suggested by security experts was the possibility of terrorists commandeering an ocean liner or cruise ship and using the passengers and crew on board as hostages to thwart capture or military intervention.

U.S. Coast Guard Commandant James Loy endorsed several counter-terrorist defense measures, explaining, "Any given ship in the hands of the wrong guy has potential to do harm," given the significance of shipping to the national economy and their presence on strategic waterways. Admiral Loy advocated close cooperation with the Customs

Service and INS to monitor and police crew rosters and cargo manifests. Loy facilitated the establishment of well trained, armed Regular and Reserve Coast Guard "Sea Marshals" who boarded ships in major harbors to inspect vessels and escort them into port under cutter protection (Johnson, St. Paul Pioneer Press, November 2001, p. 11A).

In January 2002 the U.S. Customs commissioner expressed concern about the potential of terrorist organizations to smuggle small nuclear devices by ship into major deep water sea ports. Coast Guard Commandant Admiral Loy and Customs Commissioner Robert Bonner proposed that cargo destined for U.S. ports be inspected, placed in secure containers, and certified as safe before being shipped from foreign ports. New technology was considered which would monitor the thousands of huge cargo containers that enter American ports daily. Global trade could be seriously threatened and interrupted by successful terrorist activity or incomplete inspections (Dettmer, Insight, pp. 22-23).

By October 2001, Coast Guard sea marshals were policing the dozen refineries, storage facilities, ports, ferry lines, and bridges ringing San Francisco Bay. These special investigative teams had access to manifests forwarded to the Coast Guard Marine Safety Office by foreign and domestic commercial vessels several days before their arrival. San Francisco, Oakland, New York, Houston, Seattle and other ports were protected by the Coast Guard traffic system.

Coast Guard port security duties include the supervision and inspection of hazardous cargo handling and the boarding vessels to inspect and assist harbor pilots in bringing vessels into port. Foreign and domestic ship captains generally welcome the protective security service. Selective enforcement and presence is the key to the sea marshal service because it is impossible to inspect the thousands of cargo containers that ships bring into U.S. harbors on any given day (Ritter, USA Today, p. 4A).

Defending against terrorist attacks on land, sea, public waterways and in vulnerable seaports is a daunting task for U.S. civilian, law enforcement and military authorities.

Homeland security is an integrated mission and a duty for which the Coast Guard, with its multi-mission and civil-military authority is ideally suited.

Commander Stephen E. Flynn (USCG) contributed to the analysis and expansion of the service's national security mission. Commander Flynn served as a senior fellow in the National Security Studies Program affiliated with the Council on Foreign Relations, where he directed a study about border control and global economic integration (Flynn, Proceedings, p. 75).

Flynn explained that the U.S. economic infrastructure is especially vulnerable to terrorist attack because of the high volume of international trade that comes into U.S. harbors on foreign cargo vessels. Those ships could knowingly or unknowingly house unconventional nuclear, biological and chemical weapons of mass destruction in the millions of tons of cargo containers, technologically rigged to be activated in strategic locations at designated times.

Such devices could be timed to detonate after being transported by rail or truck to strategic inland ports and transportation terminals. Commander Flynn asserted that the Coast Guard's multiple mission experience and presence on land and sea provides the trained personnel to be a first responder in what Coast Guard Commandant Admiral James Loy described as "maritime domain awareness" (Flynn, Proceedings, pp. 73-74).

Coast Guard Captains of the Port play an essential role in gathering data on ship movements and coordinating intelligence with local, state and federal law enforcement and security agencies. COTPs utilize "Coast Guard shore side and afloat assets" in their capacity as "on-scene federal incident coordinators" (Flynn, Proceedings, p. 74).

The complexity of guarding the national infrastructure against terrorism was illustrated by U.S. Attorney John Ashcroft's directive (8 October 2001) which urged law enforcement agencies across the nation to go on high alert, and warned utilities (electrical, water and nuclear power plants), railroads, trucking firms and gas and oil companies to expand their capacities to prevent or respond to terrorist attacks (Seper, The Washington Times, p. 8).

In November 2001, the FBI alerted law enforcement departments in several Western states to be on the alert for terrorist threats against strategic targets, including suspension bridges along the Pacific. Homeland Security Director Tom Ridge coordinated information between local, state and federal law enforcement agencies and security specialists in the California governor's office. Security around suspension bridges in San Diego, Los Angeles and San Francisco was stepped up and monitored by the California Highway Patrol, the National Guard and the U.S. Coast Guard (Keith, Associated Press, 1 November, 2001).

On 11 September 2001, the CGC Tahoma was visible with its distinctive red racing stripe, patrolling the New York Harbor security zone in the shadow of Manhattan skyscrapers. The distinctive stripe is present on all USCG vessels. President John F. Kennedy (1961-63), who gave an address from the deck of the CGC Eagle, is the alleged "father" of the well known stripe, the result of his proposal to enhance the visual identification of federal facilities and equipment. The distinctive stripe was officially added to Coast Guard vessels on 6 April, 1967 ("Coast Guard," inside cover, November 2001).

On that tragic September 11 day, Coast Guard Captain of the Port of New York, Rear Admiral Richard Bennis, in coordination with the Port Authority of New York/New Jersey, reopened the harbor on a selective basis to commercial vessels while additional Coast Guard units were arriving from around the nation to supplement port security forces.

Incoming vessels were boarded at sea by Coast Guard and other agency officials, and escorted through the various security perimeters. A Coast Guard C-130 cargo plane from Sacramento landed at a New York City airport with 400 pounds of blood supplies. Port security was enhanced along the Pacific Coast from California to the Alaskan oil port of Valdez.

Coast Guard bases and district headquarters throughout North America and Hawaii upgraded security, using concrete barriers, barbed wire, and additional armed personnel. Large armed cutters were stationed off strategic harbors to protect major waterways.

High risk locations on the Great Lakes were protected by Coast Guard and other law enforcement and security agencies. Coordinated teams of Canadian and U.S. Coast Guard personnel boarded foreign vessels bound for the St. Lawrence Seaway to check crews, cargo and ships manifests. Law enforcement and port security units from across the nation contributed more than 1600 active duty, civilian and Reserve Coast Guard men and women to New York City to aid local, state and federal officials in search and rescue and security operations.

On the day of the terror the Coast Guard assisted civilian sailors and local officials with the evacuation of thousands of New Yorkers from Manhattan by water. Coast Guard helicopters patrolled urban skies and coastal areas. The following day 12 cutters were patrolling New York harbor. A tent city for Coast Guard personnel was erected at Fort Wadsworth, Staten Island. Coast Guard Auxiliary boats plied the harbor waters. Coast Guard Regular and Reserve personnel delivered supplies to "Ground Zero" rescue crews (Wilder, Coast Guard, November 2001, pp. 8-11).

Coast Guard responses to subsequent events were quick and varied. On 5 January 2002, a 15 year old male crashed a Cessna piper cub aircraft into a Tampa, Florida skyscraper. It seemed to be the independent, impulsive act of a troubled teenager. A Coast Guard helicopter had tracked the unauthorized flight and motioned the young pilot to land, but got no response. Two U.S. Air Force F-15 jet fighters scrambled from a base 200 miles away, but got to the scene after the crash. The high school senior was alleged by police officials to have no ties to terrorists, but a suicide note found later included a statement sympathetic to terrorist mastermind Osama bin Laden (Chachere, Associated Press, January 6, 2002).

President Bush announced his plan for increased homeland security funding on 24 January, 2002. On 25 January the President went to Portland, Maine, where he and Transportation Secretary Norman Y. Mineta boarded the USCGC Tahoma to visit Commander Gary Smialek (USCG) and his crew. Speaking to the crew, Bush promised to increase funding to enhance Coast Guard capabilities: "The Coast Guard has a vital and important mission. I saw how the Coast Guard responded after 9/11, and know how important the Coast Guard is for the safety, security, and well being of American citizens" (Peterson, Sea Power, February 2002, pp. 16-17).

President Bush praised the Coast Guard personnel, describing them "as a fine group of people who don't get nearly as much appreciation from the American people as they should" (CNS News, 25 January 2002).

Under Bush's $10.7 billion border security plan, the Coast Guard's expanded role was to be supported with $2.9 billion, "the largest boost increase in spending for the Coast Guard," the president proclaimed, "in our nation's history." The funding was necessary because of increased assignments in port security, intelligence, vessel reconnaissance and surveillance beyond established maritime boundaries (Curl, The Washington Times, January 26, 2002).

A Coast Guard spokesperson expressed gratitude for President Bush's pledge, adding that the additional funding would provide for a more modern cutter fleet, "help with the Deepwater program, pay the large number of reservists on active duty, cover increased recruiting costs, and provide needed pay raises for our men and women" (Peterson, Sea Power, p. 17).

The homeland security mission before 9/11 had been divided between federal military, law enforcement and intelligence agencies. Coordination was difficult because laws prohibited inter-agency data sharing. After 9/11, the U.S. Armed Forces increased their commitments to homeland security, and made commendable efforts toward mutual cooperation.

Those efforts illustrated the need for training and increased expenditures for updated and new equipment for regular and reserve units. To meet the new challenges, President Bush, expanding Executive Order 13223, gave the Transportation Secretary the same authority to mobilize Coast Guard reservists as the Secretary of Defense had to call up reserve personnel in the Defense Department (DOD).

The post-9/11 Coast Guard responded to its port security responsibilities in major sea ports with increased patrol activities, using Coast Guard equipment and U.S. Navy Cyclone-class boats. Hundreds of "sea marshals" were deployed to secure ships entering U.S. ports on the West Coast. The Coast Guard intelligence data base which monitored thousands of commercial vessels operating globally was extensively utilized and shared with other military, intelligence and law enforcement agencies.

Steps were taken to secure more funding for the Deepwater program which is designed to upgrade and replace Coast Guard command and control systems, helicopters, fixed wing aircraft, and cutters.

Securing U.S. waterways and ports is a Coast Guard responsibility requiring coordination with civilian and military agencies, all the more essential after 11 September 2001 (Goure, Sea Power, February 2002, pp. 46-49). The Coast Guard solidified its relationships with the U.S. Customs Service, Federal Emergency Management Agency, Department of Defense and the U.S. Navy, Border Patrol, Immigration and Naturalization Service (INS), Federal Bureau of Investigation, local and state authorities, the Departments of Commerce, Justice and State, and agencies of the Department of Transportation, under which the Coast Guard had operated since 1967.

The Coast Guard adjusted to what U.S. Coast Guard Commandant Admiral James Loy termed "the New Normalcy" conditions for maritime security (Conroy, Proceedings, November 2001, pp. 39-40).

The need to reform and integrate border security operations was illustrated by the post September 11 INS report which revealed that of the 19 terrorists involved in the attacks, 13 had entered the United States legally, but several had remained in the nation after visa violations. In response, the Department of Justice (DOJ) presented a restructuring plan to Congress which divided INS functions into customer support (assisting legal aliens) and law enforcement, which would deal strictly with visa violations and the arrest and deportation of illegal aliens. DOJ and Congressional planners favored the complete restructuring of the INS and combining border enforcement functions into a single National Border Security Agency (NBSA) to include the INS, Drug Enforcement Administration (DEA), U.S. Customs Service, and the U.S. Coast Guard (Johnson, CNS News, January 01, 2002).

Despite the increased security duties imposed upon the Coast Guard, environmental politics intruded upon the service. Midway Island, the former U.S. Navy base of World War Two fame, became a key Coast Guard refueling depot and emergency North Pacific landing strip for civilian and military aircraft. Then, in 2000, a U.S. resort on Midway was forced to close because of expenses incurred as a result of stricter U.S. Fish and Wildlife environmental regulations. The Coast Guard depended on the island as a base for refueling during search and rescue and law enforcement missions (Post Bulletin, February 1, 2002). A Coast Guard spokesperson warned that with the closing of the resort, loss of employees and tourists, and the threatened termination of the base, "there will be no one to mind the store, and that's not in America's best interest" (Jones, CNS News, February 1, 2002).

In February 2002, a Pentagon plan to create the new office of the Northern Command under the leadership of a four star general, was revealed. The four star officer would be in charge of military personnel assigned to domestic air patrols and coastal and port security operations designed to respond to terrorist activities and biological, chemical and nuclear threats.

Secretary of Defense Donald H. Rumsfeld explained that the Northern Command would have the responsibility of coordinating U.S. Navy and Coast Guard security patrols. The Northern Command would also direct military units involved in fighting the drug war in the Caribbean and Latin America.

Civil liberties organizations opposed the plan because of their contention that military personnel are not trained to deal with civilians in law enforcement operations. Critics also asserted the use of the military for such purposes violated the Posse Comitatus Act (1878), which requires presidential and congressional approval before military forces can be utilized in domestic police activities (Dao, The New York Times, 6 February 2002). The Coast Guard provides ample precedent for the professional use of a military service for domestic law enforcement functions. Critics of such operations are not familiar with the exemplary training and functions of armed forces military police units.

During the stressful months following the terror attacks, the U.S. Coast Guard found itself handling a sensitive political and humanitarian mission in Cuba. Cuban officials expressed gratitude for U.S. donations of food after a November 2001 hurricane wreaked havoc throughout the Marxist dictatorship. Over the next year and a half the Coast Guard placed a representative in Cuba to coordinate patrol and law enforcement operations, and the FBI helped Cuban police investigate the murder of two Miami visitors. This liaison was stimulated by President Castro's offer of intelligence and medical help to the United States after the 11 September terrorist attacks, and his acceptance of the American use of the U.S. Navy base at Guantanamo as a detainment center for captured Al Qaeda and Taliban prisoners (Thompson, The New York Times, February 7, 2002).

Respect for the anti-terrorist responsibilities of the U.S. Coast Guard was illustrated by the suggestion of a U.S. airline pilot that Coast Guard personnel be used as sky marshals while in or out of uniform, and as security personnel at major national airports. The pilot reviewed the training and responsibilities of the service and commended the USCG for its two centuries of protecting U.S. borders and citizens (Fow, Letter to the Editor, USA Today, December 28, 2001).

The impact of 11 September 2001 upon the structure and mission of the USCG, and on its personnel, is incalculable. Soon after the terrorist attack, Coast Guard personnel were at "Ground Zero," the scene of the destruction, administering their expertise in that devastating and emotional environment.

Coast Guard National Strike Force teams monitored air quality levels in the damaged and unsafe building structures, or what remained of them. Coast Guard chaplains counseled and conducted religious services. Coast Guard firefighters, many of them Reservists who worked at area fire departments applied their skills to the formidable tasks. Two Coast Guard Reservists who worked for the New York Fire Department (PS2 Vincent Danz; MK1 Jeffery Palazzo) died carrying out rescue attempts. One volunteer firefighter and member of the Coast Guard Auxiliary who had served in the Marine Corps (Gregory Sikorsky) died during the collapse of buildings at Ground Zero trying to save victims (Sperduto, Coast Guard, December 200l/January 2002, p. 46).

Coast Guard firefighter Rich Hyland spent one week at Ground Zero looking for survivors, some of whom were friends from joint training sessions with the New York Fire Department. "I was there so many days," Hyland reported, and "between the debris and the smell alone, it was horrible" (Sperduto, Coast Guard, December 2001/January 2002, pp. 45-49).

PSC Robert Gryder (USCG) served in Vietnam with the United States Marine Corps, four years on active duty with the Coast Guard, and then switched to port security in the Coast Guard Reserve. The 36 year Alaskan military veteran retired from the Coast Guard one month before the September 11 terrorist attacks, after which he requested and was granted a return to active duty to assist his nation (Grisafe, Coast Guard, December 2001/January 2002, p. 27).

While serving as the Coast Guard's Liaison to the Department of Defense for Reserve Affairs at the Pentagon, Captain Louis Farrell was on duty on 11 September when the commercial passenger jetliner under the control of Middle East terrorists crashed into the Pentagon. Farrell experienced the reaction, injuries and deaths of Pentagon friends and colleagues on that horrible day (Farrell, Coast Guard, December 2001/January 2002, p. 36).

Lieutenant Commander Gilbert Granados, USCGR (Retired), was in his office on the 98th floor of the World Trade Center when the hijacked terrorist aircraft hit the buildings. Granados died in the collapse of the second tower. Lieutenant Commander Granados was a 20 year veteran of the USCG, a graduate of the U.S. Merchant Marine Academy, served in Desert Storm in the Persian Gulf, and had been assigned to several active and reserve duty stations in the New York area (Coast Guard, December 2001/January 2002, p. 34).

The Coast Guard Auxiliary supplemented active duty and reserve units after the terrorist attacks. The Auxiliary contributed thousands of hours of volunteer service patrolling ports and rivers, monitoring recreational boating, offering public boating education, and providing search and rescue standby. Auxiliary services released active duty personnel for crucial law enforcement and port security duties. After September 11, the Coast Guard Auxiliary increased its patrols on the sometimes fog bound Potomac River, adding to the security watch in the Washington, D.C. area (Coast Guard, December 2001/2002, p. 7).

The Commandant of the United States Coast Guard issued "An Open Letter To Team Coast Guard"* following the terrorist attacks upon the United States. Among Admiral J. M. Loy's inspirational remarks, were the following:

"In the wake of the terrible events of September 11th, every one of you has answered the call to action to protect and defend the liberties of a grateful nation. I am deeply proud of your superb response...We are now in the process of adjusting operations to the 'new normalcy' of American life...The mission of maritime security is not new to us...We must continue to keep watch...(aware) of our vulnerabilities, the threats to our security, and those who would seek to do us harm. Above all, we must continue to protect America at all costs. Semper Paratus" (Coast Guard, December 2001/January 2002, p. 3).

* The 1994-95 integration of Coast Guard reservists into active commands gave the Coast Guard Reserve special status among military reserve units. Team Coast Guard includes all of the USCG components: active duty, reserve, auxiliary and civilian (The Coast Guardsman's Manual, Ninth Edition, p. 30).

CHAPTER XII

AN OVERVIEW OF COAST GUARD HISTORY

The origin of the U.S. Coast Guard can be traced to 4 August 1790, when Congress established the Revenue Cutter Service (RCS) to suppress the smuggling trade. Treasury Secretary Alexander Hamilton endorsed the establishment of this naval service to assist U.S. Customs collectors in enforcing the tariff laws which provided revenue for the federal government. Not even the British Royal Navy could suppress smuggling, but the attempt to do contributed to the outbreak of the Revolutionary War (1775-1783).

President George Washington and Hamilton insisted the officers of the U.S. Revenue Service who commanded the revenue cutters be of the highest personal and professional qualities, and show respect to civilian merchant vessel crews and captains while enforcing federal laws .

President Thomas Jefferson ordered the RCS to enforce the trade embargo against rogue nations (1807). President Andrew Jackson ordered the USRCS to enforce the tariff laws when South Carolina challenged federal tariff laws (1832-1833). President Pierce ordered the cutters to enforce the fugitive slave law in the sectional Compromise of 1850.

The USRCS enforced maritime law, aided mariners in distress, chartered U.S. waters, and assisted the U.S. Lighthouse Service. The cutter crews maintained aids to navigation, marked river and harbor channels, inspected lighthouses, transported and supplied lighthouse crews, and, in northerly latitudes, used reinforced cutters to break ice.

The RCS initiated the Coast Guard's wartime affiliation with the U.S. Navy. The RCS teamed up with USN forces in the suppression of pirates and in the 19th century wars against France, Britain, Mexico, the Seminole Indians, and the Confederate States of America (King, I.H., pp. 1-3).

The U.S. Revenue Marine performed valiantly in the Civil War

(1861-65). Captain John McGowan led the Federal merchant vessel Star of the West into Charleston Harbor to supply besieged U.S. troops under Confederate fire at Fort Sumter, South Carolina, and was the first U.S. naval vessel to come under fire in the War Between the States. During the siege, U.S. Revenue cutter Harriet Lane under the command of Captain John Faunce (USRM) and the rest of the relief naval squadron came under fire. The Harriet Lane fired at a Confederate vessel, becoming the first U.S. naval vessel to fire a shot in the Civil War. U.S. Revenue Marine cutters were then ordered by President Lincoln into duty with the U.S. Navy where the Revenue Marine performed blockade and combat missions and supported infantry landings with gun fire (Strobridge, "The U.S. Revenue Marine and the Civil War," pp. 1-3).

In May 1862, the Revenue cutter Miami transported President Lincoln and several high ranking military and civilian officials down the Potomac River to a safe landing at Fortress Monroe, Virginia, where the President directed a reluctant Union general to commence artillery bombardment and an infantry assault on Confederate positions (Strobridge, pp. 6-9).

Revenue Service personnel performed landing assaults not unlike the amphibious actions of U.S. Marines and, later in history, U.S. Navy Seals. On 17 May 1890, a USRCS infantry squad stormed ashore in Cedar Keys, Florida, to bring law and order to an isolated town suffering under the tyrannical control of a mayor and his gang of thugs, some of whom were members the local police force. The Revenue Service assumed jurisdiction because the mayor was also a Customs inspector! The mission was supported by the officers and crew of the cutter McLane, a 357-ton sidewheel steamer. The wayward mayor fled the territory, eventually fell victim to an Alabama police chief in a shootout (Wells, "Crisis at Cedar Keys," pp. 41-45).

The Revenue Cutter School of Instruction for cadets and future officers featured a rigorous curriculum taught on board training and cruising vessels, and land sites. By 1900, Congress authorized the purchase of land at Curtis Bay, Maryland. Arundel Cove was the site of a boat and ship building yard and the Academy classroom building (King, I.H., pp. 154-158).

The curriculum evolved into a two year eclectic blend of cutter cruises, physical training, mathematics, history, government and the Constitution, language, composition, rhetoric, the construction of official reports, philosophy, law, navigation, commerce, marine engineering, navigation, gunnery, naval technology, steam engineering, surveying, and seamanship, ending with rigorous oral and written examinations. The instructional staff was composed of civilian and military specialists (King, I.H., pp. 159-175).

The Revenue Marine rescued imperiled mariners, enforced maritime law, and monitored aids to navigation and lighthouses. In 1789, Congress federalized the lighthouses which had existed since the British colonial period. Colonial and Federal lighthouses were built of wood, stone, steel and concrete. Managed by isolated keepers and their families, the optical evolution of illumination included wicked oil lamps with glass refractors and reflecting prisms. Sound warnings from cannons, gunfire, bells, and air sirens warned ships away from rocky shores and guided them at night, and in fog and other low visibility weather.

Lighthouses were controlled at various times in history by the Treasury Department and Commerce Department, and transferred to Coast Guard jurisdiction in 1939. Men and women served in the Lighthouse Service in peace and war, and saved the lives of people in peril on land and sea.

Lightships sailed, floated and were anchored in dangerous places where lighthouses could not be built. Lightship crews lived isolated, cramped and dangerous lives. Some vessels were torn apart in storms. Others were run down at night or in inclement weather by larger vessels. The first lightship was stationed in Chesapeake Bay (1820), the last at Nantucket Bay, replaced by a large navigation buoy in 1983 ("U.S. Coast Guard: A Historical Overview," 28 December, 2000, p. 1).

The lighthouses off Grand Marais (Minnesota) and the Apostle Islands (Wisconsin) on Lake Superior were built in 1874 of similar design to accommodate particular geographic conditions and withstand storms, high waves and winter ice (Stonehouse, Lighthouse Keepers and Coast Guard Cutters, pp. 11-14).

Lightships manned and anchored at sea in strategic and often dangerous points supplemented the aids to navigation mission. Lightship 34 served Charleston Harbor, South Carolina until the vessel was retired from duty in 1924 after 59 years of service. Built in 1865 of oak, pine, galvanized iron and copper, the gleaming white sailing ship had a length of 101 feet, beam of 23 feet, and draft of 11 feet. The illuminating apparatus consisted of 8 oil lamps and 2 lanterns with a hand operated bell fog signal ("Vessel Designation: LV 34," pp. 1-2; description in part from photo of Lightship 34 taken in 1916 in author's personal file collection).

Heroic lighthouse keepers kept harbor entries safer, and ventured out on treacherous waters to save the lives of endangered passengers and mariners who were the victims of collisions, storms, fires and acts of war. The names of many brave lighthouse keepers remain etched on the hulls of buoy tenders called, in their honor, Keeper Class cutters, built by the Marinette Marine Corporation of Marinette, Wisconsin. Designated by the letters WLM, the cutters include the Katherine

Walker, Abbie Burgess, Frank Drew, William Tate, Maria Bray, and Henry Blake (Stonehouse, Lighthouse Keepers...., pp. 49-219). Proud indeed were the men and women who wore the sturdy golden copper badges of the U.S. Lighthouse Service on their uniforms. The author acquired a replica of the badge from an antique shop in Charleston, South Carolina. The wings of the American eagle round off the top of the badge, the center of which features a lighthouse surrounded by the words, "U.S. Light House Service."

Among the service heroines, Catherine Moore, who retired from the Lighthouse Service in 1878 at the age of 84. Moore saved more than 20 lives from her post at the Black Rock Harbor Light Station in Connecticut ("Heroes...," Coast Guard, inside front cover).

In the 1960s the Coast Guard began the automation of U.S. lighthouses, but preserved the nation's earliest lighthouse in Boston Harbor to honor lighthouse keepers (Holland, F. Ross, p. 73). The magnificent black and white Tybee Island Lighthouse and light station facing the Atlantic Ocean at the entrance of the port of Savannah, Georgia, is a popular tourist attraction ("Tybee Island Lighthouse," personal file, author).

The USCG gradually replaced on-station lightships with large navigational buoys (LNB), also called "lanbys," the British name for the navigation aids (Holland, F. Ross, p. 101).

Lightship No. 103 was built in the early 20th century. It is the last surviving Great Lakes lightship and is moored at Port Huron, Michigan (Holland, F. Ross, p. 105).

Lightship duty was dangerous enough without the threat of enemy submarines. During World War One (August 1918) the crew of a lightship off Diamond Shoals, North Carolina, observed and reported by radio the sinking of a U.S. merchant vessel by a German submarine. The German vessel picked up the radio signal, surfaced, ordered the crew off the lightship, and then sank the vessel with its deck gun. The lightship's warning message allowed more than 20 ships to seek safe refuge in secure waters (Holland, F. Ross, p. 104).

The historical record reveals pre-Civil War African-American slaves, and post-Civil War former slaves, were crew members on several lightships, one of which was stationed at Royal Harbor, South Carolina. In 1870, two African-Americans, Robert Darnell and John Parker, tended the Lower Cedar Point Lighthouse on the Potomac River (Holland, F. Ross, p. 111).

The lighthouse sentinels loyally maintained the watch until rendered obsolete by automatic light systems, buoys, sonar, radar and satellite navigation (Holland, F. Ross, p. 115).

The Coast Guard accommodated contemporary lighthouse nostalgia by transferring the historic facilities to other government agencies, private organizations and historical societies. The Coast Guard leased the Presque Isle Lighthouse to a Michigan historical society, and the Cana Island Lighthouse to the Door County (Wisconsin) Maritime Museum. Several lighthouses have been transformed into inns and hostels which accommodate tourists.

Among the organizations associated with light station (lightships and lighthouses) preservation are The U.S. Lighthouse Society (San Francisco, California), The Lighthouse Preservation Society (Rockport, Maine), and the Great Lakes Lighthouse Keepers Association in Allen Park, Michigan (Holland, F. Ross, pp. 116-117).

African-Americans have served the Revenue Service and Coast Guard with distinction. Historical records reveal that officers used slaves on board Revenue cutters as cooks, stewards and seamen while, ironically, being ordered to prevent the importation of slaves into U.S. territorial waters after 1794. In the early 19th century the Revenue Marine Service captured several slave trading vessels.

After the emancipation of slaves (1863) African-Americans remained in the Revenue Service. Captain Michael A. Healy was the first African-American to earn an officer's commission in the RCS. Healy commanded the cutter Bear (1887-1895) with courage and distinction. Captain Healy enforced maritime law, performed search and rescue missions, and brought supplies and medical assistance to Alaskan natives. Healy was appointed U.S. Marshal in his Arctic and Sub-Arctic jurisdiction and aided the cause of science and navigation by making ice and weather reports and navigation charts.

A Coast Guard icebreaker is named in Captain Healy's honor.

African-Americans served in all the wars the RCS and USCG have engaged in, from the Revolutionary War to the present. They distinguished themselves in all of the services that eventually became part of the Coast Guard, including the Revenue Cutter Service, Lighthouse Service and Life-Saving Service.

Alex P. Haley (1921-1992) retired from the USCG in 1959 with the rank of Chief Journalist. The distinguished African-American author wrote histories of the Coast Guard, civil rights leaders, and slavery, and won a Pulitzer Prize for fiction in 1977. The chief petty officer commended his 20 years of Coast Guard experience, and honed his writing skills during long periods of sea duty on the USCGC Mendota ("African-Americans in the United States Coast Guard," pp. 1-8).

Master Chief Petty Officer of the Coast Guard, Vince Patton, was one of the distinguished Americans selected to carry the Olympic Torch through Washington, D.C., on its way to the 2002 Winter Games in Salt Lake City, Utah. The top ranking USCG chief petty officer served as an advisor in the office of the Coast Guard Commandant. MCPO Patton was the first African-American to achieve the top enlisted rank (U.S. Coast Guard News, pp. 1-3). In July 2002, Master Chief Petty Officer Ja M. Good became the first female MCPOCG in Coast Guard history (Office of Coast Guard Historian).

Chief Petty Officer Alex Haley was among many celebrities who served in the USCG Regular, Reserve and Auxiliary on land and sea in peace and war. From World War Two to more contemporary times, many famous people have worn the Coast Guard uniform with pride and performed with distinction. Hollywood film stars include Buddy Ebsen, Victor Mature, Caesar Romero, Beau Bridges, Gower Champion, Alan Hale, Jr., Tab Hunter, singer-actor and bandmaster Rudy Vallee, and actor-boxing champion Jack Dempsey (Wise and Rehill, pp. 159, 201, 227, 291, 296).

Other Coast Guard celebrities include Humphrey Bogart, Sid Caesar, Walter Cronkite, Charles Gibson, Arthur Godfrey, Otto Graham, U.S. Senator Sam Nunn (Armed Services Committee),* Arnold Palmer, Ted Turner, and actors Patrick Wayne and Gig Young ("FAQS: What Celebrities Once Served in the Coast Guard," p. 1).

Women have played an important role in the Coast Guard and its service antecedents. Mention has been made of women in the Lighthouse Service who contributed to the safe navigation of sea vessels and risked their lives saving fishermen, other seafarers and ship passengers in distress. Petty Officer Leslie Kraushaar (USCG) highlighted the role women play in the modern Coast Guard: "We are allowed to drive boats, shoot guns, and fly helicopters and planes. In fact, a female captain is in charge of one of our largest cutters" (USA Today, Jan. 15, 2002, p. 12A).

Women have assisted the Coast Guard since the Revolutionary War, when John Thomas joined the American army and Hannah, his spouse, assumed the position of lighthouse keeper at Gurnet Point outside of Plymouth, Massachusetts.

Historical research indicates more than 138 women were paid lighthouse keepers between 1825 and 1950, often the wives or daughters or acquaintances of keepers who needed to be replaced because of age, injury or death. As steam foghorns and electric lights replaced oil lamps and fog bells, male and female lighthouse keepers passed into history. One of the last woman lighthouse keepers was Fannie Salter who ran Turkey Point Light (Maryland) until 1947.

World War I caused the expansion of the armed services. The U.S. Navy began to enlist women in uniform in the Nurse Corps even before the war. With the outbreak of Great War which the U.S. entered in 1917, the U.S. Navy authorized women to join the Naval Reserve, and the office administrator rank of "Yeoman" was created. The Coast

Guard adopted these innovations, and twin sisters Lucille and Genevieve Baker transferred from the Navy Reserve to become the first uniformed females in the U.S. Coast Guard.

From 1941-1945 the United States was embroiled in World War Two. Lieutenant Dorothy Stratton (USN) transferred to the USCG to direct the Coast Guard Women's Reserve and what came to be called the SPARS. The role of women in the Armed Forces in general, and the Coast Guard in particular ebbed and flowed. Then, in October of 1975 President Gerald Ford signed an Act of Congress which required the service academies to admit female applicants in 1976. The U.S. Coast Guard Academy at New London, Connecticut accepted female applicants and assigned them with their male counterparts to summer training cruises on the training barque Eagle where they resided in women's quarters in the lower deck.

In 1977 the Coast Guard assigned women to ocean cutters Morgan-thau and Gallatin, each receiving a complement of two female officers and 10 enlisted women who performed their duties admirably.

Lieutenant (jg) Beverly Kelley took command of the 95-foot patrol boat Cape Newagen out of Hawaii. Later earning the rank of Com-mander, Kelley and her crew earned a Meritorious Unit Commenda-tion for outstanding achievements in law enforcement and search and rescue operations.

Over the next few decades Coast Guard women assumed the duties their ranks required. Lieutenant Commander Melissa Wall's assignments included command of a Loran Station in Alaska (1983) and a comple-ment of 26 males; and executive officer on a 210-foot cutter. By 1983, of 129 female Coast Guard officers, 35 served aboard cutters, five flew aircraft, and out of 1,747 enlisted women, 85 served on sea duty.

Lieutenant Sandra Stosz commanded an ice breaking tug in the 1980s. Lt. Cmdr. June Ryan was a military aide in the Clinton adminis-tration, and commander of an icebreaker. Chief Boatswain Mate Diane Bucci became officer in charge of the CGC Capstan. Since the 1990s, female regulars and reservists were sent to the Middle East in Operation Desert Shield-Desert Storm, enforced drug and immigration laws on boats and ships in the Caribbean (Tilley, John A., "A History of Women in the Coast Guard," pp. 1-8), and served their nation valiantly after the terrorist attacks of 11 September 2001.

Admission to Coast Guard Rescue Swimmer School has generally been limited to males who must endure exacting and strenuous physi-cal and water safety training. ASM3 Kelly Mogk was the first female graduate in rescue swimming. Mogk's courage and endurance was tested on 3 January 1989 when two Air National Guard pilots were forced to bail out of their burning F-4 Phantom jet fighter plane off the Oregon coast in windy and stormy seas.

The heavy winds and marginal visibility challenged the HH-65 res-cue helicopter which flew out from USCG Air Station Astoria. ASM3 Mogk jumped from the helicopter into the cold 20-foot waves. Mogk swam to the surviving pilot who was in hypothermia and tangled in his parachute. She got the pilot into the helicopter hoist basket, and they both were lifted to safety by the well trained crew. On her first mission, ASM3 Kelly Mogk earned the United States Coast Guard Air Medal (Spellman, Coast Guard, March 2002, back cover).

The U.S. Coast Guard has four main missions: maritime law enforce-ment, environmental protection, maritime safety, and national security and defense. The Coast Guard promotes and protects maritime com-merce and supports the economic infrastructure. The Service contributes to scientific research missions, administers a maritime communications system, enforces international agreements, and, when directed by the President, operates as part of the U.S. Navy ("The United States Coast Guard in Brief," Office of Coast Guard Historian, January 1999, p. 1).

Maritime law enforcement put the Coast Guard directly into the war against alcoholic beverages during the Prohibition era (1920 -33). The inland and ocean water patrols were not without political and legal controversy. In fair weather and foul, the Coast Guard sought out the "rum runners." The mission was dangerous and cost the lives of law breakers and Coast Guard personnel. Apprehension efforts were hazardous because "poison gas, smoke screens, and machine guns were the smugglers' common weapons" (Brown, p. 147).

One lethal incident occurred on 7 August 1927 when patrol boat CG-249 confronted a drug runner off the Florida Coast. The CG crew boarded the contraband vessel and in the arrest process suffered the murder of two Coast Guardsmen and an accompanying Secret Service agent. After a protracted and bloody struggle, the surviving crew sub-dued the smugglers and were assisted a couple of hours later by other Coast Guard craft and personnel. Two of the surviving perpetrators were brought to trial after a two year delay. One was hanged at a Coast Guard base in Ft. Lauderdale, Florida (Brown, pp. 146-160).

Coastguardsman Riley Brown traced the CG-249 incident in his book, The Story of the Coast Guard: Men, Wind and Sea, dedicated "to my shipmates, the officers and enlisted men o the Coast Guard, and to the members I knew who were killed in the line of duty..."

The author perceptively predicted the future of the Service in the book, published in 1939: "More and more obligations and duties are being imposed upon the service by the consolidation of government agencies and the formation of defense plans designed to protect North and South America from assaults by aggressor foreign nations" (Brown, p. 248).

Among the historically significant Coast Guard missions was the search for the courageous and accomplished civilian pilot Amelia Earhart and her navigator Fred Noonan. They disappeared on 2 July 1937 during the last portion of their transglobal flight. Recent scholarship suggests Earhart's aircraft ran out of fuel from 50 to 100 miles shy of her Howland Island destination in the Pacific Ocean. Historical research discovered radio messages from the flight in an age of uncertain radio communications, rough landing zones, and unreliable maps and charts.

The U.S. Coast Guard and U.S. Navy cooperated in tracking, communicating with, and ultimately searching for Earhart and Noonan. Commander Warner K. Thompson, captain of the 250-foot CGC Itasca, sailed from Los Angeles to Honolulu to Howland Island to monitor the terminal segment of Earhart's historic journey.

Coast Guard and Navy records and other recently acquired primary sources indicate that a plethora of problems plagued the pilot, Navy, Coast Guard and other federal and civilian entities involved in planning, monitoring and responding to the events.

Analysts have suggested a variety of problems, communications errors and accidents which might have been avoided. Barely perceptible easterly winds may have blown the westward flight off course. A faulty chart, based on the best information of the day, misplaced Howland Island. Clear skies should have helped guide Noonan and Earhart to their landing zone, except that the particular quadrant they were flying in developed cloud cover. Misinterpretations of the predetermined frequency levels Earhart and her naval guardians were to use for communication caused problems, as did different interpretations of what portions of which hours communications was to occur by which parties. There were conflicts over whether and when radio-telephone (voice) or Morse Code should be utilized. Noonan and Earhart were not trained in Morse Code. Faulty transmission batteries plagued the Howland Island site.

Earhart's radio communications equipment may have been faulty, and a high-quality transmission device on the aircraft had been installed by technicians not affiliated with the company that produced it. Problems with aircraft design may have contributed to Earhart's injury and death upon impact with the water. A faulty fuel ejection intake system may have facilitated the rapid flooding and sinking of the aircraft.

An extensive, sophisticated six-day search of hundreds of square miles of ocean by the CGC Itasca, military aircraft, and several U.S. Navy ships failed to discover the lost aviators or their aircraft (Long, E.M. and M.K. Long, pp. 195-235).

The significant contributions of the Coast Guard as part of the Navy in World Wars One and Two were surveyed in previous chapters. The compliment paid to the sea services by naval historian and Admiral Samuel Eliot Morison after World War Two could be applied to the Coast Guard from its Revenue Service days to the present: "Let us remember the gunboats, minecraft, destroyer escorts, PTs, beaching and other lettered craft....and small cutters. These, largely commanded by Reservists, were forced to perform functions and make long voyages for which they had not been designed...the operation of them under the most hazardous conditions are beyond praise; but we may not forget that (at the beginning of the war) the Navy was woefully deficient in escorts and small craft, and should resolve to never be caught short again" (Beck, pp. 225-226).

Admiral Morison concluded, "America will always need sailors and ships and shipborne aircraft to preserve her liberty, her communications with the free world, even her existence" (Beck, p. 226).

Coast Guard archives provide a plethora of primary sources for naval historians. In July 1981, Captain R. F. Bennett (USCG), Captain of the Port of Charleston, sent a letter to the director of the South Carolina Historical Society on behalf of the commander of the 7th Coast Guard District and the commandant. In the letter Captain Bennett explained his purpose: "...to gratuitously present a copy of a history of the Coast Guard in the Sixth Naval District during World War II." Captain Bennett concluded, "because of the significance of this two-volume collection to future students of military history....it is my pleasure to provide a copy for your organization" ("During World War Two." Vols. I and II, 1946. Unpublished papers, The South Carolina Historical Society).

The content file of the papers includes a survey of the ports and shipping in the naval district, background on submarine patrols, Charleston area cutters, aircraft and Coast Guard facilities, port security and law enforcement responsibilities and missions, mobilization assignments, military operations of regular, auxiliary and reserve personnel, and coordination activities with civilian and military port officials in South Carolina and Georgia. Merchant marine inspection, beach, harbor and sea patrols, intelligence gathering, aircraft (including blimp) patrols, aids to navigation, public relations, and a variety of incident reports were chronicled, including explosives, fire fighting, and the sinking of a German submarine (U-Rathke) by the USCGC Icarus.

The donated Coast Guard file included official Coast Guard photographs of personnel and incidents, including the following:

1. A Navy-Coast Guard-Marine Corps presentation of a medal for heroism to Richard J. Cariens, MM1, USCGR, for his response to an Army boat explosion in Charleston Harbor.

2. An award presented to Coast Guard firefighters and port security personnel by Charleston Fire Department officials for containing a pier fire (6 October 1944).

3. The awarding of the rank of Chief Yeoman to SPAR Elizabeth S. Ryder (June 1945), and

4. A company of Coast Guard officers and enlisted members of the Mounted Beach Patrol accompanied by trained dogs on patrol in South Carolina ("During World War Two," Files 324/514, The South Carolina Historical Society, Charleston).

Charleston Harbor is noted not only for being the site of the outbreak of the Civil War (1861-1865) at Fort Sumter, but it is host to two distinguished warships at Patriot's Point Naval and Maritime Museum in Mount Pleasant, South Carolina: the aircraft carrier USS Yorktown and the USCGC Ingham (WPG-35). Both vessels saw duty in World War Two (in which the CGC Ingham sunk a German submarine) and in Indochina during Vietnam War.

On 7 December 2001 the CGC Taney hosted the 60th Pearl Harbor Anniversary Memorial Ceremony at the Inner Harbor, Baltimore, Maryland. The Taney was in the custody of the Baltimore Maritime Museum, and is the last surviving ship which was present during the Japanese attack on Pearl Harbor (7 December 1941). Pearl Harbor survivors, the 229th U.S. Army Band and Coast Guard Commandant Admiral James Loy joined in the celebration. In his speech, Admiral Loy compared the 9/11/01 attack on the U.S. with Pearl Harbor and alluded to the sacrifices of veterans and American resolve.

A Maryland National Guard helicopter dropped a wreath in the harbor, a USCG Honor Guard directed a gun salute, and a U.S. Navy Band musician chief petty officer played taps (Craft, "Last Surviving Cutter," Coast Guard, February 2002, p. 7). In New Orleans, Louisiana on 7 December 2001, the National D-Day Museum opened a new exhibit, and Coast Guard units from the 8th District furnished a platoon and color guard for the parade, marching with representatives from all the military services (Farris, "Parade Marks Exhibit Opening," Coast Guard, February 2002, p. 6.)

In 1946, just after World War Two and with the commencement of the Cold War between the Communist and non-Communist nations, U.S. Coast Guard officers were sent to train South Korean naval personnel and establish a Korean coast guard. With the invasion of South Korea by Communist North Korea (June 1950) USCG officers were ordered to evacuate the Korean peninsula (Price, "The Forgotten Service in the Forgotten War," pp. 1-2). The Korean War (1950-1953) was diplomatically termed a "conflict" or "police action" by the international community and led to the entry into the war of Chinese troops in support of North Korea.

Coast Guard cutters on Pacific ocean station status remained on duty carrying U.S. Weather Bureau meteorologists to monitor weather conditions. Coast Guard cutters provided guidance and assistance to military and commercial maritime, air, and communication links. The cutters conducted search and rescue and medical service missions for merchant crews and military personnel, and contributed to the United Nations war effort dominated by U.S. military forces.

The Coast Guard and U.S. Navy cooperated in the Pacific region. The Navy donated several destroyer escorts which the USCG commissioned. The vessels carried weather balloons, anti-aircraft weapons, and depth charges. Pacific Ocean station duty required diligence and seamanship to handle gale force winds, 20 to 50 foot waves, and frigid seas. Seaplane tenders and 255-foot vessels supplemented the cutter armada. More than twenty cutters served in the Korean theater performing search and rescue duties and escorting United Nations troop and supply vessels (Price, "The Forgotten Service... pp. 2-4).

Among its search and rescue missions, Coast Guard aircraft and vessels participated in the dangerous and costly rescue of the crew of a U.S. Navy P2V patrol plane shot down off the China coast in January 1953. The rescue attempt was threatened by Chinese military intervention. A Coast Guard PMB-5A seaplane crashed with survivors on board while attempting to take off in high seas. Four U.S. Navy and five Coast Guard crew members perished in the cold waters, or may have been captured and executed by the Chinese. The U.S. Navy destroyer Halsey Powell rescued the surviving seamen. The Gold Lifesaving Medal was posthumously awarded to the missing Navy and Coast Guard personnel (Price, "The Forgotten Service...," pp. 4-5).

Coast Guard personnel were stationed in South Korea during the war at a LORAN Station in Pusan. The Pusan station and other Loran sites in the Far East directed the merchant ships and air traffic. Logistical support was provided by the U.S. Air Force and U.S. Army (Price, "The Forgotten Service...," p. 6). In 1952 the Coast Guard established a Merchant Marine Detail in the port of Yokohama (Japan) to monitor the increased cargo traffic necessitated by the Korean War ("Coast Guard Korean War Chronology," Office of Coast Guard Historian).

During the Korean War, President Harry Truman authorized the Coast Guard to enhance port security in major U.S. ports, prevent sabotage, and facilitate the safe loading of merchant vessels, particularly those ships delivering military supplies and ammunition to U.N. forces in Korea. The Coast Guard was authorized to fund and expand the Reserve component in port security units. Not without controversy, the Coast Guard investigated the background of merchant seamen, harbor pilots, and civilian port employees and withdrew licenses and certification from alleged security risks.

Reminiscent of concerns and measures taken after the 11 September 2001 terrorist attacks upon the U.S., the Cold War era Coast Guard and other government agencies were concerned about the danger of a foreign freighter detonating a nuclear device in a major port. Beginning in 1951, vessels entering U.S. anchorages had to give notice of destination and cargo at least one day in advance of estimated arrival. The vessel names were given to Captains of the Port. Coast Guard patrol boats and boarding parties identified and inspected suspicious vessels. Coast Guard explosives loading teams assumed the hazardous duty of inspecting and supervising the handling of dangerous cargo. Trained units checked for nuclear devices and biological and chemical weapons (Price, "The Forgotten Service...," pp. 5-6).

Military operations in the Korean conflict ended with the cease-fire agreement of 26 July 1953. The Coast Guard decommissioned destroyer escorts, ocean and search and rescue stations and air detachments, and resumed its traditional peacetime missions. Cold War fears stimulated the expansion of port security duties. Male and female reservists returned to civilian life, and many remained active in Reserve units. To maintain the visibility and viability of the Coast Guard, and using the Korean War as a guide, commanders and commandants stood ready to contribute Coast Guard knowledge and equipment and participate in future combat situations (Price, "The Forgotten Service...," pp. 6-7).

The Vietnam War gave the Coast Guard its next opportunity to serve with the U.S. Navy and the other Armed Forces in combat. The U.S. Revenue Marine Service and its successor, the U.S. Coast Guard, served in all U.S. wars from 1790 to the present, described in previous chapters of this book. Combat and wartime service included the Quasi-War with France, the War of 1812, the Mexican War, Civil War (War Between the States), Spanish-American War, World War One, World War Two, Korea, Vietnam, the Persian Gulf, several Latin American-Caribbean support missions, and deployment at home and overseas after the terrorist attack upon the United States on 11 September 2001.

Many observers and analysts are unaware of the global participation of the Coast Guard in military operations. The military visibility of the Coast Guard was illuminated after the 9-11 tragedy. After 9/11, national appreciation of the Coast Guard national security and border protection mission was enhanced. Supporting the national security mission is the Deepwater recapitalization program. Without the revitalization of Coast Guard aircraft and deep water cutters capable of off-shore operations at 50 nautical miles or more, the Deepwater mission capability would be diminished.

The Coast Guard performs laws enforcement, military, humanitarian and diplomatic missions in its Deepwater capacity. That mission includes migration and drug interdiction which are significant components of the national security mission. The International Ice Patrol, search and rescue, marine pollution enforcement, and military service are significant elements of national security.

Smaller than the New York City police department with a comparable budget, the USCG is asked to superintend a much larger geographic area with more operational diversity. Within the Department of Transportation, the Coast Guard had to compete for

federal funding and yet carry out defense and military roles more related to the missions of the Department of Defense, which the Coast Guard is administered by when under the jurisdiction of the U.S. Navy in times of war.

Therefore, the Coast Guard must design assets which allow the service to carry out these multi-task responsibilities. Its medium and high endurance cutters, communications systems, and aircraft date from the 1960s through the 1980s for the most part, so the naval service faces obsolescence in its aircraft and ocean fleet. These support systems are invariably used in corrosive, dangerous and challenging environments. The maintenance costs are high. Cutting edge technology is essential if the USCG is to continue to carry out its contemporary responsibilities (Sanial, Proceedings, November 2001, pp. 76-77).

Resource protection, potential terrorism, and weapons of mass destruction have been added to the Coast Guard agenda, as the service continues to protect the lanes of maritime commerce essential to the national and global economies while carrying out security and military missions in coordination with federal law enforcement, the Border Patrol, U.S. Customs, the Immigration and Naturalization Service, and U.S. Army, Navy and Air Force (Sanial, pp. 77-79).

The success of joint Navy-Coast Guard, and international boarding and inspection teams in the Persian Gulf since 2001 significantly reduced the export of illegal Iraqi petroleum ("Interview," Sea Power, March 2002, p. 16).

Lieutenant Commander Gregory J. Sanial (USCG) assessed the relationship between the Deepwater and National Security missions of

---

* Although noted military historians Dunnigan and Nofi mentioned the military mission of the Coast Guard in previous books, they listed Senator Nunn among those members of Congress who had never served in the Armed Forces (**Shooting Blanks**, William Morrow and Co., Inc., 1991, p. 157). Senator Nunn served in the USCG on active duty from 1959-1960 and in the USCGR from 1960-1968 (Office of Coast Guard Historian).

the Coast Guard, and concluded that "the future of the Coast Guard as an armed force rests on its ability to secure funding for Deepwater procurement." Sanial regrettably speculated that "it may take a catastrophic accident or disaster to focus national attention on the capability gap in the aging Deepwater fleet" (Sanial, p. 79).

The Homeland Security mission of the Coast Guard, as one analyst put it, threatens to "embroil the Coast Guard in a political storm as it struggles to meet short-term mission requirements and maintain focus on long term goals" in its domestic civilian and military responsibilities (Kelley, M. R., Cmdr., USCG, "The Shoal Waters of Homeland Security," Proceedings, May 2002, p. 65).

In a 1998 address to the Naval War College, Coast Guard Commandant Admiral James Loy discussed new age security threats, "conveyed to our shores in ways not effectively countered by traditional naval forces (which may) draw near civilian vessels...and mingle with legitimate commercial and recreational traffic....best combated by the combination of military discipline and law enforcement authority" manifested by the Coast Guard tradition (Kelley, "The Shoal Waters...," p. 66).

U.S. Coast Guard and Navy cooperation has increased national security. The history of cooperation between the two naval services facilitated the arming of Coast Guard cutters with Navy technology, including guns, fire-control, missile defense, refueling systems, and updated communications equipment (Kelley, "The Shoal Waters...p. 67). Coast Guard Commandants and Navy Chiefs of Naval Operations have worked together to enhance the National Fleet concept "in which both services maintain their cultures and capabilities but...remain interoperable and complementary...." with "the Coast Guard providing smaller maritime security for peacetime....and general purpose shallow draft warships..." adjacent to continental waters and "non-U.S. coastal locations such as Guantanamo Bay, Cuba," and other locations where U.S. Navy ships and bases need enhanced port security (Kelley, "The Shoal Waters....," p. 68). Contemporary Coast Guard responsibilities will necessitate more resources and expanded budgets (Kelley, Proceedings, May 2002, p. 70).

The Coast Guard cooperates with other government agencies in carrying out its multiple missions, including the Maritime Administration (MARAD). Directors of MARAD have come from the ranks of merchant marine officers and graduates of the U.S. Maritime Academy.

Illustrative of the command experience in MARAD is Captain William G. Schubert, unanimously confirmed by the U.S. Senate in November 2000. Schubert earned a U.S. Coast Guard Unlimited Master License (1979) and served as an officer in the U.S. Naval Reserve.

MARAD, an agency of the U.S. Department of Transportation, is responsible for meeting the nation's commercial shipping requirements, maintaining repair and ship building facilities, and monitoring port facilities and water and land transportation systems. After 11 September 2001, the Maritime Administration more closely coordinated its port security responsibilities with the Coast Guard and the Transportation Security Administration (TSA)

Early in 2002, Secretary of Transportation Norman Mineta named retired Rear Admiral Richard E. Bennis (USCG) associate undersecretary of transportation for land and maritime security at the TSA. Admiral Bennis directed the Coast Guard response to the 9/11 terrorist attacks in New York City. Bennis assumed the responsibility for land and seaport security in the United States in coordination with MARAD (Hessman, James D. and Gordon I. Peterson, Sea Power, May 2002, pp. 11-12).

After appointing former Pennsylvania governor Tom Ridge the Homeland Security Director, the Bush administration demonstrated a willingness to cooperate with Congress in establishing a cabinet level post for the new agency. In May of 2000, Congress introduced legislation to establish a Cabinet department which would control and coordinate the existing federal agencies of U.S. Customs, Border Patrol, and the Coast Guard, and elements of the 50 or more agencies involved in domestic security. Supporters of the legislation asserted that mandated coordination of all homeland security departments would increase efficiency, improve communication and intelligence exchange, and lessen bureaucratic turf battles (Kiely, USA Today, May 3, 2002, p. 4A).

After 9/11, the full range of Coast Guard search and rescue duties continued. On 22 May 2002, a USCG helicopter joined a Navy vessel in the successful rescue of the crew of a U.S. submarine which caught fire and flooded off the California coast (The New York Times, "Crew Is Rescued... ," May 23, 2002, p. A-18). On the same day, Coast Guard cutters, helicopters and other patrol craft provided port security and escorted U.S. Navy warships into New York Harbor to celebrate Fleet Week and the commemoration of lives lost in the 9/11 terrorist attacks on the World Trade Center ("Fleet Week..." and "A Moment of Solemnity." The New York Times, May 23, 2002, pp. A-1 and A-27).

CHAPTER XIII

MISSIONS OF THE USCG

Throughout this text the missions and duties of the U.S. Coast Guard have been described as events unfolded in historical context. In this chapter, Coast Guard duties and missions will be discussed in contemporaneous detail with illuminating examples and descriptions of the daily responsibilities of the maritime service.

Given the limited number of Coast Guard vessels and the extensive global patrol region, officers and crew must manifest maximal seamanship skills in the operation of cutters and craft on land, sea and in the air.

During World War Two, the FS-315, a Coast Guard manned Army freighter, survived mountainous seas and 150 mile per hour hurricane winds because of the superior seamanship skills of the crew. Five other navy vessels sank, including the destroyer USS Warrington with the loss of most of the crew of 390 officers and men, a minesweeper, two Coast Guard cutters and a lightship, with heavy losses.

The Atlantic hurricane hit in mid-September, 1944. The four officers and 21 crew members of the FS-315 nearly capsized several times in the 36 hour storm. After being towed to Miami by merchant marine and military vessels, it took three months of repairs to render the battered vessel seaworthy.

The 750 ton freighter was 32.7 feet wide and 176.5 feet long with a 9.5 foot draft. Its two poweful diesel engines were disabled in the storm. Armament included a 40mm. gun mounted aft and two machine guns on the bridge. Commanding officer Lieutenant David Oaksmith (USCGR) was an experienced officer who inspired the confidence of his shipmates.

The vessel rolled to and fro in the storm and rose almost vertically against the towering swells. Sea water flooded the engine room despite battened down hatches, but the ship and crew remained on the surface of the sea and survived. Lieutenant Oaksmith received a commendation for his leadership and was rewarded with a destroyer-escort command (Gault, "Destiny Rode the Wind," pp. 8-13).

Drug enforcement on the high seas is a major Coast Guard responsibility. Charles M. Fuss, Jr., chronicled the maritime war against drug smuggling from 1970-1990. The author served the U.S. government for more than 30 years as a member of the U.S. Navy, Marine Corps and National Fisheries Service. His diverse experience led to an appointment to the Office of National Drug Control Policy in 1989, where he developed interdiction policies for federal lawn enforcement and military agencies.

Fuss chronicled the dangerous missions carried out by the Coast Guard and other federal border and drug enforcement units. Fuss described gun battles and the skilled seamanship required of crews attempting to subdue the crews of contraband vessels and avoid deliberate ramming. The daring, coordinated operations of USCG cutter crews and aviators, Border Patrol and Customs officers, and the DEA were gathered from government files, interviews with government officials and incarcerated smugglers, and the author's own personal experiences (Fuss, Sea of Grass, pp. xi-xviii, 14-16, 145-147, 152-154).

Given the high speed capability of many drug smuggling vessels, a pursuing Coast Guard cutter may take hours or a full day to catch up with its target. Cutter deck guns are intimidating in appearance and sound and may persuade drug running vessels to stop for boarding. If the suspect vessel fails to stop, gun fire into the engine may cut fuel lines and disable the vessel. Sharp shooters on Coast Guard helicopters add to the fire power.

On occasion, smugglers have fired back at or over the heads of Coast Guard crews, and have tried to ram the cutters while discarding bundles of contraband which usually float to the surface, providing incriminating evidence.

Light machine guns and even missiles have been discovered aboard captured vessels. Some contraband skippers have set their vessels on fire and tried, with various degrees of success, to scuttle them (Halberstadt, pp. 43-47).

By 1990, the successful interdiction of maritime drug shipments forced the smugglers to shift their routes from the sea to aircraft, and to land routes through Mexico (Fuss, 278). In 1994 federal law enforcement and military interagency task forces were coordinated on government organizational charts. Coast Guard Commandant Admiral Robert F. Kramer was designated the interdiction coordinator (Fuss, p. 285).

In the Fall of 2000, Lt. (jg) Anna Slaven in command of the cutter Chase out of the port of San Diego searched a suspicious vessel for 15 hours before finding 1.5 tons of cocaine hidden in six feet of ice under a cargo of sharks. The commander and crew were suspicious of the tiny boat 100 miles off shore in the Pacific and a crew dressed in jewelry and polo shirts without standard fishing gear. Slaven and her 11 person crew were honored by Defense Secretary William Cohen. Coast Guard officials informed inquisitive reporters about the nonlethal techniques and technology the service uses to stop escaping vessels and subdue crews: sharpshooters who hit engines and outboard motors, small "sting ball" hand grenades that disorient crews, and nets which wrap around stern propellers ("Coast Guard Praised for Cocaine Busts," Associated Press, Post Bulletin, 29 September, 2000).

At approximately 6:30 a.m, 18 January, 2000, a Coast Guard cutter returning from homeland security patrol spotted a grounded shrimp boat. The boarding team discovered 9,000 pounds of marijuana worth $ 7 million. Customs and Border Patrol officers assisted the Coast Guard in unloading the contraband at Port Isabel, Texas. Three men who tried to escape on foot after reaching shore in a life raft were arrested ("Station Makes Year's Largest Bust," Coast Guard, March 2000, p. 2).

Despite the splendid record of interagency cooperation and achievement, departmental rivalries continued. Administrative functions sometimes appeared unmanageable, exacerbated by the ebb and flow of politics and pubic opinion, and the difficulty of affecting the supply and demand equation (Fuss, pp. 285-286).

Nonetheless, the diligence of the USCG and federal allies resulted in impressive tally sheets. By the end of 2002, 658 lives were saved; 8,164 SAR missions were completed; 1500 migrants had been interdicted; and nearly 20,000 pounds of marijuana and 70,000 pounds of cocaine had been confiscated due to the effective policing and patrolling of 131 Security Zones ("On Patrol," Coast Guard, April 2002, p. 4).

The diversity of Coast Guard duties is illustrated by its Antarctic mission. Residents of McMurdo Station in Antarctica were pleased to observe the Coast Guard icebreaker Polar Sea arrive in the land of the summer midnight sun with mail and supplies. Breaking through the ice to serve polar communities in the North and South are among the much appreciated Coast Guard missions ("Breaking the Ice," Associated Press, St. Paul Pioneer Press, January 2, 2001).

Polar patrols in Arctic, Antarctic and subarctic waters are among the many Coast Guard responsibilities. The monitoring of icebergs is an important mission because of the hazard they pose to military and commercial vessels. The National Ice Center (NIC) in Suitland, Maryland coordinates its activities with the National Oceanic and Atmospheric Administration (NOAA), the U.S. Navy, and the U.S. Coast Guard. On 21 May 2002 the NIC reported that an iceberg designated D-17 broke off the Antarctic Ice Sheet. The iceberg was as large as a small Caribbean island (34.5 miles in length, 6.9 miles in width). It was observed in a satellite image.

The previous week, iceberg C-19, the size of Chesapeake Bay, broke away and floated out to sea, joining iceberg B-22 which broke away the previous March and was estimated to be about the size of the New England state of Delaware. Some observers argued that these incidents foreshadowed an increase in global warming, but contemporaneous measurements revealed that the ice in parts of the Antarctic continent was getting thicker (Schmid, R. E., "Iceberg Breaks Away From Antarctica," May 21, 2002).

The Coast Guard protects recreational and commercial boaters when storms and seas are raging. Crab fishermen commuting from Yaquina Bay, Oregon, into the Pacific and back often confront changing seas. Breakers smash over the bar which stands between the bay and the ocean, threatening boats, crews, cargo and equipment. The Yaquina Bay Coast Guard Station places search and rescue craft in the vicinity in bad weather. Properly geared surf crews stand ready to rescue fishing crews and respond to the 600 distress calls sent out annually.

Fishing boats and crews hurled into the rocks by crashing surf have been rescued by Coast Guard swimmers and lifeboat, surfboat and helicopter crews. The life saving fleet in the summer of 2000 consisted of a 52-foot lifeboat, one 30-foot and two 44-foot boats, and a 21-foot safeboat, all of which require regular maintenance to be ready when called (Cameron, "Standing Watch," American Legion Magazine, July 2000).

Another fishing zone which is the beneficiary of Coast Guard surveillance lies in the tropical Bahamas, east of Florida and north of Cuba. It was there that a U.S. Fisheries Service agent assisted by the Coast Guard used a proper mix of diplomacy and threatened fire power to avert an international incident in contested lobster waters in October 1972.

Responding to shooting incidents between Cuban, Bahamian and Cuban-American fishermen, the U.S. Coast Guard cutter Diligence (WMEC-616), under the command of Commander David R. Markey, proceeded to the Flamingo Cay region of the Bahamas with fisheries agent Charles M. Fuss, Jr. on board. They were joined at the scene by the 95-foot cutter Cape Fox (WPB-95316) and an HH-52 Coast Guard helicopter which landed on the flight deck of the Diligence, menaced by missile carrying Cuban patrol boats.

Tense radio and on board negotiations with fishing boat captains resulted in a demilitarized zone. Eventual diplomatic settlements over continental shelf zones with adjoining political entities averted further confrontations and violence (Fuss, "Lobster War...," Naval History, June

2002, pp. 46-49).

Search and Rescue (SAR) missions constitute a major Coast Guard responsibility dating back to 1831, when the Secretary of the Treasury directed revenue cutters to patrol the coast to aid sea seafarers in distress. The colonies and states traditionally directed salvagers to train volunteer crews and aid shipwreck victims, a prerequisite before these "wreckmasters" could claim legal control of salvaged vessels and goods.

The 19th century witnessed increased immigration to the Eastern shores of the United States, and commensurate increases in passenger ship wrecks closer to surf driven coast lines. Brave volunteers saved many lives, but losses stimulated the creation of a federal life saving service which dates to 1848. Stations, boats, equipment, lighthouse keepers and revenue service officers and crews cooperated in rescue operations, aided by wreckmasters and insurance underwriters.

After the Civil War, the Life Saving Service (LSS) was established along the Great Lakes, Eastern Seaboard, and New England in harbor regions which attracted lake and ocean traffic. LSS Districts were staffed by well trained personnel and inspectors who were gradually federalized. Heroic rescues aided by domestic and foreign vessel crews became the stuff of maritime legend.

By the 1930s, deep ("Blue water") cutters expanded SAR operations onto the high seas, aided by amphibious aircraft, to monitor transatlantic ships and aircraft. In 1939 the Coast Guard Auxiliary was created, which provided well trained volunteer civilians to supplement Coast Guard full-time personnel in the performance of SAR, boating safety, and law enforcement functions ("Search and Rescue," Coast Guard Historian's Office, Updated: January 1999).

Search and rescue missions are inherently risky, and sometimes claim the lives of rescuers. Such was the case in February 1997 when three Coast Guard petty officers died in the rough seas of the Pacific Northwest off the Washington coast. Their 44-foot lifeboat capsized three times, leaving only one survivor. While Coast Guard personnel searched for their missing colleagues, a Coast Guard helicopter rescued the U.S. Navy lieutenant who made the distress call from his sailboat as it was breaking up on a rocky shore line ("Coast Guard Looks at Deaths of 3 in Lifeboat," The New York Times, February 16, 1997).

Another attempt to rescue the military personnel of a sister service was more successful. In the evening of 9 March 2002 a commercial helicopter carrying two civilians who worked for the U.S. Marine Corps crashed into the Atlantic 35 miles off the Georgia coast. One U.S. Marine and two Coast Guard helicopters were dispatched to the scene. A Coast Guard cutter rescued one survivor who died en route to a hospital.

The search by Coast Guard and Marine rescue units for the second missing person continued overnight and into the next morning, when a U.S. Marine helicopter carrying five rescue personnel crashed into the sea 30 miles from shore. A Coast Guard cutter was on site within 7 minutes and rescued all but one of the searchers. The survivors were flown to a Georgia hospital (CNN.com/U.S. News, "Two Dead, One Missing in Georgia Helicopter Crashes," March 9, 2002).

In April 2002 the Coast Guard rescued another member of the U.S. Armed Forces. A Navy crewman collapsed on board the USS Elrod, 40 miles northwest of Virginia. Coast Guard Air Station Elizabeth City, New Jersey, responded to the request for medevac assistance. An HH-60 Jayhawk was dispatched at 10:32 p.m., picked up the Navy crewman at 11:40 p.m., and flew the injured sailor to Portsmouth Naval Hospital ("Coast Guard Medevacs Navy Crewman," USCG Public Affairs, 25 April 2002).

Sometimes the Coast Guard rescues victims of another kind. In April 2002 a Coast Guard helicopter SAR crew searched the radar screen 30 miles from Hawaii looking for an abandoned tanker. The Asian crew of the Indonesian tanker crew had abandoned the vessel during a fire and were rescued by a cruise ship, minus their two year old mascot terrier. The Coast Guard helicopter crew found the vessel and dropped pizza and granola bars to the dog which had been without food for almost three weeks. The Coast Guard then radioed the shipping company which had been searching for the ship. The dog was subsequently rescued (Associated Press, "Dog Rescued After 19 Days On Abandoned Ship," Post Bulletin, April 22, 2002).

In December 2001, Captain W. Russell Webster, Chief of Operations, First Coast Guard District, Boston, contributed an article to the distinguished naval periodical, Proceedings. Webster explained the deleterious effects of 24-hour watches on personnel who serve in critical search and rescue group operations centers, and cited the study done at the Group Woods Hole Station in Massachusetts by the Coast Guard Research and Development Center in Groton, Connecticut.

From 1998 to 2001, Group Woods Hole handled an annual average of 1250 SAR and 1500 law enforcement cases in a 3,000 square mile maritime region. The study concluded that the long watches impaired safety and health. Captain Webster contended the extended watches and the pressure of dangerous duty threatened personnel and the Coast Guard mission, and was responsible for low service retention rates which necessitated the use of over-extended and inexperienced crews. Webster and the R and D Center concluded more personnel were needed, and 12 hour watches should be maximum (Webster, "Too Tired to Tell?," Proceedings, December 2001, pp. 61-63).

In a follow-up article in the same periodical, Captain Webster supplemented his conclusions using as examples the exemplary responses of the Coast Guard Woods Hole operations center to the fatal crash of John F. Kennedy's private plane with three persons on board (16 July 1999); and the crash of EgyptAir Flight 990 on 31 October 1999 with the loss of 217 passengers and crew.

The Atlantic Ocean crashes were national media events. Despite the tragic outcomes, Captain Webster credited the Coast Guard, U.S. Navy, the U.S. Air Force, and a variety of federal and state agencies and officials with timely and professional responses, effective interagency planning and communications, and the use of secure military command posts: Coast Guard Air Station Cape Cod, Massachusetts; Naval Station Newport, Rhode Island; and the Quonset Air National Guard Base (Rhode Island).

Media management, monitoring the fatigue and mental health needs of rescue personnel, and informing and assisting the relatives of victims were other facets of the operations, according to Webster. The cutter Hammerhead (WPB-87302) returned to Woods Hole with the Kennedy family after burial at sea services for the victims (Webster, "The Next Disaster...", Proceedings, September 2001, pp. 48-51).

The ever-present danger to search and rescue and patrol personnel is illustrated by the deaths of Coast Guard Petty Officers Scott Chism and Chris Ferreby in March 2001. Their boat was swamped by high waves in the frigid waters of the Niagara River. Boatswains Mate Third Class Ericka Robinson served on active and reserve duty in the Coast Guard and was an experienced coxswain. Robinson published an article critical of the base communications procedures and the absence of electronic positioning radio beacons (EPIRBs) in the 22-foot rigid hull inflatable patrol boats. Despite valiant efforts by Coast Guard and civilian law enforcement personnel, the petty officers died after being rescued (Robinson, "We Always Must Be Vigilant," Proceedings, February 2002, pp. 28-29).

Coast Guard vigilance was vindicated when Tropical Storm Allison struck Houston, Texas, causing the disastrous flood of 9 June 2001. The hurricane came ashore at Galveston on June 5, bringing heavy rain, and 60 knot winds. It hit Houston taking a toll of 22 lives and $ 5 billion in infrastructural damage.

Area Coast Guard bases joined military and civilian responders to save lives and property in dangerous urban conditions of downed power lines and limited visibility. Coast Guard small boats and helicopters rescued 200 people, many severely injured and some handicapped. Air Station Houston and Group Galveston teamed up to answer distress calls even though emergency workers living in the areas of devastation had to worry about the fate of their own families (Wyman, "Deep Trouble,"

Coast Guard, November 2001, pp. 13-16).

On August 23, local, state and federal officials turned out to honor the heroes. Coast Guard Commandant Admiral James Loy and other officers presented achievement medals and letters of commendation. U.S. Secretary of Transportation Norman Mineta expressed his pride in the Coast Guard, and added: "Because of what you do every day of the year, the world is a safer place now than it was yesterday, and it will be a safer place tomorrow than it was today" (Wyman, "Deep Trouble," p. 16).

Keeping mariners safe is the job of highly trained Coast Guard swimmers who leap into heavy seas and shark infested waters from helicopter platforms. They are rated Aviation Survival Technicians (ASTs), number in the hundreds, and have been compared to the elites of the other military services. The ASTs are the core which remains after most aspirants drop out of the 4 month training program. When not on missions, the daily training includes 10 mile runs, weight lifting, calisthenics and swimming (Grant, Associated Press, Post Bulletin, July 3, 2000).

The Coast Guard is responsible for missions in addition to search and rescue. Ice operations ("Ice Ops") include ice breaking and tracking North Atlantic icebergs, sometimes coordinated with Navy military operations. Civilian vessels also break up winter ice. The Coast Guard is the only federal agency assigned to the task since the U.S. Navy turned its icebreaking vessels over to the USCG.

Icebreaking serves military and commercial purposes. Icebreaking cutters operate on coastal waters, rivers and the Great Lakes. Coast Guard icebreakers are used to support polar scientific expeditions and resupply stations in the Arctic and Antarctic.

The Coast Guard operates the Vessel Traffic Service which provides information to ships underway in congested sea lanes and U.S. ports. The Marine Safety Office investigates ship collisions, sinkings, and fires. The MSO enforces maritime safety regulations and issues mariner licenses. A special Coast Guard unit of about 100 specialists inspects bridges located in navigation lanes.

Recreational Boating Safety is monitored by active-duty regular and reserve personnel, and the trained civilian personnel of the Coast Guard Auxiliary who also assist in search and rescue and security patrols. Auxiliary personnel approximate the number of active-duty (regular) Coast Guard.

Environmental protection has been a Coast Guard function since the 1970s. The service coordinates its activities with the Environmental Protection Agency (EPA).

Approximately 100 specially trained Coast Guard personnel make up the Strike Force unit. Stationed on the Atlantic, Pacific and Gulf Coasts these highly trained specialists respond at home and overseas to oil spills, toxic waste accidents, and other environmental disasters. They are often away from their home base. Their cumbersome equipment and astronaut suits provide protection in toxic environments and in volatile shipboard fires (Halberstadt, USCG: Always Ready, pp. 83, 86, 88, 89).

The Coast Guard Marine Environmental Protection program has 18th century antecedents. The Refuse Act of 1899 was an early response to pollution enforced by the Revenue Cutter Service and the Army Corps of Engineers. The Federal Water Pollution Control Act of 1972 furnished the Coast Guard with its contemporary mandate. The Fishery Conservation and Management Act of 1976 extended U.S. offshore fishing jurisdiction into a 200-mile zone which the U.S. Coast Guard enforces ("Environmental Protection," Coast Guard Historian's Office, 12/28/00).

Even before the Refuse Act of 1899, Congress directed the Revenue Cutter Service to prevent the illegal cutting of coastal Florida timber reserves which provided the sturdy oak trees for the hulls of naval and commercial vessels. Timber poachers were tracked in the narrow inland rivers and channels of tropical Florida, a catalyst for the acquisition of steam powered revenue cutters to supplement sail-powered boats and ships.

After the U.S. purchase of Alaska from the Russians (1867), the U.S. Revenue Service assumed the responsibility of enforcing conservation, fishing and sealing laws, and policing the territory on land and sea. The USRS brought supplies and medical services to isolated settlements and supported scientific expeditions in the high latitudes. After 1915, the USCG continued its varied missions, and increasingly enforced oil pollution and fishing laws whether the violators were domestic vessels or foreign fishing, cargo and tanker ships illegally encroaching in or polluting U.S. sovereign waters.

Marine oil pollution was monitored by the USRS as early as 1885, and by the Coast Guard with the Oil Pollution Act of 1924. International oil pollution laws gradually expanded Coast Guard efforts. Oil pollution responsibilities led the Coast Guard to develop innovative pollution detection and removal technologies and techniques. Coast Guard expertise led to nautical engineering modifications which made oil tanker navigation, loading and unloading safer. The Coast Guard developed shipboard firefighting and prevention strategies, enforced legal sanctions and imposed fines on polluters.

Since World War Two, the Coast Guard has been involved in joint responses with several federal agencies, including the Departments of Interior, Justice, Agriculture, Transportation, and the Nuclear Regulatory Commission.

One of the worse spills the Coast Guard and other government agencies ever had to deal with was the oil spill from the grounded U.S. tanker Exxon Valdez. The vessel struck a reef 75 miles from a Trans-Alaskan pipeline terminal in Prince William Sound on 24 March 1989 (details of which are covered in Chapter 9). The damage to the ecosystem, fishing and tourism, and the cleanup costs were extensive. Thousands of animals were killed. More than 300 miles of shoreline were contaminated. Extensive litigation ensued over the next several years.

The Coast Guard response, in coordination with other agencies and the oil industry, was complex and inevitably successful (Canney, "The Coast Guard and the Environment," Coast Guard Historian's Office, pp. 1-8).

Coast Guard pollution strike forces operate in the United States and overseas. In January 2001, the USCG sent a 10 member team to respond to a 160,000 gallon petroleum spill from a grounded Ecuadorean tanker. Ironically, the oil spill threatened the very ecosystem that naturalist Charles Darwin studied. Darwin's Galapagos Islands studies led to the formulation of his controversial evolutionary theories ("Galapagos Spill Moves Toward Center of Archipelago," The New York Times, AP, January 23, 2000, pp. A1, A8).

The environmental protection mission of the Coast Guard is one of the service's most complex and vital responsibilities.

Other responsibilities include the interdiction of drug and migrant (immigrant) smuggling. Night vision goggles and sophisticated radar are important enforcement tools. Coast Guard patrol boats and helicopters join in high seas chases and coordinate their activities with U.S. Customs, the Immigration and Naturalization Service, other federal, state and local law enforcement agencies and port officials. High speed deployable interceptor boats which look like recreational vessels are in the Coast Guard arsenal, as are surveillance aircraft.

The Florida coast, and Gulf and Caribbean waters are the hot spots for immigrant smuggling. Migrant smugglers charge thousands of dollars per passenger. They squeeze their human cargo into small fast boats, using darkness as a shield in their break for U.S. waters. The smugglers try to evade federal officials because the punishments for migrant smuggling and trying to escape arrest are not as severe as is the case for drug smugglers. Detained smugglers can be the beneficiaries of sympathetic ethnic juries. Since the inception of the Cold War, it has been the policy of the U.S. to automatically grant asylum to Cubans who make it safely to U.S. territory, another incentive to ignore the warnings of pursuing patrol boats.

Evasion attempts lead to challenging and dangerous situations which put smugglers, their cargoes and Coast Guard crews at significant risk, especially boarding parties, and crews of small, vulnerable rigid hull inflatable boats (RHIBs).

Most illegal immigrants from Latin America do not have the money to hire experienced smugglers with high speed boats, and depend on unseaworthy rafts which require the Coast Guard to chase them down to enforce immigration law, and carry out what often turns into search and rescue missions.

Coast Guard cutters and pursuit aircraft use gunfire to damage the motors and engines of fleeing vessels carrying illegal drugs, but are reluctant to fire into crowded boats carrying illegal immigrants. To respond, the Coast Guard has been developing non-lethal equipment to immobilize boat engines, propellers and crews (Shaw, "Catching Up With Migrant Smugglers," Proceedings, July 2002, pp. 43-45).

The law enforcement functions of the Coast Guard are increasingly dangerous and varied, especially since the 11 September 2001 terrorist attacks on the U.S. and the established need for enhanced port security. To meet the challenge, Coast Guard law enforcement detachment teams undergo rigorous physical training and compete with other civilian and military law enforcement agencies in friendly competition at law enforcement schools and training sites. Coast Guard tactical teams endure rigorous field training on obstacle courses which require reservists and regulars to master rappelling down 70 foot towers, climbing high walls, running with 150 pound loads, and engaging in simulated shoot outs which require split-second timing. Strict evaluations, rewards and penalties are awarded for success or error. Coast Guard tactical law enforcement teams have responded to a variety of situations, and have teamed up with their service counterparts in joint missions, including U.S. Navy units enforcing UN sanctions in the Persian Gulf (DeMarino, "A Little Office Rivalry," Coast Guard, May 2002, pp. 10-15).

Coast Guard rescue swimmers have trained with U.S. Secret Service agents to protect and if need be save the lives of U.S. presidents and former presidents in marine environments. President G.W. Bush, Jr., and former President George Herbert Walker Bush, Sr., for example, have enjoyed recreational boating and fishing in visits to the family lake home on the rocky shores of Maine. Always on watch at those sites are Secret Service agents and Coast Guard personnel, ready to protect, serve, and if necessary, rescue the nation's leaders (Casey, "Safety on the Rocks," Coast Guard, February 2002, pp. 19-23).

Intelligence gathering is an important task for all law enforcement agencies. Intelligence gathering can be compromised by agency insiders who may be motivated by revenge, ideology, money or blackmail. In April 2002, the Webster Commission, a Justice Department task force concluded there were serious encroachments into the security systems of the National Security Agency, FBI, and CIA, as well as military intelligence agencies. Sensitive information was turned over to the former Soviet Union by a renegade FBI agent.

The report revealed that since the 1930s, foreign agents had penetrated every national security agency except the U.S. Coast Guard (Rodriguez, "Perfect Gray Suit...," Insight, May 6, 2002, pp. 16-17).

Given that record, and in light of the significant role the U.S. Coast Guard has played in national security since its origins and after 11 September 2001, some analysts have suggested the USCG intelligence contribution should be expanded.

Ensign Wallace L. Cannon (USNR) made just such a suggestion in a leading naval journal in 2002. The former enlisted U.S. Navy intelligence specialist spent one year supporting Coast Guard drug enforcement missions, and provided professional expertise to the FBI. Ensign Cannon advocated the creation of an enlisted Intelligence Specialist (IS) rating in the Coast Guard. Cannon contends such a rating would enhance Coast Guard intelligence missions by establishing a corps of regular and reserve officers and enlisted personnel in the field, rather than continuing with the transitional assignments that have been characteristic of service.

Ensign Cannon asserted that the IS rating would be an asset in Coast Guard port security, law enforcement, and drug and migrant interdiction. Trained intelligence personnel in the Coast Guard and Navy, Cannon concluded, could form effective teams in maritime missions. The training of IS personnel could take place at military and civilian law enforcement centers which specialize in intelligence gathering and interpretation (Cannon, "Coast Guard Needs Enlisted Intel Specialists," Proceedings, February 2002, pp. 70-71).

Effective maritime intelligence is essential for the protection of U.S. commerce and national security. In 2002 it was estimated that ships carried 95% of the national trade volume to and from 350 sea ports, 50 of which control 93% of the trade. The most significant sea ports are in vulnerable urban locations.

The multiple missions of the Coast Guard illustrate the crucial role the service plays in providing coastline and port security. Security experts have speculated that a ship under the control of a terrorist crew could detonate a nuclear or biochemical device in a crowded harbor, ram a bridge or oil tanker, or sink the vessel in a busy channel to block military and merchant vessels. The terrorist take-over of a crowded cruise ship could have devastating consequences.

Federal, state and local agencies need to coordinate effective intelligence operations to monitor and deny resources intended for use by terrorist organizations, and take preemptive action to thwart aggression (Walsh, "Seaport Security: The Impossible Dream?," Proceedings, February 2002, p. 89).

On 23 May 2002 the USCG and FBI warned of the possibility of terrorist teams of scuba divers and swimmers striking at major U.S. seaports and strategic rivers and bays. Federal agents contacted scuba diving shops, schools and instructors to get profiles of suspicious students, including anyone who expressed interest in underwater demolitions equipment and techniques ("Coast Guard: Attack from Divers, Swimmers Possible," USA Today, June 10, 2002, p. 7A).

The following month, Homeland Security Director Tom Ridge warned of international terrorist interest in maritime operations and port security. Ridge claimed port authorities were warned, and the Coast Guard had outlined protective procedures ("Coast Guard Alerts All U.S. Ports to Possible Attack By Terrorists," The Oakland Tribune, June 10, 2002).

In a related public information disclosure, Coast Guard Commander Jim McPherson informed the media that the USCG planned to use helicopters to drop bomb sniffing dogs and their handlers on to suspicious ships at sea to search for explosives and chemical weapons ("Coast Guard Warns of Sea Attack," Washington Post, AP, June 10, 2002).

Retired Coast Guard Captain Bruce Stubbs calculated that the proposed Department of Homeland Security would be more effective than the disparate operations of its independent parts. The combination of agencies would allegedly be more efficient and less expensive because prior to consolidation, the Border Patrol, Customs Service and Coast Guard, had separate budgets, intelligence and communication centers, and boats and aircraft.

The Coast Guard, Stubbs contended, was not a good fit in the Department of Transportation. Its multi-mission experience and military organization, he argued, would be better suited in the proposed Homeland Security department (Stubbs, "It's the Right Thing To Do," Proceedings, July 2002, pp. 35-36).

Some critics of the proposed Homeland Security agency amalgamation feared it would threaten the funding for the Coast Guard Integrated Deepwater Systems (IDS) Program. Commander Paul J. Roden (USCG), as Deputy of the Office of Systems Deepwater Integration, contended the funding would be enhanced. Roden explained that the Congress and Department of Defense would realize that traditional Coast Guard missions and its Deepwater assets would enhance port security, intelligence gathering, ship inspection, and drug and immigrant interdiction.

Commander Roden predicted that improved Deepwater assets would be more easily integrated with U.S. Navy systems, functions and technology, and federal and local law enforcement (Roden, "The Shoal

Waters of Homeland Security," Proceedings, July 2002, pp.14-16). "The multi-mission design of Deepwater assets," Roden concluded, "enables the Coast Guard to respond to threats (and protect the U.S.) infrastructure in our ports and harbors as well as far out to sea" (Roden, Proceedings, July 2002, p. 16).

Some political factions have favored more lenient immigration enforcement, but Coast Guard Commandant Admiral James M. Loy believed continued border control was an essential part of the anti-terrorist security mission of the federal government and the USCG because some illegal immigrants could be terrorists.

After the 11 September 2001 terrorist attacks, the U.S. Coast Guard and U.S. Navy increased their mission coordination. Teams of Coast Guard law enforcement detachments (LEDETs) rode on Navy ships to board vessels suspected of carrying illegal contraband, which includes weapons of mass destruction (WMDs), drugs, and illegal immigrants (Hessman, "The Maritime Dimension," Sea Power, April 2002, pp. 65-66).

Lieutenant Commander Mark Steven Kirk (USNR) appreciated the Coast Guard role in port security and national defense. Speaking as a member of Congress and a Navy intelligence officer, Representative Kirk declared the war on terrorism necessitated the upgrading of Coast Guard fixed wing aircraft, helicopters and cutters. Kirk said the Coast

Guard plays a critical role in port security at home and deep water security missions beyond the 12 mile limit overseas. A tramp steamer, Kirk warned, could be carrying armed terrorists and a weapon of mass destruction, and the U.S. must have a naval force able to meet that challenge at sea or inshore by major port facilities (Kirk, "The Best Defense...", Sea Power, June 2002, pp. 11-19).

The Ninth Coast Guard District increased its Great Lakes security presence within hours after the 11 September terrorist attacks. District Commander Rear Admiral James Hull ordered the formation of a maritime task force and called up the Reserve. The Coast Guard Auxiliary provided extra support at air and sea stations and in maritime safety offices. The Coast Guard coordinated its surveillance and patrol activities with Canadian maritime officials, the Canadian Coast Guard, and local, state and federal law enforcement agencies. The actions were essential and effective. The Great Lakes Coast Guard district covers 12 nuclear power plants, three international bridges, the ports of Chicago, Milwaukee, Duluth and Superior, and a 1500 mile maritime border (Dechant and Fawcett, "D9 Steps Up Great Lakes Security Presence," Coast Guard, December 2001-January 2002, p. 13).

The strategic and economic importance of the Great Lakes maritime region and the Midwestern states contained therein, illustrates the importance of the United States Coast Guard in the northerly region of magnificent scenery, beautiful summers, and picturesque, frigid winters.

Lake Superior's Twin Ports of Superior (Wisconsin) and Duluth (Minnesota) is one of the oldest Revenue Service and Coast Guard jurisdictions. The earliest documentation of a lighthouse under the control of the Lighthouse Service dates to 1818. Revenue cutters enforced the treaty with Britain which ended the War of 1812-14. The Duluth lifeboat station began its maritime life saving missions in 1895. The Steamboat Inspection Service inspected merchant ships and seafaring equipment in 1913. The icebreaker USCGC Escanaba began clearing channels through the lake ice for merchant vessels in 1932.

Duluth maintains a Marine Inspection Office (MIO) which coordinates its activities with the U.S. Army Corps of Engineers. The Coast Guard posts a Captain of the Port in the harbor city. The Duluth-Superior ports host hundreds of U.S. and foreign merchant ships each year, as do the smaller ports on the Western Lake Superior shore which extends to Canada.

Coal, wheat and taconite is sent by train and truck to the Twin Ports for shipment east. Huge domestic and foreign cargo vessels and ore carriers carry goods to and from the Twin Ports, making Duluth-Superior one of the top twenty ports in the U.S. in tonnage, despite the fact that winter ice closes the harbor for 3 months out of the year.

The CGC Sundew (WLB-404) served the Twin Ports and Lake Superior in law enforcement, search and rescue, icebreaking and as a buoy tender.

The Duluth Coast Guard station is the home of an aids to navigation team and an electronic support detachment which maintains shore and shipboard electronic equipment in the Twin Ports and area stations. An active Coast Guard Auxiliary teaches boating safety courses in the Northland, and supports other Coast Guard missions as needed. Coast Guard stations in Michigan along the Upper Peninsula support the Lake Superior area with their traditional responsibilities.

Lake Superior search and rescue stations are located in the Minnesota ports of Duluth and Grand Marais; Station Portage in Dollar Bay, Michigan; and Bayfield, Wisconsin near the Apostle Islands, north of Ashland ("The United States Coast Guard in the Northland," Marine Inspection Office Duluth, and The Coast Guard Historian's Office, 12/29/2000).

Ninth Coast Guard District personnel are called "Guardians of the Great Lakes." The 9th District boundaries include the shores and major rivers of the states of New York, Pennsylvania, Illinois, Ohio, Indiana, Minnesota, Wisconsin and Michigan. In January 2001, 2,000 active duty Coast Guard personnel were supported by nearly 5,000 Auxiliary, 600 Reserves, and 70 civilians in 92 units and 48 stations, with 200 small boats, 2 air stations and 2 air facilities, two LORAN stations and 10 cutters. The events of 11 September 2001 modified those figures, increasing the number of active duty personnel whose ranks were augmented by increased recruitment and the call up of reservists.

More than 7,000 search and rescue missions are launched annually in the Ninth District. Three 180-foot buoy tenders serve as icebreakers. The 290-foot CGC Mackinaw performs traditional Coast Guard missions, including icebreaking duties. The 21st century has already witnessed the keels of the next generation of buoy tenders being laid in Marinette, Wisconsin. World War Two era cutters which have served so long and so well are scheduled to be replaced by 225-foot Juniper and 175-foot Ida Lewis class cutters equipped with the latest nautical technology.

The Ninth District Coast Guard units maintain more than three thousand aids to navigation and serve in eight marine safety offices under nine Captains of the Port. Combat trained port security units from the district have been deployed to global crisis zones, including the Persian Gulf and Haiti ("Ninth Coast Guard District," USCG Historian's Office, Updated: January 9, 2002; and "Ninth Coast Guard District," Updated: June 11, 2002).

The Commander of the Ninth Coast Guard District as of May 18, 2002 was Rear Admiral Ronald F. Silva, who succeeded Vice Admiral James D. Hull. Prior to his Great Lakes command, Admiral Silva was Chief Engineer and Assistant Commandant for Systems, where he was responsible for USCG engineering and logistics.

The Connecticut native graduated from the U.S. Coast Guard Academy in 1971, and served on three cutters at sea as well as several shore commands. Besides earning an advanced degree in engineering, the military engineer earned several meritorious, commendation and achievement medals, and a number of other personal and unit awards ("Ninth Coast Guard District: The Admiral's Corner," USCG Historian's Office, 6/19/02).

The Ninth Coast Guard District office is categorized as the Atlantic Area on the organization charts, with headquarters in Cleveland, Ohio. The other Atlantic Area districts are First (Boston), Fifth (Portsmouth, Va.), Seventh (Miami) and Eighth (New Orleans).

Pacific Area districts include the Eleventh (Alameda, California), Thirteenth (Seattle), Fourteenth (Honolulu) and Seventeenth in Juneau, Alaska ("U.S. Coast Guard: Units and Locations." Coast Guard Historian's Office. Updated: 11 June 2002).

The District Commanders serve under the Commandant of the

U.S. Coast Guard, Headquarters Washington, D.C. The first Coast Guard Commandant, Commodore Ellsworth P. Bertholf assumed leadership command in 1915, and led the USCG through World War I. The honored veteran of the U.S. Revenue Cutter Service received a Congressional Gold Medal of Honor for carrying out a dangerous Alaskan relief expedition. There was nothing in Commodore Bertholf's USRCS record to indicate why, early in his naval career, he had been court-martialed and dismissed from the Naval Academy (C. Douglas Kroll, Commodore Ellsworth P. Bertholf).

On 30 May 2002 Admiral Thomas H. Collins became the Commandant of the U.S. Coast Guard, succeeding Admiral Loy. Collins had previously served as Vice Commandant and Commander of Pacific Districts Eleven and Fourteen. Collins developed effective drug and immigration interdiction responses, and assisted in the development of the modernization of Coast Guard air and sea craft for the Deepwater System project. Collins served as a cutter officer and commander.

A 1968 Coast Guard Academy graduate and member of the Humanities Department faculty, Admiral Collins earned two graduate degrees and several Coast Guard medals and awards ("Admiral Thomas H. Collins, Commandant, U.S. Coast Guard," Coast Guard Historian's Office, Updated: Friday, June 14, 2002).

The multiple missions of the U.S. Coast Guard require skilled enlisted personnel, experienced officers, and dedicated Coast Guard commandants. The Coast Guard has been fortunate in its leadership and mission achievements.

The national security, life saving and law enforcement missions of the Coast Guard have always been significant, now more than ever. To underscore that point, within two months of his retirement as commandant and appointment as deputy director of the Transportation Security Administration, Admiral James Loy was named TSA director. In the July 2002 announcement, Transportation Secretary Norman Mineta explained Loy's promotion to the media: "Admiral Loy amply demonstrated his ability to motivate and manage a large federal agency when he was commandant of the Coast Guard. Jim Loy is the right man for this job at the right time" (Shahbandar, "TSA Chief Steps Down," CNSNews, July 18, 2002).

Maritime safety, ship inspection, illegal drug and immigration interdiction, aids to navigation, search and rescue, port security, and national defense are the main missions of the United States Coast Guard.

National and international waters have been boiling since the terrorist attack on the United States on 11 September 2001. The Coast Guard met the challenge and forged new task oriented relationships with the Defense Department and local, state and federal law enforcement. The

Coast Guard was heralded as an integral part of the evolving Department of Homeland Security (DHS).

Since Revenue Service days, the Coast Guard has had the multiple responsibilities of being a military service and having jurisdiction over civilians while enforcing national and international law.

New challenges await the smallest naval service. Coast Guard responsibilities will be increased under the Department of Homeland Security. As always, the Coast Guard is ready to carry out its missions in U.S. territorial and international waters.

The Coast Guard is well prepared to meet its traditional and contemporary responsibilities, enriching its heritage and illuminating its motto, "Semper Paratus."

CHAPTER XIV

PAST, PRESENT AND FUTURE

Former philosophy professor, education secretary, and drug czar William J. Bennett analyzed the post-September 11 war on terror in his book, Why We Fight. The prolific author paid an exemplary compliment to the U.S. Coast Guard response to the terrorist attacks, which, he said, "...gave fresh meaning to the Coast Guard motto, Semper Paratus. Without benefit of a central command, without training manuals, without field exercises, (the Coast Guard) was able to deploy its forces with lightening speed... seize the attention of the press...and read from a single script. Its tactics and its instincts were models of rapid mobilization" (Bennett, William J., Why We Fight, p. 17).

When General Colin Powell retired as Chairman of the Joint Chiefs of Staff, he was proud to be honored by the Pentagon senior non-commissioned officers who bestowed upon him honorary enlisted positions in each of the armed services, including "honorary master chief petty officer" in the U.S. Coast Guard (Powell, My American Journey, p. 586).

As important as the Coast Guard mission is for national security, port security, and drug and immigrant interdiction, its historic function has been the protection of life and property, and search and rescue. Government officials and observers of the Coast Guard have enunciated their appreciation of that role. In the wake of the planned creation of the Homeland Security Department, several members of Congress expressed their concern that SAR (search and rescue) functions not be diminished.

The historical significance of SAR is masterfully chronicled in Rescue at Sea, written by Captain John M. Waters, Jr. (USCG). The Coast Guard Academy graduate experienced maritime combat in World War Two. In his post-war career Captain Waters participated in several thousand sea and air rescues, most of the latter performed in H-52 amphibious helicopters which are no longer used by the Coast Guard.

Captain Waters served as chief of Coast Guard SAR in the 1960s, and initiated many new principles, procedures and techniques. The contributions of Captain Waters to air and sea SAR have been documented and published for the use of the Coast Guard and the other U.S. armed services. Other international rescue organizations have utilized the techniques and lessons learned from Captain Walter's adventurous and prolific career in search and rescue and law enforcement operations. Upon retirement from the USCG, Captain Waters was named director of Public Safety in Jacksonville, Florida, and clinical professor at the University of Florida in the School of Medicine.

Many changes came to the Coast Guard in his long career, among them, Captain Waters observed, "women in the cockpit and on the bridge. Just as the oar-powered surfboats of the nineteenth century disappeared with the advent of fast motor craft and helicopters, the seaplanes and ocean station vessels gave way to long-range helicopters, jet aircraft, and improved navigation and safety techniques. The amphibious helicopter, just coming into its own in 1966 (has been) replaced with helicopters unable to land on the water...a perhaps regressive change dictated by high aircraft development costs" (Waters, Rescue at Sea, pp. xi-xii). Captain Waters chronicled the courage and skillful aviation techniques of amphibious helicopter pilots in countless missions, endorsed the seaworthiness of the successful aircraft, regretted the termination of their use, and insisted that the amphibious choppers increased the safety of crews and rescue swimmers, and asserted that with the amphibious vehicles, and the potential failure of the contemporary hoist mechanism, recovery success rates would be enhanced (Waters, pp. 150-157).

With the advent of long ranged rescue helicopters which can not land on the water, the role of rescue swimmers and the rescue-basket hoist procedures became essential. The courage and danger to helicopter crews and rescue swimmers was well illustrated in January 1989, when the crew of an HH-65 chopper from Coast Guard Air Station Astoria (Oregon) set out over frigid waters and 20 foot waves to rescue a downed U.S. Air Force F-4 fighter pilot. With limited visibility, Lieutenant Commander Bill Peterson and his crew lowered rescue swimmer ASM3 Kelly Mogk into the mountainous seas. Suffering injury and hypothermia herself, Petty Officer Mogk somehow managed to untangle the semi-conscious aviator from his parachute, and get him back into the helicopter. Mogk had to wait in the cold waters, partially disabled by a back injury, for another Coast Guard helicopter to eventually return and rescue her. ASM3 Mogk, the first female swimmer in the Coast Guard, and the first woman certified from the Navy Rescue Swimmer School (Pensacola, Florida), was subsequently awarded the coveted Air

Medal, and was honored in a Washington, D.C. ceremony by President George Herbert Walker Bush, a decorated World War Two military aviator (Waters, pp. 158-160).

Lieutenant Troy Beshears, Lieutenant Commander Brian Moore, AST1 John Green and AMT1 Michael Bourchard of Coast Guard Air Station New Orleans each received a Distinguished Flying Cross for their dangerous rescue of 51 people from a flaming oil rig in the Gulf of Mexico on 5 July 2000. The courageous rescue team even stayed on station when the rig exploded sending a 100 foot fire ball above the oil rig platform ("Heroes..." Coast Guard, Air Station New Orleans, June 2002).

BMC Joseph A. Habel earned the Coast Guard Medal for heroic duty for the courageous rescue he and his utility boat crew performed in Chesapeake Bay on 25 January 2000. Sleet, snow, 10 foot waves, and frigid waters did not prevent Chief Habel and his team from rescuing four members of a stranded tugboat crew ("Heroes..." Coast Guard, Station Cape Charles, Va.).

Concerned that the multi-mission responsibilities of the Coast Guard might necessitate the diminution of some traditional tasks, Captain Waters warned that "law enforcement does not necessarily have to be sacrificed for SAR, or vice versa. In an emergency response organization, some jobs can be handled during waits between more urgent calls, thus reducing nonproductive standby time. This ability to respond to multiple requirements has contributed largely over the years to the Coast Guard's reputation for economy and efficiency" (Waters, pp. 315-316).

Since 11 September 2001, increased responsibilities for the critical missions of homeland defense and national security have made Captain Water's prophetic advice all the more significant. Coast Guard personnel serve as military personnel trained for naval warfare, humanitarian life savers, and experts in port security. Environmental protection, constabulary duties, and national security are among the many responsibilities of the maritime service. Most of the seafaring officers are U.S. Coast Guard Academy graduates who are well trained in the laws of the sea and engineering. Critics of Coast Guard education and the Academy curriculum contend that officers and enlisted personnel know far too little of the substantive history of the service, limiting the perspective necessary for comparative analysis and planning and professional writing (Stubbs, "We Are Lifesavers...Warriors," Proceedings, April 2002, pp. 50-53).

The academic study of the history of the Coast Guard is said by critics to be "the services most overlooked and underused operational asset" (Wells, Proceedings, August 2002, p. 46). The failure of the Coast Guard to emphasize and publish its history promotes its unfortunate low profile and may impact upon federal funding and the recruitment of high quality enlisted personnel and officer candidates (Wells, "History... Semper Paratus," Proceedings, August 2002, pp. 46-48).

The time of the neglect of the study of Coast Guard history may be ending. In 1999 the Foundation for Coast Guard History (FCGH) was created to assist the Historian of the Coast Guard, encourage Coast Guard historical research and studies, and enhance public education in USCG history, concepts and issues (Thorsen, "...Coast Guard History," Proceedings, pp. 48-49).

Senator Edward M. Kennedy served on the Senate Armed Services Committee for 20 years. The Massachusetts solon gained a familiarity with the Coast Guard from his service on the SASC and his life in a maritime state. The USCG administers the Integrated Support Command Base in Boston. Protection against terrorist attacks requires, Kennedy asserted, well trained and well led men and women in the Coast Guard, Navy, Marine Corps, Army and Air Force.

Kennedy credited the Coast Guard for its essential homeland security mission, but said underfunding and expanded missions have placed burdens on the service and have impacted negatively on drug interdiction effectiveness. Senator Kennedy championed the necessity of increased funding for the Coast Guard to secure the support and resources needed to meet the needs of the service's expanded responsibilities (Hessman and Peterson, "Precision...Professionalism," Sea Power, pp. 9-12).

The renewed appreciation of the Coast Guard was illustrated by the presentation of the Navy League's 2001 Admiral Burke Leadership Award to Admiral James M. Loy shortly after his retirement.

Admiral Burke (USN) was noted for his professionalism, leadership and ethics. Former Coast Guard Commandant Loy, the newly appointed chief operating officer of the Transportation Security Administration (TSA) accepted the honor from Timothy O. Fanning, President of the Navy League of the United States . The NLUS has given its annual award to a litany of military luminaries who have exemplified "the highest standards of the United States and the Navy League." Admiral Loy and Team Coast Guard were lauded by the NLUS for rapid and reassuring responses to the 11 September attacks. Fanning asserted the Coast Guard response was "their finest hour" and Admiral Loy was "one of the greatest sea-service leaders of the post World War II era" (Hessman,"Former Commandant Loy....Receives Award," Sea Power, August 2002, p. 1).

National NLUS President Fanning credited the Coast Guard with being the primary federal agency for maritime law enforcement and security, and said the naval service was chronically under staffed and underfunded, given its responsibility over "25,000 miles of coastline to patrol, 350 ports," and thousands of "foreign flag ships, many of them carrying hazardous materials," some of which come "from countries identified by the U.S. State Department as having terrorist links..." (Fanning, "Unanswered Questions," Sea Power, August 2002, p. 5).

Admiral Loy's distinguished career included Vietnam where his patrol boat provided transportation and cover for military amphibious landings north of the Demilitarized Zone which separated North and South Vietnam. On Commandant Loy's watch (1998-2002) the U.S. Coast Guard expanded its drug and immigration interdiction operations, tactics, strategy and technology, and achieved several high water marks. Among the singular events: the deployment of the CGC Chase to the Persian Gulf to support the United Nations oil embargo against Iraq; Operation New Frontier which initiated the use of special pursuit boats and armed helicopters; training teams sent to the former Soviet Republics of Azerbaijan and Georgia to develop and train national coast guards; the development of coordinated pollution control and response plans with Russia and Mexico; a National Strike Force response to an oil spill in the Galapagos Islands; the combining of BM/QM and ET/FT ratings, and the creation of OS and IT rates; the global circumnavigation of the CGC Sherman; the largest Coast Guard port security operation since World War Two in response to the 9/11 terrorist attacks on the United States; and the drafting of a terrorist resolution which was passed by the International Maritime Organization (Coast Guard, "Adm. Loy: Saying Goodbye," July 2002, pp. 7-9).

On Admiral Loy's command, the next generation of Great Lakes icebreakers is being built. Manitowoc Marine Group's Marinette Marine Corporation awarded a contract to ABB Marine to produce electric propulsion systems scheduled for delivery in 2005. The new vessel will be named after the older cutter Mackinaw. The state of the art icebreaker was scheduled to have a 360-degree steering capability, and have no mechanical gears ("The Industrial Base," Sea Power, August 2002, p. 31).

The events of 9/11 have expanded the operations and strategies of the Coast Guard. Some innovative assignments seem as innocuous as they are significant.

The Marine Safety Field Office (MSFO) in Cape Cod, Massachusetts created a Coast Guard bicycle patrol. Coast Guard enlisted personnel steer mountain bikes along the marinas and bicycle paths of the harbor area. Their duties include security and pollution watches and monitoring and instructing civilians about safe boating.

Coast Guard visibility and better communication with the public has been enhanced by the bicycle patrol. Public comfort levels are accommodated by the uniform of the day: bike shorts, helmet and golf shirt. No weapons on board, although that policy might be questioned if and when the patrol is required to do heavy duty law enforcement, or apprehend a suspected or active terrorist.

The bicycle patrol personnel have explained that they have cultivated better relations with sports and commercial fisherman, boat owners, local police and fire departments, harbor masters and area military bases.

The petty officers of the MSFO reach out to people, publicize the Coast Guard mission, and use their marine science training to protect the physical environment (Thomas, "Pedal Pushers," Coast Guard, July 2002, pp. 28-31).

The articulation of Coast Guard, U.S. Marine, and civilian law enforcement units into symbiotic security force operations provides a cohesive whole to national security training and operations. In the Spring of 2002 Coast Guard boat crews from a maritime safety and security team led by a tactical law enforcement unit cooperated with the USMC in rigorous terrorist training exercises in the harbor waters off the coast of Charleston, South Carolina. U.S. Marines and Coast Guard personnel coordinated security and search operations on board Coast Guard cutters and on shore in Operation Harbor Shield, a model for subsequent training missions. The training experience was considered valuable for domestic and foreign ports, and for the protection, said General Douglas V. O'Dell (USMC), of naval installations and vessels. Commander Gary Merrick (USCG), the Charleston area commanding officer, agreed that the training experiences gained by the cooperative exercises enhanced port security. The operations also improved relations and communication with local and state law enforcement agencies (Carr and Crawford, "Partners in Protection," Coast Guard, July 2002, pp. 16-22).

The U.S. Coast Guard has long fostered relationships with the international community. The USCG has established and trained the naval forces of other nations. The coast guards of the Bahamas and other Caribbean countries and the U.S. Coast Guard have been reciprocal beneficiaries because these contacts have led to cooperative law enforcement, search and rescue, and security operations in the tropical waters. The International Training Division (ITD) of the U.S. Coast Guard instructs foreign crews in law enforcement, boarding, ship handling, weapons, firefighting, damage control, and drug interdiction (Burns, "Building International Friendships," Coast Guard, July 2002, pp. 13-14).

In the summer of 2002 Coast Guard Commandant, Admiral Thomas Collins signed an $11 billion contract with Lockheed Martin and Northrop Grumman executives to construct elements of the Integrated Deepwater System (IDS). Rear Admiral Patrick M. Stillman (USCG) was the first executive officer for the largest recapitalization program in Coast Guard history.

Admiral Stillman's Coast Guard career has included ship and shore assignments. Stillman commanded the Coast Guard Barque Eagle and served as commandant of cadets at the U.S. Coast Guard Academy. The USCGA graduate (1972) earned two Masters degrees and was chief of Atlantic Area Operational Forces.

The Deepwater program objective is to modernize the cutters, helicopters, aircraft, data gathering and communications systems of the Coast Guard. Among the aircraft innovations are the Bell Textron XV-15 tilt-rotor vertical lift aircraft and several UAV unmanned aerial vehicles.

The traditional Hamilton class high endurance cutters commissioned more than three decades ago are scheduled to be replaced by the new class of NSC (National Security Class) cutter within a ten year period. The Coast Guard mission requires the service to articulate even more closely than in the past with the U.S. Navy and U.S. Customs and the Border Patrol. Admiral Stillman described the mission and asset coordination plans with the Navy which is monitored by the Nav-Guard (Navy-Coast Guard) Board.

The Coast Guard history, Stillman contended, illuminated the importance of naval service as a sentinel of the law in home (brown) and international (blue) waters, a tradition traced to Alexander Hamilton's creation of the first vessels of the Revenue Marine Service. Closer cooperation with international navies and coast guards are also planned, Stillman explained, including the sale of Navy and Coast Guard assets overseas which will stimulate commerce, upgrade allied fleets, and facilitate the coordination of international maritime safety, law enforcement, and national security missions (Hessman and Peterson, "A Performance Based System of Systems," Sea Power, August 2002, pp. 12-16).

Admiral Thomas H. Collins, the 22nd Coast Guard commandant, assumed command of the Service on 30 May 2002. Soon after taking his new post, Admiral Collins set the course for the 21st century Coast Guard. Commandant Collin's objectives included the implementation of safe and effective tactics, integrated logistics and communications systems, staff development to ensure highly trained and motivated personnel, better maritime domain capabilities, maximum intelligence and reconnaissance capabilities, administering and expanding the Integrated Deep Water System Program and the modernization of Coast Guard ship, shore and air assets, and facilitating more effective partnerships with military, law enforcement, and civilian agencies responsible for public safety, national security, and commerce.

The Commandant asserted that Coast Guard personnel, whether active-duty, reservists, auxiliarists, or civilians would be a top priority, along with morale and safety issues, and recruitment. Education, training and professional development will be a top priority in the increasingly technologically sophisticated Coast Guard.

Coast Guard personnel, Commandant Collins insisted, must know and appreciate the history of the Service, and understand what and why they do what they are called upon to do in the multi-mission tasks ahead (Collins, "Commandant's Direction 2002," Sea Power, August 2002, pp. 9-10).

The interdiction of undocumented aliens and illegal drugs was listed as a significant priority on Admiral Collin's agenda because of increased concern about crime and national security in an era of increased terrorist threats. The Coast Guard Sea Marshal program is an important aspect of commerce and maritime security because of the expected increase in the export and import trade in the next few decades.

President George W. Bush frequently acknowledged the enhanced significance of the Coast Guard. Bush visited several Coast Guard stations and expressed his support for significant increases in Coast Guard funding and the numbers of Regular and Reserve personnel (Hessman, " A Constellation of High Honors...Challenges and Opportunities...," Sea Power, July 2002, p. 1).

CHAPTER XV

THE TWENTY-FIRST CENTURY COAST GUARD

The twenty-first century posed new challenges for the Coast Guard and reaffirmed the importance of its traditional missions.

From the founding of the U.S. Revenue Cutter Service in 1790, to the creation of the Coast Guard in 1915, and the migration of the Service from the Departments of Treasury (1790) to Transportation (1967) to the Department of Homeland Security (2003), the USCG has served the nation at home and overseas in war and peace.

Coast Guard port security missions began during World War I, continued through World II and the Cold War, and have been enhanced since the 9.11.01 terrorist attacks upon the United States.

Under the authority of the Espionage Act (1917) the federal government assigned Coast Guard Captains of the Port (COTPs) with port security responsibilities in major U.S. ports. Under the COTPs, Coast Guard missions included aids to navigation (ATN), search and rescue (SAR), foreign and domestic ship inspections, explosives loading, firefighting, environmental protection, and the prevention of enemy espionage and sabotage activities.

COTP offices were initially established in New York, Philadelphia, and Norfolk, and in Sault Ste. Marie (Michigan) on the Great Lakes (Beard, 2004, pp. 238-252). Appendix G contains primary source material that illustrates World War II activities in just the port of Charleston (South Carolina).

A COTP office was subsequently established in the Twin Ports of Duluth (Minnesota) and Superior (Wisconsin) at the western end of Lake Superior. The Twin Ports COTP was strategically significant during World War II because of commercial and shipbuilding activities, the shipping of iron ore and coal to steel plants, and the transportation of corn and wheat.

In wartime and periods of international tension Coast Guard missions have been articulated with the U.S. Navy at home and overseas. Such was the case in World Wars I and II, the Korean and Vietnam wars, and in the Middle East during the Gulf War of 1991 and the anti-terrorist wars in Iraq and Afghanistan wars which commenced in 2001 and 2003 respectively. During the War on Terror, Coast Guard personnel have served in the United States and overseas and earned medals and commendations. In April 2004 Coast Guard Petty Officer (DC3) Nathan Bruckenthal was killed in combat in Iraq in Operation Iraqi Freedom.

Since 9.11.01, the Coast Guard established even closer relations with the other U.S. Armed Forces, and with federal, state, and local law enforcement and other public safety agencies and civilian port authorities. The USCG conducts joint missions with Customs, Border Patrol, and Immigration units, and the Departments of State and Defense. The missions include vessel tracking, monitoring and vessel boarding in an era of increased maritime awareness.

National concern about port security affected domestic and foreign politics in February 2006 when the Bush administration approved a contract which would have allowed DP World (DPW) based in the United Arab Emirates (UAE) to operate port facilities in New Orleans, Miami, Baltimore, New Jersey, Philadelphia and New York. DPW acquired the port operations in a purchase from a London firm.

Federal officials had investigated and approved the deal, despite the revelation that President Bush had not known about it, and U.S. Coast Guard officials initially were concerned with alleged port security lapses and potential risks. During Congressional hearings Coast Guard officials revealed that the USCG had revised that assessment after further investigation. Congressional and public outrage at the security implications of a Middle East nation with former ties to terrorists managing port facilities in the United States resulted in the Bush administration's withdrawal of the offer to the UAE owned company.

Congress insisted on more transparent procedural guidelines for future contingencies. Critics of the cancelled deal thought it was shortsighted and counterproductive because since 9.11.01 the UAE had been a helpful and moderate Middle East ally, and the UAE port of Dubai welcomed U.S. military vessels ("UAE Firm...U.S. Ports," 2006).

Port security protection is an ongoing challenge in the United States because of its more than 360 major ports, thousands of miles of navigable waters and coast lines, and thousands of visiting commercial vessels carrying millions of cargo containers each year. Less than 6% of the containers were directly checked, although advanced technology and trained dogs assisted Coast Guard and Customs officials in the task.

Vessels are monitored and tracked and U.S. Customs and Coast Guard officials are stationed as inspectors in key foreign ports where ships are loaded for American ports.

The southern and western ports and borders of the United States are generally the busiest for Coast Guard and Customs enforcement activities. But since 9.11.01 Great Lakes ports are more thoroughly monitored. Smuggling and terrorist activities have been detected. Weapons and money caches were found. Islamic extremist groups were monitored and arrests were made.

The Coast Guard in the Ninth (Great Lakes) Coast Guard District has worked closely with U.S. and Canadian law enforcement officials and Canadian Coast Guard personnel in ship inspections, law enforcement, and other defense and port security matters. Canadian and Coast Guard security teams board vessels and ride along in patrol vessels and cutters in the "Shiprider" program to maximize jurisdictional outreach and security operations.

Great Lakes port infrastructure like nuclear power plants and strategic Sault Ste. Marie canal locks would be attractive terrorist targets, as would the port of Cleveland, the headquarters of the Ninth Coast Guard District. In 2006 the Ninth District commander was Rear Admiral Robert J. Papp. Rear Adm. Papp was responsible for 6700 miles of shoreline and the 1500-mile international border with Canada.

Rear Adm. Papp worked closely with U.S. and Canadian commercial, law enforcement and naval officials to secure the Great Lakes. Papp expressed concern about the 2000 illegal immigrants apprehended on his watch between 2004 and 2006.

Describing the security concerns of the Great Lakes region, Adm. Papp asserted, "We no longer work hard for only nine months." Even the iced-over Great Lakes has been used as a transportation corridor for legal and illegal activities in the long winter months, requiring the constant diligence of Coast Guard, Customs, Immigration and Border officials (Hilburn, "Border Crossings, 2006, pp. 26-32).

During the Civil War, World Wars I and II, and since 9.11.01, the Canadian and U.S. governments have modified the Rush-Bagot Agreement (1817) to allow heavy weapons and deck-mounted guns on Great Lakes Coast Guard vessels. During World War II the U.S. Navy had armed training vessels on the Great Lakes. In recent years, Coast Guard personnel have been trained to use M60 machine guns if necessary on the Inland Seas

Port security is a crucial mission. Armed Coast Guard helicopters patrol petrochemical facilities and look for oil leaks, spills and even dam breeches. The Coast Guard established protective security zones around U.S. Navy vessels, other military facilities, and commercial air terminals adjacent to water. The Coast Guard monitors commercial vessels, fuel tankers and cruise ships from helicopters and watercraft. Coast Guard "Sea Marshals" board vessels at sea to investigate security and safety situations. The U.S. Coast Guard Auxiliary provides thousands of trained civilians who assist the USCG in SAR, ship safety, ATN, and security patrols in maritime regions. Auxiliary personnel use privately owned water and aircraft and some Coast Guard boats.

Coast Guard Reservists are assigned to active duty units as part of their monthly and annual service. Reservists have served with enlisted personnel in overseas assignments, including the Persian Gulf. To enhance port security skills and operations, Coast Guard personnel have trained at Army and Marine bases and Navy diving schools.

Modern, high technology patrol craft provide versatile platforms for Coast Guard personnel at large and small Coast Guard stations. The enclosed 47-foot small boat is self-righting and can withstand hurricane force winds and twenty-foot seas. Port security teams at small and large boat and cutter stations use armed Defender Class SAFE (Secure All-around Flotation Equipped) boats that can mount heavy weapons (Beard, 2004, pp. 254-255, 342, 346-347, 122-133).

Coast Guard Reserve and Regular units deployed on armed patrol boats to the waters off the Guantanamo Bay U.S. Navy Base (Cuba) to support the U.S. Navy Joint Task Force and U.S. Marine units guarding incarcerated terrorist suspects at the Guantanamo detention facility ("En Patrulla in Cuba," 2006, pp. 58-59).

Ocean-going Coast Guard cutters perform law enforcement, SAR, and national defense missions. The law enforcement missions include fisheries enforcement and drug and illegal immigration interdiction. To carry out the missions, armed, well-trained Coast Guard boarding teams are supported by cutters, small fast boats, and armed helicopters that shoot to disable the engines on contraband carrying vessels.

During a Caribbean narcotics patrol in 2006, the crew of the USCGC Escanaba seized 104 bales of contraband from a vessel off the Honduran coast. Like the Escanaba, the CGC Spencer took cocaine off a sailing vessel south of Jamaica, arrested two smugglers, and transferred the suspects to the CGC Venturous, out of St. Petersburg (Florida). The crew pf the Venturous transferred the suspects and the contraband to Customs and Drug Enforcement officers at St. Petersburg.

On the same patrol the Venturous interdicted three overloaded sailboats and 200 migrants and took them to Haiti ("Cutters Stop U.S. Bound Cocaine Shipment," 2006).

In the spring of 2006, out of the northern Michigan homeport of Charlevoix, the USCGC Acacia made its last run as a Lake Michigan buoy tender. The area of operation (AOR) of the Acacia included Lake Michigan as far south as Chicago, and north to Green Bay and Sturgeon Bay in the scenic Door Peninsula region of Wisconsin.

The 62-year old World War II era 180-foot Coast Guard cutter was scheduled to be decommissioned in May. Built in Duluth (Minnesota) and launched in 1942, the CGC Acacia is the last of the "180's" on the Great Lakes ("Acacia Makes Final Run," 2006).

On the Great Lakes, where the Coast Guard is referred to as "The Guardian of the Inland Seas," the venerable 290-foot USCGC Mackinaw (WAGB 83), built in Toledo (Ohio) in 1944 sailed for more than 60 years. The World War II era Mackinaw was decommissioned in 2006. With the support of the homeport city of Cheboygan (Michigan) and adjacent Mackinaw City, the CGC Mackinaw was scheduled to become a museum ship. The old cutter Mackinaw was joined by the new USCGC Mackinaw (WLBB 30) in October 2005 and completed its last mission in the spring of 2006 before it was decommissioned. The new CGC Mackinaw is designated as a GLIB, or Great Lakes Ice Breaker ("United States Coast Guard Cutter Mackinaw...," 2005-2006).

The new CGC Mackinaw was launched into the Menominee River from Marinette (Wisconsin) Marine's shipyard on 2 April 2005. The state of the art high technology 240-foot cutter is an icebreaker and buoy designed to carry out all of the Coast Guard missions. Like its 60-year old namesake, the new CGC Mackinaw served in ATN, SAR, icebreaking, commerce, public relations, and homeland security missions ("Making A Splash," 2006).

The 180-foot USCGC Sundew, home-ported in Duluth (Minnesota), was decommissioned on 27 May 2004. The Marine Iron and Shipbuilding Corporation in Duluth launched the Sundew in February 1944. The CGC Sundew, now a museum vessel stationed at Duluth's Canal Park, was replaced by the USCGC Alder (WLB-216), a high technology 225-foot buoy tender and icebreaker ("USCGC Sundew...," 2006).

The Marinette Marine Corporation in Wisconsin launched the CGC Alder in February 2004. After sailing through all of the Great Lakes the Alder sailed into its homeport of Duluth on 16 October 2004. The advanced technology of the multi-mission cutter includes computer navigation; remote monitoring systems; radar; sonar; environmental protection devices; controllable pitch thrusters, propeller, and rudder; satellite navigation; and computer generated charts. The 13-foot draft vessel carries two 3100 hp Caterpillar diesel engines, a 22-foot rigid hull inflatable boat, a 24-foot aluminum workboat, and heavy and light armament. The ship is run by a 50-crew member complement, including 8 officers and 42 enlisted personnel ("USCGC Alder," 2006).

The USCGC Woodrush is on the list of venerable World War II era cutters. Home-ported in Duluth prior to replacement by the Sundew, the Woodrush performed its Coast Guard missions admirably, and added to the legacy of the 180-foot buoy tenders. Among the many noble CGC Woodrush missions was the 24-hour race across storm-tossed Lake

Superior in November 1975. USCGC Woodrush Commander Jimmy Hobaugh and his crew went into the eye of the November gale in an unsuccessful attempt to locate and save the crew of the doomed MV Edmund Fitzgerald. In 1988 Captain Hobaugh became Group/Base Commander and COTP at Sault Ste. Marie, Michigan ("Hobaugh Takes Command...," 1988).

The Coast Guard and its predecessor agencies have long supported the placement of women in positions of responsibility. The Coast Guard was the first military service to put female personnel in command of gunboats.

On 16 July 2004 Vice Adm. Vivien S. Crea assumed command of the Atlantic Area that includes the Ninth Coast Guard (Great Lakes) District. Vice Adm. Crea, a Coast Guard aviator, has flown helicopters, the C-130 Hercules Turbo-propeller surveillance and cargo plane, and the Coast Guard Gulfstream II jet aircraft ("Vice Admiral Vivien S. Crea," 2006).

Continuing that tradition, Lt. (jg) Jeanine McIntosh became the first African-American female aviator after her graduation from the Corpus Christi (Texas) U.S. Naval Air Station in June 2005. After completing her C-130 training, Lt. McIntosh was assigned to Air Station Barbers Point in Hawaii ("Golden Wings," 2006).

The exemplary training and leadership of Coast Guard personnel was exemplified in the response of the service to the tragic 2005 Gulf Coast storm Hurricane Katrina. Coast Guard helicopter aviation crews and small boat and cutter personnel entered the flooded areas of flooded New Orleans (Louisiana) and Mississippi and saved more than 33,000 victims (Ripley, "Hurricane Katrina...," 2005).

Coast Guard Regulars, Reservists and Auxiliary responded from units all over the nation, as did regional Coast Guard personnel who had to worry about their own families and homes.

Katrina hit on 29 August and by 1 September the Coast Guard had 25 cutters, 48 aircraft, and hundreds of sailors from environmental response, safety, SAR and strike teams on site. By the end of the mission, more than 4,000 Coast Guard personnel had served in the region under the leadership of Vice Adm. Thad Allen.

Vice Adm. Allen coordinated Coast Guard operations with federal, state and local officials, public safety and law enforcement units, and other United States military teams. Aids to Navigation teams replaced or repaired more than 2,000 ATN markers to keep water channels and ports safe. Civilian and military environmental response units were kept busy in the dangerous and chaotic situations which involved regional oil and gas facilities and hundreds of boats and ships (O'Berry, "Katrina Hurricane Heroics," 2006),

Vice Admiral Allen's leadership skills contributed to his appointment as U.S. Coast Guard Commandant in 2006. Vice Adm. Allen was prepared to assume command from Admiral Thomas H. Collins, whose tenure as commandant secured the legacy of the Coast Guard and prepared the service for its expanding responsibilities at home and overseas.

Meanwhile, Coast Guard missions continued. A Coast Guard C-130 landed at USCG Air Station Sacramento (California) with its 7-person crew after returning from a 30-day tsunami relief mission in East Asia in 2005 ("Water Relief," 2006).

Boatswain's Mate First Class Beth Shade operated a 47-foot motor lifeboat during training drills in the turbulent surf off the Washington coast in the Pacific Northwest ("Team Coast Guard," 2006). The USCGC Bear plied through 15-foot waves off the west coast of Africa in a 90-day deployment as part of a security cooperation mission with the U.S. Navy in 2005 ("African Surfari," 2006). And Coast Guard petty officers ferried members of a science team from an Arctic Ocean ice floe back to the CGC Healy during a scientific mission ("Arctic Summer," 2006).

The Coast Guard performs its missions at home and abroad, adding to the legacy of the service motto, "Semper Paratus: Always Ready."

"Acacia Makes Final Run." U.S. Coast Guard, April 17, 2006, and military.com headlines, April 20, 2006.

"Arctic Summer." Coast Guard, Issue 1, 2006, pp. 40-41.

Beard, Tom (editor-in-chief). The Coast Guard. Foundation for Coast Guard History, and Hugh Lauter Levin Associates, Inc., 2004.

"Cutters Stop U.S. Bound Cocaine Shipment." U.S. Coast Guard,

April 17, 2006, and military.com headlines, April 20, 2006.

"En Patrulla in Cuba." Coast Guard, Issue 1, 2006.

"Golden Wings." Coast Guard, Issue 1, 2006, p. 24.

Hilburn, Matt. "Border Crossings," Seapower, April 2006.

"Hobaugh Takes Command of Group Sault Ste. Marie Coast Guard." Houghton Gazette, July 12, 1988 (UW-S, JDHL, Coast Guard History).

"Making A Splash." Coast Guard, Issue 1, 2006, pp. 22-23.

O'Berry, PA1 Mike (USCG). "Katrina Hurricane Heroics," Coast Guard, Issue 1, 2006, pp. 46-47.

Ripley, Amanda. "Hurricane Katrina: How the Coast Guard Gets it Right." Time, October 31, 2005, pp. 50-52.

"Team Coast Guard." Coast Guard, Issue 1, 2006, p. 15.

"UAE Firm to Operate Six Major U.S. Ports." World Tribune, February 13, 2006.

"USCGC Alder (WLB-216), Duluth, Minnesota." United States Coast Guard, April 20, 2006.

"USCGC Sundew (WLB-404)." Wikipedia, 26 March 2006,

"United States Coast Guard Cutter Mackinaw (WAGB 83 and WLBB 30)." Courtesy of Keith Stokes, photographer and Webmaster, and the United States Coast Guard, 2005-2006. Information on the 2 April 2006 launching of the WLBB 30 Mackinaw is courtesy of Keith Stokes, the USCG, and the Manitowoc Marine Group, Marinette, Wisconsin.

"Vice Admiral Vivien S. Crea." Flag Officer Biographies, U.S. Coast Guard Headquarters, March 14, 2006.

"Water Relief." Coast Guard, Issue 1, 2006, pp. 12-13/

EPILOGUE

The history, philosophy and mission statement of the United States Coast Guard is an extensive and exciting story. The chronological context of the USCG begins in the late 18th century with the founding of the U.S. Revenue Marine in August of 1790, under Secretary of the Treasury Alexander Hamilton.

The sail powered cutters of the USRM were commanded by revenue officers trained in life-saving, salvage and law enforcement. The officers had to be good seamen to operate in coastal waters in all seasons and every kind of weather. The USRM transported government officials and documents and suppressed the slave trade, smuggling, and piracy.

The term "cutter" comes from England and was applied to Revenue Marine vessels because of the usual two-masted sail rigging, and the association of schooners with revenue collection as opposed to naval warfare. The first 10 cutters requested from Congress by Hamilton were 36 to 40 feet in length, to be manned by six sailors, a lieutenant and a captain. The lengths of the Revenue cutters expanded with the Revenue Marine missions, eventually ranging from 56 to 110 feet of deck length. The construction of the early sailing ships was done in U.S. Navy yards or by private contractors chosen by the service (Chapelle, The History of American Sailing Ships, pp. 176-180).

By 1837, steam-powered cutters were being requested. Several were built in the 1840s. Steam cutters continued the missions begun by the sailing ships, including channel buoy placement, and the transportation of food, water and other supplies to lighthouses (Chapelle, pp. 210-211). In 1863, during the Civil War, the U.S. Revenue Marine was officially changed to the U.S. Revenue Service (Chapelle, p. 217).

The Revenue Cutter Service set the Coast Guard precedent for supporting geographic exploration and weather and marine research. In 1849, U.S. Naval Observatory superintendent Lieutenant Matthew Fountaine Maury (USN) authorized the Revenue cutter Taney to assist in the laying the first U.S. transatlantic cable. Lieutenant J. C. Walsh, the Taney commander, made depth soundings each 200 miles across the ocean using sounding twine units sixty thousand feet in length (ten thousand fathoms), marked at 100 fathom points, secured to a standard cannonball weighing 32 pounds. The task made more difficult because of surface drift and subsurface currents. With the outbreak of the Civil War, Lieutenant Maury left Washington, D.C., and the U.S. Navy. Maury made the difficult decision to contribute his considerable knowledge of ships, seafaring, physical geography, meteorology and marine science to the navy of the Confederate States of America (Hearn, Tracks in the Sea, pp. 197-199).

The USRCS was officially designated the U.S. Coast Guard in 1915. The USCG was launched upon the heritage of the Revenue Marine Service and its missions of life saving, aids to navigation, maritime law enforcement, and participation in the nation's wars under the periodic jurisdiction of the United States Navy.

The illustrious history of the Coast Guard includes secret missions in support of national economic, political and security interests. Captain Gretchen G. Grover, a U.S. Naval Reserve officer, researched the unpublicized role the Coast Guard, Navy, Army, and the Departments of Commerce and Interior played in the Pacific before and during World War Two.

In 1935, the Coast Guard cooperated with other federal agencies to colonize certain Pacific Islands with Army engineers and native Hawaiians assigned to monitor and deter Japanese expansion. In 1942, U.S. military search teams discovered two of the Hawaiian settlers had been killed in a Japanese attack upon one of the islands.

The USCGC Duane (WPG-33) unloaded supplies, equipment and personnel on isolated Howland Island in 1935. The newly constructed Howland airfield was intended for the use of Amelia Earhart and her navigator Fred Noonan on their ill-fated 1937 flight. Earhart's insufficient training in radio procedure contributed to the sea crash that claimed their lives.

Captain Grover (USNR) concluded from her research that Commander Warner K. Thompson of the USCGC Itasca made errors which prevented him from effectively communicating with Earhart en route, and finding her in the SAR mission after the disappearance (Grover, "The Coast Guard's Pacific Colonizers," pp. 43-47).

Conspiracy theorists have long suggested that Earhart may have been on a surveillance mission searching for Japanese bases and military activities in the Pacific. The Roosevelt administration denied it. Captain Grover added fuel to the speculative fire with her contention that "the covert purposes of the federal government in sending the colonizing expeditions to the equatorial islands, and in encouraging the Earhart flight, merged into a recognizable pattern" (Grover, p. 45).

Recent historical studies have illuminated the wartime contributions of the Coast Guard. Navy Seals isolated on dangerous Vietnam missions welcomed the Coast Guard cutters which made their way up dangerous channels to drop off food and military supplies (Dockery, Navy Seals, p. 56).

After the 11 September 2001 terrorist attacks upon the United States, intelligence expert Bill Gertz chronicled President Bush's plan for a new cabinet level Homeland Security Department. The HSD was to be composed of the Border Patrol, Secret Service, Customs Service, Immigration and Naturalization Service, and several other agencies (Gertz, Breakdown, pp. 123-124). Gertz cited the comments of the Coast Guard commandant in a secret meeting with intelligence officials in 2002. Admiral James Loy outlined the vulnerability of U.S. ports to terrorist attack, and the need for better assessments of international maritime threats to America. The Commandant stressed the need for the acquisition of more adequate information about ships, cargo and terrorist suspects to enhance the effectiveness of Coast Guard investigators. Admiral Loy emphasized the importance of the development and acquisition of advanced technology and more effective systems of gathering and coordinating intelligence data (Gertz, pp. 155-156).

Admiral Thomas H. Collins, the 22nd Commandant of the U.S. Coast Guard, is well aware of what needs to be done, having served under Admiral Loy as vice commandant. Admiral Collins clarified his intention to use increased federal appropriations to increase the numbers of active duty and reserve personnel, acquire Deepwater replacement assets, and meet aircraft, ship, boat, and shore station maintenance and replacement needs.

Among the planned acquisitions were 90 boats for the Marine Safety and Security Teams (MSSTs), 160 new Sea Marshall billets, and increased numbers of personnel for small boat stations.

The valiant Coast Guard C-130H long range aircraft supported SAR and law enforcement missions for more than 30 years. Between 2001 and 2005 the Coast Guard planned to replace the 27 aging aircraft with the Lockheed C-130J.

Other venerable Coast Guard craft needed replacement because of deterioration and high maintenance costs. The icebreaker Mackinaw (WAGB-83) plied the Great Lakes since its World War Two commissioning in 1944. In 2001, Marinette Marine Corporation received an $ 82 million contract to construct a state of the art icebreaker to continue the distinguished Mackinaw name.

Eight Coast Guard Vessel Traffic Service stations were scheduled for technological upgrades to facilitate more secure and effective information exchange between commercial vessels and the traffic centers (Thorsen, "Annual Reviews: The U.S. Coast Guard," pp. 98-99).

Since 9/11, the expanded role of the USCG in homeland defense and national security required the installation of upgraded electronic support. The Electronic Support Measures (ESM) facilitate the detection of threats to U.S. citizens, military assets and personnel, and the domestic infrastructure. Coast Guard Hamilton-class high endurance cutters (WHECs) have been the beneficiaries of the upgraded electronic systems, called AN/WLR-1H(V)7 countermeasure receiving set modification kits.

Electronic warfare (EW) systems on the newest Coast Guard cutters were scheduled to be enhanced by the ESM systems to improve early warning, rapid response and interdiction capabilities. The systems are intended to increase maritime security, national defense, and cutter maritime awareness.

The ESM systems identify communications sources and facilitate network connectivity (data sharing) with other vessels, units and stations. The sophisticated ESM systems process data automatically, increase intercept probabilities, and assist the Coast Guard in carrying out its increasing multi-mission responsibilities (Ilsemann, "Upgraded ESM for Coast Guard Cutters," pp. 77-78).

The vulnerability of coastal port cities to terrorist attacks was exemplified by the diligence shown since 9/11 in monitoring and responding to perceived threats. On 12 September 2002, a Liberian flag merchant vessel was ordered out of the port area of Newark, New Jersey and back to sea by the Coast Guard. Traces of radioactivity in the cargo holds were noted in an inspection. Navy SEALS assisted the Coast Guard as did USN radiation specialists from the Groton (Connecticut) submarine base ("Navy SEALS Inspecting Radioactive Ship...," Fox News, September 12, 2002).

The following day, the U.S. Coast Guard and Air Force academies at New London, Connecticut and AFA, Colorado, were temporarily closed to the public upon the recommendation of the Bush administration. The alert level was raised because of possible attack warnings. Officials of the U.S. Military Academy (West Point, N.Y.) and the U.S. Naval Academy (Annapolis, Maryland) were not requested to change their alert status ("Military Academies Closed to the Public," Post Bulletin, 4A).

New Coast Guard "SWAT" units were commissioned after the 9/11 terror attacks, and took their posts beneath New York City's Brooklyn Bridge and other strategic national sites ("New Coast Guard SWAT Unit," The Washington Times, NWE, Sept. 23-29, 2002, p. 1).

Regulations and procedures established since 9/11 have impacted upon American pleasure boaters who now must navigate security zones policed by the Coast Guard and local law enforcement agencies. Security perimeters have been established around nuclear plants, oil refineries, and other strategic infrastructure sites. Unwary, ignorant, or suspicious boaters experienced the approach of lights, screaming sirens, armed Coast Guard helicopters and sea craft, and local police boats. Boaters have been ordered to stop and accept the boarding of inspection teams.

Especially well patrolled are security zones around water filtration, energy and power plants, and U.S. Navy ships. The harbor areas of San Francisco, San Diego, Miami, Chicago, and Boston have been extensively patrolled, as has the port of New York City.

Congress appropriated a 13% increase over its $ 5.7 billion dollar fiscal 2002 budget to pay for the additional personnel and patrol boats necessary to increase inspections and respond to port security needs ("Pull Over, Sailor," The Wall Street Journal, August 9, 2002, pp. W1 and W4.

The Coast Guard and Navy have overlapping interests in coastal (littoral) security and defense capabilities. The naval services have cooperated in missions and planning for littoral security. Each service needs to improve and increase the small craft and patrol boats necessary for those duties.

Rear Admiral George R. Worthington (USN, Ret.) has argued that the Navy needs to increase its funding, equipment and training to face enemy terrorists and combatants in littoral regions. Worthington traced the ebb and flow of Navy funding for smaller patrol boats, and regretted that the Navy turned over so many of its small, littoral defense patrol craft over to the Coast Guard after the Gulf War (1990-1991).

Admiral Worthington, a former Navy SEAL, recommended that littoral craft be outfitted with rigid-hull inflatable boats and rubber raiding craft suitable for SEAL and U.S. Marine missions, and berthing room for special forces. Worthington said several such craft could perform missions with more economy, flexibility and less target risk for military personnel than one large, expensive. guided missile destroyer.

To increase Navy littoral defense capacities, Admiral Worthington concluded that a variety of vessels and fast attack boats should be built. Worthington advocated multi-hulled vessels with a 4,000 mile range, 40 knot average speed, operable in heavy seas. The vessels should support unmanned aerial vehicles; communications connectivity with sea, air and land units; have fire support systems; and possess rearming and refueling capacities for helicopters and sea craft.

The Coast Guard was commended for its role in national defense. The admiral alluded to the Coast Guard Deepwater program and its need for more craft to "enhance its posture in the littorals as well as homeland defense" (Worthington, "We Have the Craft for Littoral

Warfare," Proceedings, October 2002, p. 128).

Former surface warfare officer Captain James F. Kelly, Jr. (USN, Ret.) contended that new national defense needs require an expansion of the role of the U.S. Armed Forces. Captain Kelly asserted it was time to amend or abolish the U.S. Posse Comitatus Act which limits the use of federal troops in domestic law enforcement.

Kelly noted that the U.S. Coast Guard and state national guard units activated by governors have law enforcement jurisdiction. Those forces could benefit from the added presence of responsive and well-trained military personnel from the Army, Navy, Marines and Air Force. Domestic emergency responses in the age of terrorism could be improved, Kelly insisted, by well trained and technologically advanced Armed Forces, each of which has law enforcement components (Kelly, James F., "Broaden Armed Forces' Roles....," Proceedings, October 2002, p. 2.).

Major General David M. Mize, United States Marine Corps, expressed his admiration for the Coast Guard in a 2002 issue of the distinguished naval magazine, Proceedings: "On 2 August, U.S. Representative Henry Coble (North Carolina), a retired Coast Guard Reserve captain, cut the ribbon to officially open the USCG Special Missions Training Center (joined by the commandants of the USCG and the USMC) at venerable Courthouse Bay. We consider this the down payment on a useful and robust partnership which is already having a positive impact in the war on terrorism...Semper Paratus! Semper Fidelis!" (Mize, "The New Coast Guard," Proceedings, September 2002, p. 40).

Management expert Neil Ruenzel served in the Marine Corps and retired from the Coast Guard. Ruenzel's eclectic background gave him the perspective to offer friendly criticism, compliments, and suggestions for the Coast Guard post-9/11 homeland security mission.

Reviewing Coast Guard history, Ruenzel commended the service's often unheralded role in maritime safety, law enforcement and war, in concert with, but subordinate to the U.S. Navy. Ruenzel said the Coast Guard needs to specialize, lobby Congress about its capacities and contributions, emphasize its military assets, and establish public relations contacts to maintain and foster its relevance. Reunzel compared the Coast Guard to the other armed services, and attributed its often second class status to the failure of retired officers to tout the service needs and missions from positions of corporate and political authority.

The USCG, Ruenzel concluded, has tried too long to maintain its multi-mission purpose; and it has too proudly and counterproductively emphasized its role as peacetime generalists. The modern era, the analyst asserted, requires specialization targeted for specific constituencies. What the Coast Guard needs, according to Ruenzel, is a clarified mission and more "cohesive definition and doctrine" (Ruenzel, "Searching for

Relevance," Proceedings, October 2002, pp. 56-58).

Perhaps the attention visited upon the Coast Guard by virtue of its essential homeland security mission will contribute to a renewed appreciation of the nation's oldest naval service.

Nonetheless, the Coast Guard's uniqueness is its multi-mission, civilian/military responsibilities. The humanitarian side of the assignment accounts for its early progressivism on enlistments and personnel assignments. Ethnic minorities served in the Revenue Marine and have distinguished themselves in the Coast Guard.

Women have served gallantly in the naval service since its earliest days as Lighthouse Keepers. In that capacity women braved stormy seas to save the lives of mariners in distress. Women have served in the Coast Guard in regular and active duty responsibilities. The World War Two service of the SPARS is forever etched in Coast Guard lore.

In 1977, the Coast Guard led the other armed forces in integrating female enlisted personnel on board ships, and giving female officers command of patrol boats and ships.

Today, female officers and enlisted personnel are represented in every rank and rate in a wide range of sea and shore assignments. Master Chief Petty Officer Diane Bucci exemplifies the role model. Bucci served on ship and shore duty in a 27 year career and was the first female boatswain's mate Master Chief in the Coast Guard.

MCPO Bucci enlisted in the USCG in 1975 in the deck seamanship career track. In 1988, she assumed command as officer in charge of a 65 foot harbor tug stationed at Fort Belvoir (Virginia), patrolling the Potomac and Chesapeake Bay in search and rescue and security duty. Her shore commands included Coast Guard Stations St. Inigoes (Maryland) and Cortez (Florida).

Master Chief Bucci served as an advisor on women in the armed services to the Defense Department, as Atlantic Area Command Master Chief, and was assigned to Coast Guard Headquarters in Washington, D.C. Chief Bucci's husband retired from the Coast Guard as a boatswain's mate master chief. Master Chief Petty Officer Diane Bucci retired in July of 2002, and said: "I've enjoyed my career. I've never seen myself as a trail blazer, and I wouldn't change a thing" ("Women Reach New Heights in Military Service," USAA Magazine, August/September 2002, p. 16).

The author of this text corresponded with Rear Admiral W. J. Holland, Jr. (USN, Ret.), to commend him as editor-in-chief of the excellent photographic and narrative history, The Navy, and express appreciation for his references to the Coast Guard. Admiral Holland responded: "Thank you for your very kind words about our book, The Navy. As for mentioning the Coast Guard, like the Marine Corps, no book about the Navy is complete without reference to (the USCG) and the vital part played at least since World War II" (personal correspondence from Rear Adm. Holland, 11 January, 2002).

This modest history of the U.S. Coast Guard cannot do the distinguished service justice. The earliest and smallest of the naval services of the United States, from its beginnings as the Revenue Marine to the present, the Coast Guard has been assigned multi-mission maritime safety, law enforcement and military defense tasks.

On an average day, the Coast Guard saves 10 lives; aids 192 people in maritime distress; saves $ 3 million in property; seizes more than 470 pounds of cocaine and marijuana worth $ 10 million; investigates 6 marine accidents; conducts 144 law enforcement boardings; inspects 60 commercial fishing vessels; checks for port security and safety in 100 large ship boardings; processes more than 200 seaman documents; interdicts 14 undocumented aliens; and services 135 navigation aids ("During An Average Day," USCG Atlantic Area and Ninth Coast Guard District Home Page, 9/11/02).

The historic and contemporary missions of the Coast Guard have earned it the service motto, "Semper Paratus." How the motto was chosen remains obscure, but Captain Francis Saltus Van Boskerck wrote the lyrics and music which accompanies the motto.

Captain Van Boskerck wrote the words in 1922 while on the cutter Yamacraw, stationed in the port of Savanna (Georgia). He later composed the song with the assistance of two Public Health Service dentists (Drs. Nannestad and Fournier) in Unalaska, Alaska, five years later.

Captain Van Boskerck enlisted in the Revenue Cutter Service in 1891. He served at sea and shore stations on the Atlantic and Pacific Coasts, and commanded the famous cutter Bear in the Bering Sea and Arctic Ocean.

During World War One he was the first USCG officer to report the position of a German U-boat. In the 1920s, Boskerck pursued rum runners off the Carolina and Florida coasts; attended the Naval War College; and became commander of the Great Lakes District.

"Semper Paratus" has been etched on Revenue Marine and Coast Guard ensigns since 1910.

Captain Van Boskerck illuminated the honored motto and secured its place in naval history with his riveting lyrics and music (Krietemeyer, The Coast Guardsman's Manual, pp. 82-83).

"Semper Paratus." Always Ready. The Coast Guard motto is the ongoing description which defines the multi-mission military service as it sails forth to meet new challenges.

As January 2003 ended, the Coast Guard announced it was sending forces into the Persian Gulf in what appeared to be the second phase of the 1990-1991 Gulf War against Iraqi dictator Saddam Hussein.

Some news accounts described the Coast Guard mission as the first time its forces had been sent into a potential war zone since the Vietnam War. The assertion overlooked the fact that Coast Guard personnel participated in the early Gulf War and remained in the Persian Gulf performing port security and ship boarding duties with other military units in subsequent years.

The initial January 2003 Coast Guard deployment was another stage in the on-going war against international terror. News reports revealed that eight high-speed patrol boats and 1400 Coast Guard personnel were involved in the mission to protect U.S. Navy ships, oil tankers, military command vessels and other strategic targets from, among other things, suicide bomb threats.

The United States Coast Guard has had to rise to new challenges throughout its history. Since the 9/11/01 terrorist attacks on the United States, the Coast Guard proved its ability to enhance that legacy.

ABOUT THE AUTHOR

Thomas P. Ostrom served in the USCGR from 1961-69, and had basic and advanced training at the USCG Base, Alameda, California. He served subsequently in the Port Security Reserve Unit in Duluth, Minnesota, and participated in monthly and active duty assignments each summer, earning petty officer rank.

Mr. Ostrom taught history, anthropology and geography at Rochester Community College in Rochester, Minnesota for thirty two years, has written a regular column for the Rochester "Post Bulletin" and has been a political pundit on KROC-AM radio.

Ostrom was born in Superior, Wisconsin. He received his BA and MS degrees from the University of Wisconsin-Superior. He did graduate and post-graduate work at Ball State University, the University of North Dakota, Winona State University, and the University of Minnesota in Minneapolis.

He is a member of The Foundation for Coast Guard History, Navy League, the U.S. Naval Institute, and the National Maritime Historical Society.

APPENDIX A

HISTORICAL CHRONOLOGY OF THE U.S. COAST GUARD

1789 (7 Aug.) U.S. Lighthouse Service established under the Treasury Department.

1790 (4 Aug.) Congress authorized the creation of the Revenue Cutter Service and the construction of ten cutters assigned to enforce tariff laws.

1801 (3 Feb.) Treaty with France ended the undeclared "Quasi War" in which the Revenue Cutter Service performed valiantly, capturing several enemy vessels.

1812 The cutter fleet was ordered into war with the U.S. Navy in the War of 1812 against Britain.

1833 (Jan.) The Revenue Cutter fleet was used to enforce tariff laws in the port of Charleston, South Carolina after merchants refused to pay duties on imports.

1838 (7 July) Steamboat Inspection Service placed under the Justice Department.

1845 (19 Feb.) Lighthouse Service placed under the Revenue Marine Bureau.

1846 (Nov.) Cutters used in riverine and blockade missions in the Mexican War.

1848 (14 Aug.) Life-Saving Service created to rescue coastal seafarers in distress.

1852 (30 Aug.) Steamboat Inspection Service placed under the Treasury Department.

1861 (12 Apr.) Cutter Harriet Lane fires first naval shot in Civil War against a Confederate vessel in Charleston Harbor, South Carolina.

1876 (31 July) Cadet training for Revenue Service cadets begins at the forerunner of the U.S. Coast Guard Academy.

1878 (18 June) U.S. Life-Saving Service placed under the Treasury Department.

1884 (5 July) Bureau of Navigation established under the Treasury Department.

1890 Cutter Bear crew purchases reindeer from Russian officials in Siberia and introduce the animals to Alaska to enhance the diet of Inuit and Indian populations.

1903 (14 Feb.) Steamship Inspection Service and Bureau of Navigation placed under the Department of Commerce.

1905 The Revenue Cutter Service Yard is established in Baltimore, Maryland at Curtis Bay.

1909 (23 Jan.) A sinking passenger ship uses radio for the first time in a distress call to Revenue cutters.

1913 The cutters Miami and Seneca begin the International Ice Patrol after the sinking of the passenger ship Titanic (1912).

1915 (28 Jan.) The U.S. Coast Guard is officially created with the consolidation of the Life Saving Service and the Revenue Cutter Service under the Treasury Department.

1916 (1 Apr.) Coast Guard aviation begins with the acceptance of Coast Guard officers into U.S. Navy flight training at Pensacola, Florida.

1917 (6 Apr.) With U.S. entry into World War 1, the Coast Guard is ordered to become part of the U.S. Navy in wartime, and returned to the Treasury Department in 1919.

1918 Coast Guard cutters participate in search and rescue operations in the Atlantic in World War 1. The cutter Tampa was sunk (26 Sept.) by German U-boat torpedoes while escorting an Allied convoy with the loss of the entire crew.

1919 (27 May) Lt. Elmer Stone (USCG) made the first military transatlantic crossing in a naval NC-4 aircraft.

1919 (Dec.) Coast Guard patrol boats begin the "Rum War" against rum runners at the start of Prohibition.

1920 (24 Mar.) The first USCG Air Station is operational at Morehead City, North Carolina.

1925 (18 May) The U.S. Coast Guard Band is founded.

1939 (23 June) The Coast Guard "Reserve" is formed as a non-military unit to assist recreational boaters, becoming the Coast Guard "Auxiliary" in 1941.

1939 (1 July) The Lighthouse Service is incorporated into the Coast Guard.

1940 (10 Feb.) Cutter Duane initiates the Coast Guard weather patrol. In 1976 weather patrol cutters were replaced by electronic buoys and satellites.

1940 (27 June) The Espionage Act of 1917 is invoked by President Franklin Roosevelt, giving the USCG a new Port Security mission.

1941 (30 June) The Coast Guard Reserve military component was formed. Of the 240,000 members of the Coast Guard in World War Two, most were Reserve personnel.

1941 (1 Nov.) The USCG was transferred to U.S. Navy control for the duration of World War Two, and then returned to Treasury Department jurisdiction on I Jan. 1946.

1942 (21 Feb.) USCGC Spencer sinks a German submarine.

1942 (28 Feb.) The Bureau of Marine Inspection is transferred to the Coast Guard.

1942 (27 Sept.) Petty Officer First Class Douglas Munro (USCG) rescued U.S. Marines from Guadalcanal and received the Medal of Honor posthumously.

1942 (Dec.) The Coast Guard Women's Reserve (SPARS) was organized. During World War Two 10,000 female personnel served in the USCG.

1943 The Loran-A (long range electronic aids to navigation system) was initiated.

1944 (29 June) The first shipboard landing of a helicopter on the deck of USCGC Cobb. The U.S. Navy assigned the Coast Guard to develop helicopter operations for Search and Rescue (SAR) and Anti-Submarine Warfare (ASW).

1945 (29 Jan.) The USS Serpens, a U.S. Navy warship manned by the Coast Guard, blew up at Guadalcanal with the loss of the entire crew. In World War Two, Coast Guard crews manned 650 vessels for the Navy and Army, and sank 11 enemy submarines.

1946 (1 Jan.) The USCG was returned to the Treasury Department after World War Two.

1948 (17 Mar.) The cutter Acacia and icebreaker Mackinaw opened ice passage from Buffalo, New York, up to then the earliest opening date for commercial maritime shipping on the Great Lakes.

1950 (25 June) The Korean War (1950-53) began. In 1946 a U.S. Coast Guard team went to South Korea to train the Korean Coast Guard which became the National Maritime Police. When the Korean War erupted, the Coast Guard performed support duties in the Pacific Ocean, ran several U.S. Navy destroyer escorts, manned regional Loran stations, including a station in Pusan, South Korea.

1957 (July-Sept.) Coast Guard cutters Spar, Storis, and Bramble navigated the historically sought Northwest Passage across the North American Arctic.

1965 (March) The USCG begins its involvement in the Vietnam War, during which 8,700 Coast Guard personnel served.

1965 (24 July) U.S. Navy turns all of its icebreakers over to the U.S. Coast Guard.

1967 (1 April) The Coast Guard ends its 177 year history under the Treasury Department and is transferred to the Department of Transportation.

1967 (6 April) The famous racing stripe ("slash") becomes official, and is added to all Coast Guard vehicles, buildings, stations, signage, stationary, cutters, boats and aircraft.

1969 (15 Feb.) Several CG cutters were given to the South Vietnam government. In all, 56 Coast Guard cutters served in Vietnamese waters during the Vietnam War.

1969 (August) Coast Guard icebreaker Northwind accompanied a supertanker on an historic voyage through Arctic waters across the North American coast.

1973 USCG Pollution Strike Teams are created to police maritime oil and chemical pollution.

1975 (November 10) The cargo carrier Edmund Fitzgerald sinks on Lake Superior. The USCG is involved in rescue efforts and subsequent investigations and hearings.

1976 (April) Coast Guard fisheries enforcement extends to the 200 mile offshore zone.

1976 (July) USCG Academy becomes the first military academy to admit women.

1976 (1 Oct.) USCG uniforms are officially changed to a distinctive shade of blue.

1979 (12 April) Lt. (jg) Beverly Kelly takes assumes command of the USCGC Cape Newagen. Lt. Kelly was the first female commander of a military ship.

1980 (April) The largest migration of Cuban migrants left their island nation resulting in the Coast Guard rescue and monitoring of more than 200,000 refugees on the high seas.

1983 (7 Dec.) Four Coast Guard cutters begin surveillance patrols around the island of Grenada to support the U.S. military intervention.

1986 (4 August) The USCG activates the Maritime Defense Zone coordinating a continuing cooperative defense role with the U.S. Navy.

1989 (24 March) The oil tanker Exxon Valdez runs aground in Prince William Sound, Alaska. U.S. Coast Guard Strike Teams and investigative units responded to the largest oil spill in American history.

1989 (July and October) Coast Guard cutters Shearwater and Cushing seize a total of more than 15,000 pounds of cocaine in high seas interdictions and arrests.

1990 (4 Aug.) The USCG celebrated 200 years of maritime service.

1990 (Aug.) Active Duty and Reserve Coast Guard personal deployed with other U.S. and allied military personnel in Operation Desert Shield and Desert Storm in the Persian Gulf, Red Sea and Gulf of Oman in response to the Iraqi invasion of Kuwai and subsequent military action in Saudi Arabia. The U.S. Transportation Secretary and the Commandant of the U.S. Coast Guard committed boarding teams to support law enforcement and port security duties in the Persian Gulf War.

1991 (June) Coast Guard Port Security Units (PSUs) return to the U.S. from the Persian Gulf War. Some Coast Guard Law Enforcement Detachments (LEDETs) remained in the theater of operations.

1991 (1 July) A Coast Guard Law Enforcement Detachment from the CGC Rush stationed on the U.S. Navy warship Ingersoll made a coordinated high seas capture of a contraband vessel carrying 70 tons of hashish.

1993 (Jan.) The Coast Guard initiated the largest search and rescue mission in its history of response to a massive exodus of Haitian refugees.

1994 (12 Aug.) Adm. Robert Kramek, Commandant, USCG, approved the creation of "Team Coast Guard," which integrated the reserves into the operation mission and administrative processes of the regular Coast Guard.

1994 (19 Aug.) Operation Able Vigil monitored the massive Cuban refugee migration.

1994 (22 August) USCGC Polar Sea became the first U.S. surface vessel to reach 90 degrees North, expanding the previous record of the USCGC Polar Star which reached 84 degrees 59.7 minutes North (25 Aug. 1991).

1995 (17 Aug.) The USCGC Conifer made the largest maritime cocaine seizure in U.S. history, seizing 12 tons of the illegal contraband from a single vessel.

1995 (31 March) Coast Guard Communication Area Master Station Atlantic sends a final Morse Code message and then signed off, ending more than a century of telegraphy communication.

1996 (17 July) TWA Flight 800 crashed off New York City. Coast Guard search and rescue units found no survivors.

1996 (1 Oct.) The largest counter-narcotics operation in Coast Guard history, Operation Frontier Shield) commences.

1997 (15 March) Operation Gulf Shield begins. Beach patrols, the first since World War Two, monitored remote areas on the Gulf of Mexico-Texas to interdict narcotics smuggling.

1997 (2 Nov.) USCGC Baranof arrested Cuban exiles off the coast of Puerto Rico, preventing an assassination attempt on Cuban dictator Fidel Castro.

1997 Operation Frontier Shield seized more than 200,000 lbs. of illegal drugs.

1997 USCG training teams conducted 75 missions to foreign nations.

1998 (27 Aug.) Air and sea units of the USCG intercepted a Chinese vessel carrying 170 illegal immigrants.

1998 (Dec.) USCG cutters and the USCG International Training Detachment (ITD) went to the Dominican Republic to instruct that nation's navy in drug interdiction technique,

1998 USCGC Chase was ordered to the Persian Gulf to support the LIN embargo of Iraq.

1999 (18 June) USCG Midgett (WHEC-726) deploys from Seattle to join the USS Constellation Battle Group, supplementing U.S. Navy forces.

1999 Operation New Frontier commenced with the use of armed USCG helicopters and rapid pursuit boats to interdict illegal drug shipments.

2000 (1 Feb.) USCG units conducted SAR operations in after the crash of Air Alaska Flight 261 off the California coast.

2001 (11 Sept.) The USCG responds with rescue and port security operations after the international terrorist aircraft attacks upon the Twin Towers in New York City, the Pentagon in Washington, D.C., and the crash of a hijacked civilian airliner in Pennsylvania.

2001 (Sept. and Oct.) The USCG initiates the tactical deployment of "Sea Marshals" to monitor, police and protect foreign and domestic commercial shipping in strategic U.S. port areas.

2001 (December) USCG Commandant, Admiral J.M. Loy issued "An Open Letter To Team Coast Guard" in which he praised the responses of Coast Guard personnel to the 11 September terrorist attacks upon the U.S. Adm. Loy reminded members of the service that "the mission of maritime security is not new to us."

2002 (9 March) Two Coast Guard helicopters, one cutter, and one U.S. Marine Corps helicopter joined in search and rescue operations off the Georgia coast in response to a downed civilian and a downed USMC rescue helicopter. Several civilian and military personnel were rescued. Two died and one was missing.

2003 (3 January) USCGC Boutwell left Alameda, California to join other CG vessels and personnel in the Persian Gulf and Mediterranean Sea in support of Operation Iraqi Freedom.

(6 August) Department of Homeland Security Secretary Tom Ridge honored
Coast Guard male and female enlisted and officer personnel for their contributions to domestic security and Operation Iraqi Freedom

2004 (24 April) DC3 Nathan Bruckenthal (USCG) killed in combat in Iraq in support of Operation Iraqi Freedom.

Information for the Coast Guard historical chronology was acquired from this textbook, The Coast Guardsman's Manual (Ninth Edition), and the Coast Guard Historian's Office
and Coast Guard (Magazine), May 2004.

APPENDIX B

COAST GUARD TERMINOLOGY

Abaft: astern; toward the stern; to the rear of.

Abeam: at right angle (90 degrees) away from the heading or course of the ship.

Absent without leave: unauthorized absence; AWOL.

Accommodation ladder: portable flight of steps down the side of a ship.

Admeasure: to measure the capacity of a ship or other vessel or container. The Coast Guard appoints admeasures for merchant ships which constitutes the official data from which fees and the cost of licenses are calculated.

Admiral: highest naval rank, equivalent to a general in the other armed services. An officer of four star rank. Rear admirals wear two stars; vice admirals three. Fleet admirals five stars. Admirals of all ranks are authorized to fly flags containing the stars of their rank, and are therefore called flag officers.

Admiralty law: laws applied to maritime cases, ships, jurisdiction.

Adrift: loose from moorings or dock.

Aerographer: officer involved in weather forecasting. Enlisted weather specialist is called an aerographer's mate.

Aground: resting on or touching the ground or the bottom of a river or other body of water

Aids to navigation: devices which assist navigation; markers, lights, bell, buoys, fog horns, radio and other electronic transmissions, loran stations.

All hands: entire ship's crew or company; all officers and enlisted personnel.

Aloft: above a ship's uppermost solid structure; overhead.

Amidships: midships, middle portion of ship; along the line of the keel.

Amphibious: capable of operating on sea or land.

Anchor: a device to hold a ship or boat fast to the bottom; act of dropping the anchor.

Anchorage: suitable place for ship to anchor; a port or harbor area.

Anchor chain: heavy linked chain, line or wire connecting the anchor to the ship.

Anchor light: light(s) displayed by ship at anchor; also called riding lights.

Athwart: athwartships; at right angles to the fore and aft center line of a ship or boat.

Antisubmarine warfare (ASW): techniques used against enemy submarines.

Awash: a portion of a ship or vessel so low that water flows across the surface.

Aye, aye: response to order or command indicating it will be acted upon.

Azimuth: angle measured clockwise between north and the sighted object.

Backwash: water thrown aft by turning of a ship's propeller.

Bail: dip water out of a boat;

Ballast: heavyweight or water in the hold of a vessel to maintain stability, trim or draft.

Bar: shallow water obstruction to navigation composed of sand, gravel or other sediment.

Bark (barque): a vessel with three or more sail masts.

Barnacle: small marine animal that attaches to the sides and bottoms of hulls and piers.

Barometer: instrument that measures atmospheric pressure.

Barrier ice: edge of an ice shelf.

Bathymetric chart: a chart indicating depths of water by contour lines and shading; a bottom contour chart.

Bathythermograph (BT): depth sensing device which obtains water temperatures.

Batten down: to cover, fasten down; to close off a water-tight door or hatch.

Battery: ship's guns.

Battle stations: one duty listed in crew member watch, duty and station billet.

Beach patrol: patrol along a beach which warns of danger, sabotage or contraband.

Beam: width or breadth; athwartships width of a vessel.

Bearing: direction of object from observer expressed clockwise from 000 to 360 degrees.

Beaufort Scale: a table or chart indicating wind velocities.

Belay: to cancel an order; to stop; to secure a line.

Below: below decks; below the main deck.

Bend: a category of knots used to join two lines together.

Berth: space assigned to a vessel for mooring or anchoring.

Bilge: lower part of a vessel where seepage and waste water collect.

Bilge pump: used to clear or empty the bilge of water.

Bill of lading: document showing information on the shipper and the cargo.

Billet: assigned duties of a crew member.

Binnacle: stand or structure used to house a magnetic compass.

Blinker: lamp or lamps used to send flashing light messages.

Bluejacket: naval enlisted person below the rank of chief petty officer.

Boarding party: crew members who board a ship for social, military, inspection or law enforcement purposes.

Boat fall: rigging used to lower or hoist a ship's boats.

Boat: water craft smaller than a ship; small, open or closed over deck propelled by oars, sail or engine. Term applies to larger vessels which navigate inland rivers and lakes.

Boatswain: pronounced "bosun;" warrant or petty officer in charge of deck work and crew.

Boatswain's chair: board secured by line on which worker sits aloft or over the side.

Boatswain's locker: compartment where deck gear is stowed.

Boatswain's mate (BM): petty officer who supervises deck force seamanship duties.

Boatswain's pipe: small, shrill whistle used to give orders or calls.

Bollard: wooden or iron post on wharf or pier to which mooring lines are secured.

Boom: projecting spar or pole for extending sails, mooring boats and handling cargo.

Boot camp: recruit training center.

Bow: forward section of vessel.

Bow number: hull number painted on the bow of a ship for identification.

Boxing the compass: naming compass points and quarter points in proper order.

Breakdown lights: red lights on the foremast which denote ship breakdown, or search for crew member overboard.

Breakwater: a structure built or used to break the force of waves in a port or anchorage.

Breeches buoy: device for transferring personnel between ships or from ship to shore.

Bridge: raised platform from which ship is steered and navigated.

Brig: prison or incarceration facility on a shore station or ship.

Brightwork: metal work which is kept polished and not painted.

Broach to: suddenly turning into the wind or thrown broadside in surf.

Broadside: at right angles to the fore and aft lines of a ship.

Bulkhead: walls or partitions within a ship. Bunker: fuel storage space.

Bunker crude: black, unrefined or slightly refined crude oil burned in merchant ships.

Buoy: floating marker anchored to the bottom which indicates navigational information by shape or color; may be lighted or unlighted or equipped with sound devices; may provide mooring for a vessel.

Buoy tender: vessel designed for serving buoys and other aids to navigation.

Burdened vessel: vessel required to take action to avoid collision under the Rules of the Road. The other "privileged vessel" must maintain its course and speed.

By your leave (Sir/Ma'am): a courteous greeting expressed by a junior in rank when overtaking a senior while walking, usually accompanied by a salute.

Cadet: a student officer of the United States Coast Guard Academy.

Caliber: diameter of a gun's bore in inches or centimeters. Used also to specify barrel length. A 3-in./50 gun has a bore diameter of 3 inches, and a barrel length 50 times the bore, or 150 inches.

Call sign: In communications, a group of numerals and letters which identifies a base, station, activity or command.

Can buoy: cylindrical, green metal buoy which marks the left side of a channel entering from seaward.

Captain of the port: Coast Guard officer responsible for port security in a certain port.

Cardinal point: one of the four principle compass points, North, East, South or West.

Cargo documentation: papers required on a ship for entering or leaving port, including manifest, crew list, stores, bills of lading, tonnage and other required marine certificates.

Cast off: order given to throw off the mooring lines.

Chain locker: compartment where chain cable is stowed.

Challenge: a demand for identification or authentification. Response may be transmitted by a number of acceptable means of communication or coded signals.

Channel: marked deeper portion of a harbor or waterway through which vessels navigate

Chaplain: ordained member of the clergy commissioned as an officer.

Chart: map showing land and submarine geographic features; a navigational aid.

Chartroom: compartment near bridge containing navigational equipment, maps, charts.

Chief petty officer (CPO): the highest enlisted pay grades (E-7, E-8, E-9) of CPO rank, including chief petty officer, senior chief petty officer, and master chief petty officer. A Master Chief Petty Officer of the USN and USCG represents enlisted personnel in the office of the highest ranking naval service officers.

Chevron: v-shaped mark on uniform which denotes a military specialty or rate.

Chopper: slang for helicopter.

Chronometer: a particularly accurate timepiece used for navigation.

Cleat: metal deck fitting with anvil shape to which lines are secured.

Clipper: general name for a fast sail-powered ship.

CO: commanding officer of a station, base or ship.

Coast Guard: a federal military organization charged with enforcing laws and protecting life and property on the high seas and in U.S. coastal and internal waters. The service originated under the Treasury Department in 1790. In 1967 it became part of the Transportation Department. After the 11 September 2001 terrorist attacks upon the U.S. some observers suggested the USCG should be in a separate agency with Customs, the Border Patrol and the Immigration and Naturalization Service. In time of war the USCG serves under the U.S. Navy and the Department of Defense.

Coast Guard Academy: military training institute for Coast Guard officers located in New London, Connecticut.

Coast Guard Auxiliary: see Team Coast Guard
Coast Guard Regular (Active Duty): see Team Coast Guard

Coast Guard Reserve: see Team Coast Guard

Coast Guard Yard: location of shipyard for ship and boat construction and repair located at Curtis Bay, Maryland.

Colors: the national flag. The ceremonies of raising and lowering the flag.

Commandant: the top ranking officer in charge of the U.S. Coast Guard at the service headquarters in Washington, D.C.

Commissioned officer: military officer granted a commission by authority of the President of the United States and confirmed by Congress.

Combat information center: the section of a ship equipped to collect tactical information

Compass: instrument which indicates geographic direction.

Complement: number of ranks, ratings, officers and enlisted personnel determined necessary to operate the ship effectively and carry out assigned duties.

Coriolis force: the deflection of wind and water caused by the earth's rotation.

Counter flood: to take water into a ship's tanks or compartments to reduce list or inclination of bow or stern. Must be done carefully because the process reduces buoyancy.

Courts-martial: military court which tries serious offenses.

Coxwain: enlisted helmsman in charge of a boat. Pronounced "kok-sun."

Crow's nest: lookout stand high up on a mast.

Cutter: Coast Guard vessel 65 feet or more in length. A type of sailing vessel. A cutter is a type of rig used on sailing vessels. The original U.S. Revenue Service vessels used the rig, so were called cutters.

Damage control: measures taken to establish watertight integrity, stability, and offensive power; to control list and trim, make rapid repairs, and extinguish or limit the spread of fire; to remove contamination and care for wounded personnel.

Davit: shipboard crane used for hoisting and lowering boats and other weighted objects.

Davy Jones locker: the bottom of the sea.

Dead reckoning: navigator's estimate of ship's position from the course steered and distance traveled.

Deck: floor of a ship, numbered from top down; the weather deck is exposed to the elements.

Deep six: throwing objects over the side; use of lead line to determine six fathom depth.

Depth charge: explosive charge dropped from ship, used against enemy submarines.

Derelict: abandoned vessel at sea still afloat.

Diesel: oil burning, internal combustion engine used on ships and boats.

Destroyer (DE): ocean escort; frigate; small, ocean going multipurpose warship.

Ditty bag: bag used by sailors for stowage of personal articles or laundry.

Doldrums: sea areas straddling the equator consisting of calm water and light breezes.

Doper: Coast Guard slang for a drug smuggling vessel.

Double bottoms: water tight subdivisions of ship, next to keel between outer and inner bottoms.

Draft: depth of water from the surface to the ship's keel; ship's depth below the waterline.

Ebb tide: tide flowing out to sea from shore; a falling tide.

Engineer officer (EO): officer responsible for the ship's machinery, fuel and water.

Ensign: colors, national flag; a junior commissioned naval officer.

Even keel: floating level; no list.

Executive officer (XO): directly subordinate to the commanding officer; in charge of ship administration, routine and personnel.

Executive petty officer (XPO): enlisted person directly subordinate to the officer in charge; in charge of ship administration, routine and personnel.

Fake down: coiling a line so each fake of rope overlaps and clears the line for running.

Fantail: the after (rear) most topside deck of a ship.

Fast Ice: sea ice that remains along the coast; landfast ice.

Fathom: six-feet unit of length.

Fender: canvas, rope, cork, plastic or rubber device used over the side to protect a ship when along side a pier or another vessel.

Field strip: to disassemble a piece of ordnance or weapon for routine cleaning and oiling.

Fire control: shipboard system of directing gun, missile or torpedo fire; compartment where fire-control functions are controlled.

Flagstaff: vertical spar at the stern of a ship on which the ensign is hoisted.

Flank speed: speed increase over standard speed; maximum speed.

Fleet: naval organization of ships and aircraft under one commander.

Flood tide: rising tide flowing toward land; incoming tide.

Flotsam: floating wreckage or debris.

Flying bridge: aloft of the pilothouse; a lookout station.

Forecastle: pronounced "foke-sul." Abbreviated "fo'csle." Upper forward deck on ship.

Forward: toward the bow.

Foul: jammed; not clear.

Founder: to sink.

Freeboard: height of the side of a ship from the waterline to the main deck.

Full speed: greater than standard speed but less than flank speed.

Funnel: ship's smokestack; stack.

Fuselage: the body of a vehicle; body to which wings and tail of an aircraft are attacked.

Gale: winds between a strong breeze and a storm recorded in knots.

Galley: ship's kitchen.

Gear: term for rope, line, blocks, fenders, personal gear.

General quarters: battle stations assigned to crew members.

Gig: a ship's boat designated for use by the commanding officer.

Glass: barometer or spyglass.

Glasses: binoculars.

GLORIA: Geographic Long Range Inclined Asdic; a towed sonar device which maps the ocean floor.

Greenwich Mean Time: solar time measured from the meridian of Greenwich, England. A navigational time reference point.

Greenwich meridian: the reference meridian for measuring longitude and time. Longitude 0 degrees. Meridian half way around the world from the International Date line.

Ground: to run ashore; strike the bottom.

Ground mount: a gun structure open or enclosed in a steel shield. Less heavily armed than turrets and less than five inch guns.

Gunboat: small, moderate-speed, heavily armed vessel for patrol and escort duty.

Gun captain: petty officer in charge of a gun crew.

Gunner's mate (GM): petty officer who supervises the repair and upkeep of ordnance.

Gunnery officer (weapons officer): officer in charge of ship's gunnery. Officer in charge of ship's armament: guns, gunnery, missiles, and other weapons and weaponry.

Gunwale: upper edge or rail of a ship or boat side. Pronounced "gun'nle."

Gyrocompass: compass used to determine true direction with gyroscopes.

Gyropilot: automatic steering device designed to hold course without a helmsman.

Halyard: line used for hoisting flags, pennants or balls.

Harbormaster: officer in charge, under the port director, of piloting, berthing, and traffic in the harbor responsible for navigational aids and hydrographic information.

Hatch: opening in the ship's deck for communications or handling stores and cargo.

Hawser: line five inches or more in circumference used for towing or mooring.

Head: compartment on a ship with toilet facilities.

Heading: direction of a ship's bow at a given moment.

Heaving line: a small line with a weight on one end; weighted end is thrown to another ship or pier to pass a larger line attached to it.

Helm: the helm proper is called the "tiller," but the term is also used to mean the rudder and the ship's wheel.

Helmsman: the person at the wheel; the person who steers the ship.

Hull: framework of the vessel with decks, plating and planking, but exclusive of the rigging, guns, mast or superstructure.

Icebreaker (WAGB, WTGB): specially designed U.S. Coast Guard vessel with a reinforced bow, protected propellers and powerful engines for operation in heavy ice with the ability to break up or put a channel in the ice to allow the movement of ships.

Inboard: toward the center line of the ship.

Inshore: toward land. If already ashore, inshore means away from the sea.

International Ice Patrol: a patrol operated by the U.S. Coast Guard in accordance with international agreements for the prevention of collisions of vessels with ice. Coast Guard aircraft supplement cutters to monitor iceberg movements as well.

International Rules: rules governing navigation on the high seas established by agreement among maritime nations. Part of the Rules of the Road. Other compilations include Inland Rules of the Road, Sailing Directions, and Pilot Rules.

Isobar: a chart line connecting points of equal atmospheric pressure.

Isobath: a contour line connecting points of equal water depth on a bathymetric chart.

Isotherm: lines connecting points of equal temperature.

Isothermal layer: a layer of water throughout which a constant temperature exists.

Jack: flag similar to the national ensign; flown at a jackstaff when in port.

Jacob's ladder: ladder made of rope or chain with metal or wooden rungs, used over the side and aloft.

Jettison: to throw goods overboard.

Junior officer of the deck (JOOD): officer or petty officer acting as assistant to the OOD (Officer of the Deck). When the ship is moored or anchored, the term "junior officer of the day" is generally used.

Keel: backbone of a ship running from stem to sternpost at the bottom.

Knot: one nautical mile per hour.

Ladder: stairs.

Latitude: the measure of angular distance in degrees, minutes and seconds of arc from 0 degrees to 90 degrees north or south of the Equator.

Leave: authorized absence of an individual from a place of duty.

Lee (leeward): direction away from the wind; winds are labeled from the direction of origin: westerly winds, the prevailing wind in the Northern Hemisphere, come from the West; north winds come from the north and blow in a southerly direction.

Liberty: authorized absence from duty for short periods of time.

Life buoy (life ring): U-shaped buoy of cork or metal to support a person in the water; a personal flotation device.

Lifejacket (life preserver): a belt or jacket of buoyant or inflatable material worn to keep a person afloat; a personal flotation device.

Lifeline: line secured to deck to hold in heavy weather.

Life raft: inflatable float craft for use in survival at sea.

Lightship: small ship equipped with distinctive light and anchored near an obstruction to navigation or in entrances or shallow water to warn ships. There are no longer any lightships in U.S. waters, having been replaced by buoys or other structures.

Line-throwing (Lyle) gun: a small caliber gun that throws a line weighted at one end a long distance; used in lifesaving, or throwing a lifeline to a vessel.

List: inclination or heeling over of a ship to one side.

Littoral: the coastal region, the seashore.

Log book: a chronological record of events, such as an engineering watch log.

Longitude: a measure of the angular distance of arc from 0 to 180 degrees from the Greenwich Prime Meridian.

Loran (Long-range aid to navigation): a navigational system that fixes the position of a ship by measuring the difference in the time of reception of two synchronized radio signals.

Magazine: compartment used for stowage of explosives and ammunition.

Main deck: highest complete deck extending from stem to stern.

Mainmast: second mast from the bow of the ship that has two or more masts, or the single mast of a ship which has only one mast.

Maritime: pertaining to the sea; maritime nations are nations which have a sea coast.

Mast: upright spar supporting signal yard and antennas on a naval vessel; the term applied to the hearing of disciplinary cases or for requests or commendations.

Master at arms (MAA): ship's police headed by a chief MAA.

Mayday: international distress signal.

Meridians: great circles of the earth that pass through the poles; longitude lines.

Mess: the compartment or location for dining.

Midchannel buoy: buoy with red and white stripes which marks the middle of a channel.

Midshipman: a student officer of the U.S. Naval Academy.

Midwatch: the watch from 0000-0400 (midnight to 4 AM).

Military Sealift Command (MSC): ocean freight, research and passenger service operated by the U.S. Navy for the Department of Defense. Formerly known as the Military Sea Transport Service (MSTS).

Mine: a submerged or surface explosive charge designed to explode against or beneath a ship. Mines may be dropped from the air, moored or allowed to drift. A ship designed to place mines is a minelayer; minesweeper vessels remove or destroy mines.

Mooring: securing a ship to a pier, buoy, or another ship; or anchoring.

Mooring buoy: a large, well anchored buoy to which one or more ships moor.

Mooring line: a line used for mooring a ship to a pier, wharf, buoy, or another ship.

Morse code: dots and dashes used in visual and radio signaling.

Motor launch: large, sturdy power boat used for liberty parties and freight.

Motor torpedo boat: high speed boat armed with torpedoes, guns and missiles.

Motor whaleboat: a small, double ended diesel powered boat.

Muster: to assemble the crew; roll call.

Muzzle bag: canvas cover fitted over a gun to shield the bore from water.

National Ocean Survey (NOS): a government agency which produces navigation charts and publications; formerly the Coast and Geodetic Survey (CGS).

Nautical mile: 6,080.2 feet; one sixth longer than a land mile.

Naval stores: oil, paint, turpentine pitch and other items used on ships.

Navigation: the art and science of conducting a ship, boat or craft from point to point.

NAVSTAR: part of the Global Positioning System (GPS), a navigation system using high altitude satellites which broadcast signals which provides position fixing.

Nonrated personnel: enlisted person who is below the rank of petty officer.

North Atlantic Drift: the North Atlantic Current; part of the Gulf Stream (from the Gulf of Mexico) which drifts North to Canada, and across the Atlantic to Britain, warming the waters in the middle and high latitudes.

Nun buoy: red, cone-shaped buoy used to mark channel on the right side from seaward.

Officer candidate: person under instruction at an officer candidate school; enlisted rank.

Officer of the deck (OOD): the officer on watch in charge of the ship.

Offshore winds: winds blowing from the land toward sea.

Oiler: a tanker vessel designed to carry and dispense fuel.

Ordnance: collective term for guns, missiles, torpedoes and bombs.

Outboard: toward the side of the vessel, or outside of the vessel.

Out of trim: to list to one side, or be down at the bow or stern.

Pack ice: offshore ice moving with current and wind, closed or open, in the form of fields, floes or blocks.

Parallel of latitude: a plane parallel to the Equator.

Patrol boat: small vessel used for escort and patrol duties.

Paymaster: disbursing officer; financial officer in charge of distributing personnel pay.

Passageway: corridor or hallway on a ship.

Peacoat: heavy topcoat worn by sailors in cold weather.

Peak tank: tank in the bow or stern of a ship used for water ballast.

Petty officer: Noncommissioned third, second, and first class and all chief petty officers rates.

Pier: a harbor structure with sufficient depth along side to accommodate vessels.

Pilot: an expert who comes aboard ships to advise the captain on how to steer the vessel in dangerous waters or harbor areas; the pilot may take charge of the helm

Pitch: the forward heaving and plunging motion of a vessel at sea.

Poop deck: partial deck over the main deck at the stern.

Port: left side of ship facing forward; a harbor; an opening in the ship's side for light.

Port security: mission of safeguarding ports, waterways, facilities, vessels, property and personnel from accidental or deliberate damage, destruction or injury; to monitor oil spills and hazardous cargo operations; enforce pollution regulations; law enforcement to prevent criminal acts, apprehend violators, and protect against espionage and sabotage.

Quarter: that part of the ship's side toward the stern.

Quarterdeck: that part of the main deck reserved for ceremonies and honors; the station of the OOD in port.

Quartermaster: assists the OOD; navigates when the ship is underway; quarterdeck watch stander in port; the helmsman in critical operations such as battle stations and entering or leaving port.

Quarters: living space of the crew; assembling of all hands at designated stations for muster, drills and inspections.

Radar (Radio detection and ranging): the method of locating objects by radio waves which are transmitted, reflected, and received, illuminated by a cathode ray screen.

Radio beacon: an electronic aid to navigation that sends out radio signals for reception by a radio antenna.

Range: distance in yards from ship to target; two or more objects in line to give direction.

Rank: grade of official standing of warrant and commissioned officers.

Rate: paygrade, level of advancement, occupational specialty, training, responsibility of enlisted personnel.

Recruit: newly enlisted person in basic training.

Red, right returning: Reminderto navigators and helmsmen that red buoys are on the right hand of channel when returning to port from a seaward direction.

Reef: chain or ridge of rocks, sand or coral in shallow water.

Registry: merchant ship's certificate indicating ownership and nationality.

Regular: full-time active duty personnel as opposed to part-time reservist.

Relative bearing: bearing or direction of an object in degrees in relation to ship's bow.

Reveille: arousing the ship's company for breakfast and the work day.

Revenue Marine (Revenue Marine Service; Revenue Cutter Service: USRCS):
early names for the U.S. Coast Guard, dating to 1790 when Treasury Secretary Alexander Hamilton created the sea service to enforce customs laws, engage in search and rescue at sea, and serve as a military naval service.

Rigging: general term for ropes, chains and gear supporting masts, yards, booms, and sails. Standing rigging are lines that provide support, but generally do not move. Running rigging move and operate equipment.

Roll: side to side motion of a ship at sea.

Rope: cordage over one inch in diameter. If smaller, known as string, line, cord or twine. It is constructed by twisting fibers or metal wire. Size is designated by diameter or circumference. Length is given in feet or fathoms.

Running lights: ship, boat or craft lights required by law when under way between sunset and sunrise.

Salvage: to save a ship or cargo from danger; to recover a ship or cargo from disaster and wreckage.

Screw: the propeller. A rotating bladed device that propels a vessel through the water.

Scupper: opening in the side of a vessel to carry off accumulated or flowing water.

Scuttle: small opening in bulkhead, hatch or deck; covering for such an opening; to sink a ship deliberately by opening seacocks.

Sea anchor (drogue): floating anchor usually made of spars or canvas used to keep the bow of the vessel to the wind, or to slow headway.

Sea buoy: buoy furthest out to sea which marks a channel or entrance; a farewell or departure buoy.

Seabag: large canvass bag for stowing sailor's clothing or gear.

Seaman apprentice (SA): rate to which a person is advanced after recruit training.

Seaman recruit (SR): the lowest enlisted rating.

Search and rescue (SAR): Coast Guard mission of finding vessels in distress and rescuing those in peril at sea.

Seaworthy: capable of being put to sea and enduring unusual sea conditions.

Secure: to make fast; to tie; order given on completion of a drill; to withdraw from duties on station.

Semaphore: code signals indicated by position of the arms or hand flags.

Service stripes: diagonal stripes on lower left sleeve of enlisted personnel uniforms denoting period (length of time) of enlistment. Each "hash mark" indicates four years of service.

Set taught: take in slack on line or take a strain on running gear.

Set course: giving the helmsman the desired course to be steered.

Set the watch: the order to station of the first watch.

Shaft alley: space within a ship surrounding the propeller shaft.

Shakedown: test, adjustment and training cruise of a newly commissioned ship.

Shellback: person who has crossed the Equator and been initiated.

Shift the rudder: order to swing the rudder an equal distance in the opposite direction.

Ship: a large ocean going vessel. A Coast Guard vessel of more than 65 feet in length. To ship over is to reenlist in the service.

Ship's company: all hands; all officers and enlisted personnel attached to a ship.

Shipshape: neat and orderly.

Shore patrol (SP): naval personnel attached to shoreside police duty to maintain discipline and to assist local police in handling naval personnel on liberty or leave.

Short blast: whistle, horn or siren blast of about one second's duration.

Shove off: an order for a boat or ship to leave a landing or mooring.

Sick bay: ship's hospital; dispensary.

Side arms: pistols or revolvers, as opposed to "small arms" which includes pistols, carbines, shotguns and rifles.

Side lights: red and green running lights on port and starboard sides respectively.

Slip: space between two piers; waste motion of a propeller or screw.

Small craft: vessels less than ship size.

Sonar(Sound navigation and ranging): device for locating objects or depth under water by emitting sound vibrations and measuring the time taken for the vibrations to bounce back from the objects or structure to the ship.

Sound: to measure water depth by a lead line; to measure depth of liquids in oil tanks, voids, compartments and tanks.

Spar: steel or wood pole serving as a mast or boom; female member of the Coast Guard in World War Two, the letters taken from "Semper Paratus" (Always Ready), the Coast Guard Motto.

Spar buoy: long, thin wooden spar used to mark channels.

Squall: a sudden stormy gust of rain and wind.

Square away: to get things in order and settled down.

Squilgee: device with rubber blade and long handle to move water off deck or glass, pronounced "squeegee."

Stack: ship's smoke pipe; funnel.

Stage: platform rigged over ship's side for repair work or painting.

Stanchion: supportive metal or wood upright.

Stand by: preparatory order to "get ready" or "prepare" for action or activity.

Starboard: right side of vessel looking forward.

Star shell: projectile that detonates in the air and releases an illuminating parachute flare

Stern: aft or back part of vessel.

Storekeeper (SK): naval petty officer stationed in the supply department.

Stow: to put gear in its proper place.

Striker: enlisted person in training for a particular rating or rate.

Superstructure: all equipment and fittings except armament extending above the hull.

Superstructure deck: partial deck above the main, poop and forecastle decks.

Swab: a rope or yarn mop.

Swash plates: plates with pierced holes fixed in tanks to limit violent liquid motion when a ship rolls or pitches in heavy seas.

Swell: wind generated waves; the heave of the sea.

Swing ship: moving a ship through the points of a compass to check the magnetic compass on different headings and construct or monitor a deviation table.

Syzygy: points of the new and full moon; the cause of spring tides.

Tachometer: mechanical device which indicates shaft revolutions.

Tackle: arrangement of ropes and blocks to give mechanical advantage; a rig of lines and, pulleys to increase hauling force; pronounced "take-el."

Take a turn: to pass around a cleat, bitts or bollard with a line.

Tanker: a ship that transports and delivers fuel. An oiler refuels ships at sea or at anchor.

Taps: lights out for the night.

Tarpaulin: heavy canvass used as a protective covering.

Team Coast Guard: the 1994-95 integration of Coast Guard Reserve into active component commands. Team Coast Guard includes all of the Coast Guard components: auxiliary, civilian employees, active duty (regulars) and reserve.

Tender: an auxiliary vessel that supplies and repairs ships and aircraft; a logistical support and repair vessel.

Thermocline: an ocean layer of rapid temperature change in a small change of depth.

Thruster: a propeller or jet at the bow or the stern that assists shiphandling by moving the bow or stern laterally.

Thwart: cross piece used as a boat seat.

Tidal current: current caused by the rise and fall of tides.

Tidal wave: a surface bulge of water caused by the gravitational attraction of the sun and moon.

Tide: vertical rise and fall of the sea caused by the gravitational effect of the sun and moon.

Tide tables: publication listing time and heights of tides at various locations published by the National Ocean Survey (formerly the Coast and Geodetic Survey).

Tiller: a metal or wood device attached to the rudder to facilitate turning.

Tompion (tamplon): plug placed in gun muzzle to keep moisture, water and foreign objects out. Pronounced "tompkin."

Tonnage: cubic capacity of a ship expressed in tons loaded and unloaded.

Topside: the upper deck or decks. A deck exposed to the weather.

Tow: to pull a vessel through the water. A cutter may tow a boat or another ship. The usual towing vessels are tug boats.

Towing lights: two or three vertical white lights on a towing vessel as required by the Rules of the Road.

Trimming tanks: balancing a ship in the water by flooding or emptying ballast tanks.

Turret: heavily armored housing containing a grouping of main battery guns which extend downward through the decks and include ammunition, handling rooms and hoists.

Uniform Code of Military Justice (UCMJ): enacted by Congress in 1950 for all of the armed forces; the basis for the Manual of Courts-Martial. Military police units of one military service have jurisdiction over members of the other services.

United States Armed Forces: a collective term for the components of the Army, Navy and Marine Corps, Air Force and Coast Guard.

United States Naval Institute (USNI: nonprofit, nongovernmental, self-supporting professional society that publishes naval periodicals and books and serves as a forum for the sea services.

United States Naval Ship (USNS): a ship owned by the U.S. Navy but not commissioned as part of the Navy. Normally manned by civilian crews, sometimes supplemented by naval personnel, and operated by the Military Sealift Command.

Veer: when wind changes clockwise or to the right.

Very well: reply of a senior enlisted in rank or officer to a junior in rank to indicate information given is understood or permission is granted.

Void: empty compartment or tank.

W: Coast Guard Commandant Admiral Frederick C. Billard (1924-1932) ordered the letter "W" placed on cutter hulls in 1926 to distinguish them from Navy designations.

WAGB: designation for icebreakers, the largest Coast Guard cutters which rang from 399 feet to 420 feet in length.

Wake: the disturbed water astern of a moving vessel.

Wake (Stern) light: dim light at the stern directed down on the wake to assist following ships to keep on station.

Wardroom: the compartment where officers lounge and dine.

Warrant officer: an officer senior to all chief petty officers and junior to all commissioned officers who derives authority from a warrant issued by the Navy or the Coast Guard. A commissioned warrant officer is the highest warrant grade commissioned under the authority of the President and confirmed by Congress.

Warship: Navy or Coast Guard ship designed to perform wartime duties and missions.

Watch: duty period, normally four hours, scheduled around the clock.

Waterline: point to where a ship sinks in the water loaded and unloaded.

Watertight door: door or hatch made with closure equipment, gasket and dogs so when closed water cannot pass through in either direction even under considerable pressure.

Watertight integrity: system of keeping ship afloat by maintaining watertightness.

Weapons officer: officer in charge of ship's armament.

Weather deck: topmost ship deck, or any deck exposed to the elements.

Whaleboat: sharp-ended, double-ended boat, high at both ends, used as a life-boat.

Wharf: harbor structure alongside which vessels moor. A wharf is generally built along the water's edge. A pier extends well out into the harbor.

WHEC: designation for 378-foot, high-endurance ocean going cutters. Their primary missions are search and rescue, law enforcement and defense readiness. They are equipped with helicopter landing decks.

Wheel: the steering wheel of a ship.

Wheelhouse: pilot house, the topside compartment where the OOD, helmsman, and quartermaster of the watch stand their watches.

William: designation "W", a ship condition set to open and operate cooling water and fire-main systems which are to be open at all times; closed only to prevent the spread of damage.

Winch: hoisting engine secured to the deck which haul lines by turns around a drum.

Windward: into the wind; toward the direction from which the wind is blowing.

WIX: the Coast Guard training cutter Eagle based at the U.S. Coast Guard Academy in New London, Connecticut.

WLB: designation for 225-foot Coast Guard sea-going buoy tenders.

WLM: designation for Coast Guard coastal buoy tenders which range from 133-feet to 175 feet in length. Inland (WLI) and River (WLR) class tenders range from 65 to 115 feet.

WLIC: the designation for 75 to 160-foot Inland class construction tenders.

WMEC: designation for 270-foot, medium-endurance cutters whose missions and equipment is similar to the larger WHEC cutters.

WPB: designation for fast, sturdy, maneuverable Coast Guard patrol boats whose duties include search and rescue and maritime law enforcement. They range in size from 87 to 110 feet in length -

WTGB: designation for the 140-foot icebreaking tugs of the Coast Guard fleet.

XO: designation for executive officer.

X-Ray: phonetic word for the letter X. Ship condition set when there is no danger of attack.

Yard: spar attached at the middle of the mast running athwartships used as a support for halyards and signal lights. A place for shipbuilding and repair, at Coast Guard Yard, Baltimore, Maryland.

Yardarm: either side of the yard.

Yaw: zigzag motion of a vessel carried off its heading by strong, overtaking seas.

Yeoman (YN): petty officer who performs administrative and clerical duties.

Yoke: ship condition set and maintained at sea and in port in time of war.

Zebra: phonetic word for the letter Z. Ship condition set to provide protection for crew and ship for battle and other emergency situations.

Zenith: that point of the celestial sphere vertically overhead.

Zigzag: straight-line variations from the base course; evasive steering.

Zulu: phonetic word for the letter Z; a time zone designation based on Greenwich Mean Time (GMT).

The Coast Guard terminology (glossary) is based upon and modified from The Coast Guardsman's Manual (Ninth Edition) and Naval Terms Dictionary (Fifth Edition). These sources are listed in the bibliography.

APPENDIX C: COAST GUARD WAR CASUALTIES

WAR	PERSONNEL	KIA	WIA	TOTAL
Quasi-War with France	unknown	unknown	unknown	unknown
War of 1812	100	none	unknown	unknown
Mexican War	71 officers	unknown	unknown	unknown
Civil War	219 officers	1	unknown	unknown
Spanish American War	660	0	unknown	unknown
World War One	8,835	111*	unknown	192
World War Two	241,093	574**	unknown	1,917
Korean War	44,143	0	0	0
Vietnam War	8,000	7***	60	67
Persian Gulf War	400	0	0	0
Iraq War	1250	1	****	****

* Coast Guard deaths from other causes (crashes, disease, accident, drownings): 81
** Coast Guard deaths from other causes: 1,343
*** MIA: I (source: Summers, H.G., Jr., The Vietnam War Almanac, p. 126)
****Unknown as of the time of this printing, the war not yet being over.

KIA = Killed In Action

WIA = Wounded in Action

MIA = Missing in Action

Source: FAQS, Coast Guard Historian's Office (Created, January 1998), Coast Guard (Magazine) May 2004.

Appendix D: U.S. Coast Guard Personnel on Active Duty

Year	Total	Officers	Cadets	Enlisted
2000	35,712	7,154	863	27,698

Women Active Duty Troops in 2000

Service	% of Women
Army	15.1
Navy	14
Marines	5.9
Air Force	19.0
Coast Guard	14.4

Source: The World Almanac and Book of Facts 2001
    Mahwah, N.J.: World Almanac Books, 2001, pp. 204 205.

In 2001, more than 2,000 Reservists were called up to Active Duty in response to 11 September Terror Attacks on the United States. Hundreds of civilian Coast Guard Auxiliary personnel answered the call and assumed supplemental public safety and surveillance activities which allowed specialized Reserve and Active Duty personnel to concentrate on expanded port security and related law enforcement duties (Office of Coast Guard Historian).

APPENDIX E

COMMANDANTS OF THE COAST GUARD

Prior to the creation of the U.S. Coast Guard in 1915, the service was called the Revenue Marine. The naval service was founded in 1790 by Alexander Hamilton. Its function was to enforce the collection of tariff revenue. The Revenue Marine also engaged in naval action against piracy and in several wars.

The first chiefs of the U.S. Revenue Marine (USRM) directed the Revenue Marine Bureau. The first Chiefs were:

Captain Alexander V. Fraser, USRM (1843-1848) Captain Richard Evans, USRM (1848-1849)

The Revenue Marine Bureau was terminated in 1849. The Revenue Marine was administered by the Commissioner of Customs until 1869 when the Revenue Marine Bureau was reestablished and headed by civilian directors:

1869-1871 N. Broughton Devereux 1871-1878 Sumner 1. Kimball 1878-1885 Ezra Clark 1885-1889 Peter Bonnett

In 1889 the heads of the Revenue Marine Service were named chiefs of the Revenue Marine Division, and initially held the military rank of captain in the U.S. Revenue Cutter Service (USRCS). The office of Captain-Commandant was created in 1908.

1889-1895 Captain Leonard G. Shepard, USRCS 1895-1905 Captain Charles F. Shoemaker, USRCS 1905-1911 Captain Worth G. Ross, USRCS, Captain-Commandant

1911-1919 Commodore Ellsworth P. Bertholf, Captain-Commandant, Chief Division of Revenue Cutter Service, which became the U.S. Coast Guard in 1915.

1919-1924 Rear Admiral William F. Reynolds, first Captain-Commandant, and later Rear Admiral-Commandant. Reappointed Commandant on 12 January 1923 with the rank of Rear Admiral effective in October of 1923, the first Coast Guard officer to attain this rank.

1924-1932 Rear Admiral Frederick C. Billard, Commandant, USCG
1932-1936 Rear Admiral Harry G. Hamlet, Commandant, USCG

1936-1945 Admiral Russell R. Waesche, Commandant, USCG-Appointed Commandant as Rear Admiral. Appointed Full Admiral on 4 April 1945, the first Coast Guard officer to attain the ranks of Vice Admiral and Admiral.

1946-1949 Admiral Joseph F. Farley, Commandant, USCG 1949-1954 Vice Admiral Merlin O'Neill, Commandant, USCG 1954-1962 Admiral Alfred C. Richmond, Commandant, USCG. Appointed Commandant as Vice Admiral. Appointed Admiral on 1 June 1960. by Act of 14 May 1960, Public Law 86-474, under which all Coast Guard Commandants automatically became Admirals.

1962-1966 Admiral Edwin J. Roland, Commandant, USCG
1966-1970 Admiral Willard J. Smith, Commandant, USCG
1970-1974 Admiral Chester R. Bender, Commandant, USCG
1974-1978 Admiral Owen W. Siler, Commandant, USCG
1978-1982 Admiral John B. Hayes, Commandant, USCG
1982-1986 Admiral James S. Gracey, Commandant, USCG
1986-1990 Admiral Paul A. Yost, Commandant, USCG
1990-1994 Admiral J. William Kime, Commandant, USCG
1994-1998 Admiral Robert E. Kramek, Commandant, USCG
1998-2002 Admiral James M. Loy, Commandant, USCG*
2002- Admiral Thomas H. Collins, Commandant, USCG

Source: Coast Guard Historian's Office

* In May 2002, Admiral Loy retired as commandant of the Coast Guard, and was immediately appointed second in command of the newly formed Transportation Security Administration. The TSA is responsible for screening airport baggage and passengers ("Coast Guard Chief Moves to Air-Safety Post," USA Today, May 31, 2002, p. 8A).

APPENDIX F

COAST GUARD DOCUMENTS

On 4 April 1997, the Russian merchant vessel **Kaplitan Man** was believed to be gathering electronic intelligence information on a U.S. nuclear submarine in the Puget Sound area near Seattle, Washington. The **Kapitan Man** was under surveillance by a Canadian navy helicopter with a U.S. Navy intelligence officer on board. The Russian vessel was alleged to have responded by shooting a laser weapon at the helicopter, injuring the eyes of the Canadian pilot and USN officer. On 7 April, a joint U.S. Coast Guard-Navy intelligence inspection team boarded the Russian vessel in the port of Tacoma. The inspection result was concisely explained by reporter Bill Gertz in "The Washington Times" dated 27 June 1997:

RUSSIAN SHIP NOT SEARCHED THOROUGHLY IN LASER INCIDENT:

The Pentagon acknowledged yesterday that Coast Guard and Navy officials failed to search all areas of a Russian vessel in a search for lasers that might have been fired at a Canadian surveillance helicopter injuring a U.S. Navy intelligence officer on board. "They were granted access to every part of the ship to which they requested access with one exception: there was a library to which the crew could not find the keys, and they did not go into that library," according to a Pentagon spokesman.

Coast Guard documents obtained under the Freedom of Information Act (FOIA) pertaining to the incident are included in Appendix F.

U.S. Department
of Transportation

United States
Coast Guard

Commander
Thirteenth Coast Guard District
United States Coast Guard

Staff Symbol: (dl)
Phone: (206)220-7110
FAX: (206)220-7119

5290
22 January 2002

Mr. Thomas P. Ostrom
207 5th Ave. SW #508
Rochester, MN 55902

    Re: Freedom of Information Act Request dated January 3rd, 2002

Dear Mr. Ostrom:

I am responding to your Freedom of Information Act (FOIA) request dated January 3rd, 2002. LTJG Melanie Bell, our FOIA coordinator, has reviewed the "1997 Kapitan Man" file and has determined that we have no documents responsive to your request. You requested "a report of or synthesis from Coast Guard officials of the Coast Guard side of things." No such report or synthesis exists.

If you have any questions regarding this matter, please do not hesitate to contact LTJG Melanie Bell at the number listed above.

        Sincerely,

        MICHAEL J. LOHR
        Commander, U.S. Coast Guard
        Acting Legal Officer, Thirteenth Coast Guard District
        By direction of the District Commander

U.S. Department
of Transportation

**United States
Coast Guard**

Commander
Thirteenth Coast Guard District
United States Coast Guard

Staff Symbol: (dl)
Phone: (206)220-7110
FAX: (206)220-7119

5290

D13-02-005

Mr. Thomas P. Ostrom
207 5ᵗʰ Ave. SW #508
Rochester, MN 55902

    Re: Freedom of Information Act Request dated January 28, 2002

Dear Mr. Ostrom:

I am responding to your Freedom of Information Act (FOIA) request dated January 28, 2001 sent to the 13ᵗʰ Coast Guard District Legal Office. You requested copies of all documents on file relating the 1997 M/V Kapitan Man incident. A legal review of the material was completed on March 20, 2002.

In response to your request, I am releasing 4 sets of documents in their entirety, consisting of 40 pages. I am also withholding 36 documents consisting of 112 pages of potentially responsive material which are exempt from release under FOIA subsections (b)(5), (b)(7)(A), (b)(7)(C) and/or (b)(7)(E) of 5 USC 552. In general, exemption (b)(5) protects records that are pre-decisional in nature, (b)(7)(A) protects records that are compiled for law enforcement purposes, (b)(7)(C) provides protection for personal information in law enforcement records, and exemption (b)(7)(E) affords protection to all law enforcement information that would disclose techniques and procedures for law enforcement investigations.

I have enclosed an index of material provided and withheld in accordance with the decision of *Vaughn v. Rosen,* 484 F.2d 820 (D.C. 1973), cert. denied 415 U.S. 977 (1974) (enclosure (1)).

Due to the minimal staff time required to respond to this request, all fees associated with this request have been waived.

I am the person responsible for the denial of your request. LTJG Melanie A. Bell, Thirteenth District Assistant Legal Officer has also participated in this decision.

5290

You have the right to appeal this denial to Commandant (G-CIM-2), U.S. Coast Guard, Washington, D.C., 20593-0001, within thirty days of your receipt of this letter. Please ensure all correspondence regarding this denial indicates the FOIA number D13-02-005.

ERROLL BROWN
Rear Admiral, U.S. Coast Guard
Commander, Thirteenth Coast Guard District

Encl. (1) Vaughn Index
    (2) Materials released under the Freedom of Information Act

U.S. Department
of Transportation

United States
Coast Guard

Commanding Officer
USCG Marine Safety Office
Puget Sound

1519 Alaskan Way South
Seattle, WA 98134-1192
(206) 217-6232

16660
April 7, 1997

ORDER 97-04 OF THE CAPTAIN OF THE PORT PUGET SOUND, SEATTLE, WA.

Master, M/V KAPITAN MAN
C/O Far Eastern Shipping Co. (FESCO)
614 Norton Building
801 Second Avenue
Seattle, WA 98104
206-583-0860/fax:206-583-0889

SITUATION: Your vessel is suspected of having materials or conditions aboard which constitute an unreasonable hazard, as a result I am concerned that your vessel, M/V KAPITAN MAN, poses a threat to the safety of the port or the marine environment.

DIRECTIONS: Under the authority of the Ports and Waterways Safety Act, Title 33 U.S. Code 1221 et. seq., and/or the Magnuson Act, Title 50 U.S. Code 191; and the regulations issued thereunder, Title 33 Code of Federal Regulations, Part 6 and 160, I hereby order the following concerning the operation of the M/V KAPITAN MAN:

Do not move your vessel or transfer any cargo until the completion of a Coast Guard examination to verify that no hazardous condition exists aboard your vessel.

PENALTIES: The Ports and Waterways Safety Act prescribes that whoever violates an order issued under the act is liable to a civil penalty of not more than $25,000 for each violation. Each day of continuing violation shall constitute a separate violation. If such a violation is willful, you are subject to a criminal penalty of not more than $50,000 and/or five years imprisonment. This criminal penalty is classified as a class "D" felony under federal law.

This order is issued without prejudice as to the initiation of civil penalty proceedings for any violations which may have previously occurred.

APPEALS: Should you be aggrieved by this order, you may, under the procedures as prescribed in 33 CFR 160.7, appeal orally or in writing to the Commander, Thirteenth Coast Guard District, Jackson Federal Bldg., 915 Second Avenue, Seattle, WA 98174. However, if the initial appeal is made orally, a written submission is required within five days of the oral presentation. While any request or appeal is pending all provisions of this order remain in effect.

16660
April 7, 1997

SUBJ: ORDER 97-04 OF THE CAPTAIN OF THE PORT PUGET SOUND

TERMINATION OF ORDER: This order will remain in effect until
cancelled by the Captain of the Port Puget Sound.

If you have questions, please contact Mr. John Dwyer at 217-6232; Fax
217-6345.

Sincerely,

M. S. Boothe
Captain, U.S. Coast Guard
Captain of the Port

Copy: VTS Puget Sound
       CCGD13(m)
       Washington State Office of Marine Safety

```
PSAR                    PORT SAFETY ACTIVITY REPORT                    25APR97

CASE NUMBER/ PS97033672 PORT/ SEAMS  ACTIVITY DATE/ 07APR97 REF CASE/
CARGO: NAME/ CONTAINERS              TYPE/ BULK SOLID - NON HAZARDOUS
OPERATION../ MOORED           NEC DESC/
LOCATION.../ TACOMA, WASHINGTON
             PIER 12
BOARD TIME / 1700    HIGH PRIORITY?/ Y               TEAM LEADER INITS/ LDS
CERT ACTION/ NONE                         VALIDATE/ X  CLOSE TO FILE/
COMMENTS.../ COMPLETED SIV BOARDING TO VESSEL, REASON: CLASSIFIED. VESSEL
             SEARCH WAS INITIATED DURING THIS BOARDING.  ISSUED (2)
             REQUIREMENTS, CLEARED NONE, & (2) REMAIN OUTSTANDING.  INSPECTION
             COMPLETE.

                                                           CI 4/25

          SEL               --- ACTIONS REPORTED ---
           1   NUMBER OF DISCREPANCIES..../   2  OUT?/ Y  LEGAL ACTIONS?/ N
           2   VPI NOTICE..................../
           3   OPERATIONAL CONTROL IMPOSED/
           4   NARRATIVE SUPPLEMENT......../

VESSELS INVOLVED:
V/K   VIN           NAME                    FLAG       SERVICE
 V  L8406690 KAPITAN MAN                    UR FREIGHT SHIP
    #DIS/  2   OUT?/ Y  LEG.ACT?/ N    LPC/ RS   NPC/ RS
    ACTIVITY TYPE(S)/ SIV BOARDING

    OTHER ENF ACTIONS: REQ LOU/   REQ SURETY BOND/   DEV LTR ISSUED/   NONE/ X
    (IF ASSOCIATED WITH AN MC CASE, RECORD IN IAPR)


    #DIS/      OUT?/    LEG.ACT?/     LPC/        NPC/
    ACTIVITY TYPE(S)/

    OTHER ENF ACTIONS: REQ LOU/   REQ SURETY BOND/   DEV LTR ISSUED/   NONE/
    (IF ASSOCIATED WITH AN MC CASE, RECORD IN IAPR)


FACILITIES INVOLVED:
V/K   FIN           NAME                    CATEGORY         LOCAL ID

    #DIS/      OUT?/    LEG.ACT?/
    ACTIVITY TYPE(S)/



                 ------------TOTAL TIME SPENT PER ACTIVITY------------
                 ------REGULAR------- ------RESERVE--------
SUBJ ACTIVITY TYPE ACTIVITY TRAIN PERS ACTIVITY TRAIN PERS  BOAT AIRCRAFT
 V1  SIV BOARDING                 14


                 ADMIN/    52.0   ADMIN/
                 TRAV /     4.0   TRAV /
```

United States Coast Guard
Port State Control Boarding Report

Vessel Name: KAPITAN MAN   Date: 07/18/97 Annual Exam Yes / (No)

Lloyds Number: L8406690 Year Built: 1985   Case Number: PS97033672

Gross Tons: 18574 Call Sign: UJCQ Vessel Type: FREIGHT Flag: RUSSIA

Deficiency Description

1. HOLE SIZE APROXIMATELY 6"x6" (3) EACH PENETRATING
MAIN WT TWIN DECK ON CARGO HOLD NO. 2 & 3 USE
FOR CABLES SUPPLYING POWER TO TRANSFORMER
FEEDING REEFERS FOR CONTAINERS IN CARGO HOLDS.
                              ILLC 66 Annex I/25
2. FIRE DOOR TO EMERGENCY ESCAPE FROM CONTROL
ROOM TO MN DECK AREA, BY FUEL OIL DAY TANK
DECK AREA, REMOVED DUE TO HINGES BROKEN.
                              SOLAS 74 Rg II 2/61
                              9 5(a)

Special Instructions: REPAIR & CORRECT ON NEXT VESSEL'S U.S.
PORT CALL.

Boarding Officer: L. D. SAZON
                  Printed name   Signature

Copy delivered to: ROBERT RAZUMNYY
                   Printed name   Signature

USCG Marine Safety Office   Phone: (206) 217-6180
1519 Alaskan Way South   Fax: (206) 217-6345
Seattle WA 98134   24 Hr: ████████

UNIT COPY   (206) 217-6232
                                   Page: 1 of 1

DEPARTMENT OF TRANSPORTATION
UNITED STATES COAST GUARD

Commanding Officer
Marine Safety Office
196 Tradd Street
P. O. Box 724
Charleston, S. C.
29402

5720

6 JUL 84

Mr. Gene Waddell
Director
South Carolina Historical Society
100 Meeting Street
Charleston, S. C. 29401

Dear Mr. Waddell:

On behalf of the Commandant and the Commander, Seventh Coast Guard District, it is my pleasure to gratuitously present a copy of a History of the Coast Guard in the Sixth Naval District during World War II. This account was prepared shortly after World War II concluded. A copy was recently discovered in our office files and was duplicated at Coast Guard Headquarters. Because of the significance that this two-volume collection may present to future students of military history in the Charleston area, it is my pleasure to provide a copy for your organization.

                    Sincerely,

                    R. F. BENNETT
                    Captain, U. S. Coast Guard
                    Captain of the Port

Encl: (1) Volume I and Volume II - History of U. S. Coast Guard in the
           Sixth Naval District during WWII

CONTENTS

NOTE: All photographs used are official United States Coast Guard photos.

BIBLIOGRAPHY, REFERENCES, SUGGESTED READINGS

BOOKS

Ambrose, Stephen E. **D-Day.** New York: Simon and Schuster, 1995.

Barzun, Jacques. **From Dawn To Decadence: 1500 Years of Western Cultural Life (1500 to the Present).** New York: HarperCollins Publishers, 2000.

Beck, Emily Morison (editor). **Sailor Historian: The Best of Samuel Eliot Morison.** Boston: Houghton Mifflin Company, 1977.

Bennett, William J. **Why We Fight.** New York: Doubleday, 2002.

Bergen, Peter L. **Holy War, Inc.: Inside the Secret World of Osama bin Laden.** New York: The Free Press, 2001.

Bishop, Hugh E. **The Night the Fitz Went Down.** Duluth, Mn: Lake Superior Port Cities Inc., 2000.

Blair, Clay. **Hitler's U-Boat War.**
Vol. I **1939-42.** New York: Random House, 1996.
Vol. II **1942-45.** New York: Modern Library, 2000.

Bovard, James. **Feeling Your Pain.** New York: Palgrave, 2000.

Brown, Riley. **The Story of the Coast Guard: Men, Wind, and Sea.** Garden City, New York: Carlyle House Publishers, 1939; Blue Ribbon Books, 1943.

Chambers, John Whiteclay II, (ed.) **The Oxford Companion to American Military History.** New York: Oxford University Press, 1999.

Chandler, David, G., and James Lawton Collins, editors. **The D-Day Encyclopedia.** New York: Simon and Schuster, 1994.

Chapelle, Howard I. **The History of American Sailing Ships.** New York: Copyright by W.W. Norton & Co., 1935. By arrangement with

W.W. Norton, published by Bonanza Books and distributed by Crown Publishers, Inc.

Cutler, Thomas J. **Brown Water, Black Berets: Coastal and Riverine Warfare in Vietnam.** Annapolis, Md.: Blue Jacket Books, Naval Institute Press, 2000.

Daniel, Clifton, (ed. in chief. **20th Century Day by Day.** New York: Dorley Kindersley Publishing, Inc., 2000.

Dockery, Kevin. **Navy Seals: The Vietnam Years** (Part II). New York: The Berkley Publishing Group, 2002.

Dorwart, Jeffery M. **Conflict of Duty: The U.S. Navy's Intelligence Dilemma, 1919-1945).** Annapolis, Maryland: Naval Institute Press, 1983.

Dunnigan, James F., and Albert A. Nofi. **Dirty Little Secrets of the Vietnam War.** New York: St. Martin's Griffin, 1999.

————. **Shooting Blanks.** New York: William Morrow and Company, Inc., 1991.

————. **The Pacific War Encyclopedia.**

New York: Checkmark Books, 1998.

————. **Dirty Little Secrets.** New York: Quill (William Morrow), 1990.

Edwards, Kenneth, (Commander, Royal Navy, World War 11). **Operation Neptune.** London: Collins, 1946.

Evans, Stephen H. **United States Coast Guard, 1790-1915: A Definitive History.** Annapolis, Md.: United States Naval Institute, 1949.

Faragher, John Mack. **The American Heritage Encyclopedia of American History.** New York: Henry Holt and Company, 1998.

Faust, Patricia L. editor, et. al. **Historical Time Illustrated Encyclopedia of the Civil War.** New York: HarperPerennial, 1991

Foner, Eric, and John A. Garraty, editors. **The Reader's Companion to**

American History. New York: Hougton Mifflin Co., 1991.

Fuss, Charles M., Jr. **Sea of Grass: The Maritime Drug War (1970-1990).** Annapolis, Md.: Naval Institute Press, 1996.

Gertz, Bill. **Betrayal.** Washington, DC: Regnery Publishing Co., 1999.

_____. **Breakdown.** Washington, D.C.: Regnery Publishing, Inc., 2002.

Gilbert, Martin. **A History of the Twentieth Century.** Vol. One: (1900-1933). New York: Avon Books, Inc., 1997.

_____. **A History of the Twentieth Century.** Vol. Two: (1933-195 1). New York: Avon Books, Inc., 1998.

_____. **A History of the Twentieth Century.** Vol. Three: (1952-1999). New York: HarperCollins Publishers, Inc., 2000.

Gregory, Barry. **Vietnam Coastal and Riverine Forces.** Northhamptonshire, United Kingdom: Patrick Stephens, 1988.

Halberstadt, Hans. **USCG: Always Ready.** Novato, Calif.: Presidio Press, 1986.

Hearn, Chester G. **Tracks in the Sea.** New York: International Marine and McGraw-Hill Companies, 2002.

Holland, F. Ross. **Lighthouses.** New York: Friedman/Fairfax Publishers, 2001.

Holland, W.J., Jr., Rear Adm. (USN, Ret.). Editor in chief. **The Navy.** Washington Navy Yard, D.C. Navy Historical Foundation, 2000.

Johnson, Paul. **A History of the American People.** New York: Harper-Collins Publishers, Inc., 1997.

Johnson, Thomas H. **The Oxford Companion to American History.** New York: Oxford University Press, 1966.

Johnson, Robert E. **Guardians of the Sea: A History of the U.S. Coast Guard,**
1915 to the Present. Annapolis, Md.: Naval Institute Press, 1987.

Kaplan, H.R. , and James F. Hunt. **This is the Coast Guard.** Cambridge, Md: Cornell Maritime Press, 1972.

Karnow, Stanley. **Vietnam: A History.** New York: Penguin Books, 1984.

Kennedy, David M. **Freedom From Fear: The American People in Depression and War, 1929-1945.** New York: Oxford University Press, 1999.

Kennedy, David M., Elizabeth Cohen, Thomas A. Bailey, and Mel Piehl. **The Brief American Pageant.** New York: Hougton Mifflin Co., 2000.

Kinder, Gary. **Ship of Gold in the Deep Blue Sea.** New York: Vintage Books, 1999.

King, Admiral Ernest J., (USN). **U.S. Navy at War (1941-1945).** Official Reports to the Secretary of the Navy. Washington: United States Navy Department, 1946.

King, Irving H. **The Coast Guard Expands (1865-1915).** Annapolis, Md.: Naval Institute Press, 1996.

Krietemeyer, Capt. George E. (USCG, Retired). **The Coast Guardsman's Manual.** Annapolis, Md.: Naval Institute Press, 2000.

Kroll, Cmdr. C. Douglas (USCG, USNR, Ret.) **Commodore Ellsworth P. Bertholf: First Commandant of the Coast Guard.** U.S. Naval Institute Press, 2002.

LaFeber, Walter. **The Clash: U.S.-Japanese Relations Throughout History.** New York: W.W. Norton and Company, Inc., 1997.

Larzelere, Alex. **The Coast Guard at War: Vietnam, 1965-75.** Annapolis, Md.: Naval Institute Press, 1997.

Leepson, Marc. **Webster's New World Dictionary of the Vietnam War.**

New York: Simon and Schuster Macmillan Co., 1999.
Long, Elgen M. and Marie K. Long. **Amelia Earhart: The Mystery Solved.** New York: Simon and Schuster, 1999.

Margiotta, Franklin D., (editor). **Brassey's Encyclopedia of Military History and Biography.** Washington, D.C.: Brassey, Inc., 1994.

Marolda, Edward J. **By Sea, Air, and Land: An Illustrated History of the U.S. Navy and the War in Southeast Asia.** Washington, D.C.: Naval Historical Center, 1994.

Marolda, Edward J., and Robert J. Schneller, Jr. **Shield and Sword: The United States Navy and the Persian Gulf War.** Annapolis, Md: Naval Institute Press, 2001, and Washington, D.C., Naval Historical Center, 1998.

McLean, Ian (editor). **The Concise Oxford Dictionary of Politics.** New York: Oxford University Press, 1996.

McPherson, James M. **Battle Cry of Freedom: The Civil War Era.** New York: Oxford University Press, 1988.

Morison, Samuel Eliot. **The Two-Ocean War: A Short History of the United States Navy in the Second World War.** New York: Little, Brown and Company, 1963.

Morris, Richard B. ed. **Encyclopedia of American History.** New York: Harper and Row, Publishers, 1965.

Noel, John V., Jr., and Edward L. Beach. **Naval Terms Dictionary.** Annapolis, Md: Naval Institute Press, 1988.

Powell, General Colin L. (USA, Ret.) **My American Journey.** New York: Random House, 1995.

Prange, Gordon W., with Donald M. Goldstein and Katherine V. Dillon. **Pearl Harbor: The Verdict of History.** New York: Penguin Books, 1991.

Reed, Chris. **Lockheed C-130 Hercules and its Variants.** Atgen, Pennsylvania: Schiffer Publishing Ltd., 1999.

Schrecker, Ellen. **Many Are The Crimes: McCarthyism in America.**

New York: Little Brown and Company, 1998.

Schwarzkopf, H. Norman, and Peter Petre. **It Doesn't Take A Hero.**
New York: Bantum Books, 1993.

Scheina, Robert L. **U.S. Coast Guard Cutters and Craft of World War II.**
Annapolis, Md.: U.S. Naval Institute, 1982.

_____. **U.S. Coast Guard Cutters and Craft, 1946-1990.**
Annapolis, Md.: U.S. Naval Institute, 1990.

Scotti, Paul C. **Coast Guard Action in Vietnam- Stories of Those Who
Served.** Central Point, Oregon: Hellgate Press, 2000.

Silverstone, **Paul H. Warships of Civil War Navies.** Annapolis, Md.:
Naval Institute Press, 1989.

Spector, David D. **Eagle Against the Sun.** New York: Macmillan, Inc.,
1985.

Stern, Philip Van Doren. **The Confederate Navy: A Pictorial History.**
Da Capo Press, Inc. (of the Peresus Books Group), 1992.

Stonehouse, Frederick. **Shipwreck of the Mesquite: Death of a Coast
Guard Cutter.** Duluth, Mn: Lake Superior Port Cities, Inc., 1991.

_____. **Lighthouse Keepers & Coast Guard Cutters.**
Gwinn, MI.: Avery Color Studios, Inc., 2000.

Strobridge, Truman R. and Dennis L. Noble. **Alaska and the U.S.
Revenue Cutter Service (1867-1915).** Annapolis, Md.: Naval Institute
Press, 1999.

Summers, Harry G. **The Vietnam War Almanac.**
Novato, Calif.: Presidio Press, 1999.

Tart, Larry and Robert Keefe. **The Price of Vigilance.**
New York: Ballatine Books, 2001.

Tindall, George B. **America: A Narrative History.** New York: W.W.
Norton, & Company, Inc., 1988.

Tucker, Spencer C. **The Encyclopedia of the Vietnam War: A Political, Social & Military History.** New York: Oxford University Press, 1998.

Urdang, Laurence, (editor). **The Timetables of American History.** New York: Simon and Schuster Inc., 1996.

Walker, Spike. **Coming Back Alive.** New York: St. Martin's Press, 2001.

Waters, Captain John M. (USCG, Ret.). **Rescue at Sea.** First edition, D. Van Nostrand Co., Inc., 1966. Second edition, Annapolis, Md: United States Naval Institute, 1989.

Willoughby, Malcolm F. **U.S. Coast Guard in World War II.** Annapolis, Md.: United States Naval Institute, 1957.

Wise, James E., and Anne Collier Rehill. **Stars in Blue.** Annapolis, Md.: Naval Institute Press, 1997.

ARTICLES, PERIODICALS, AND PUBLIC DOCUMENTS

Public documents came from the Coast Guard Historian's Office, 2100 2nd St. SW, Washington, D.C. and from the CGHO Web site and are so designated in the text. Periodicals and other articles are cited and arranged in alphabetical order by author or title. Abbreviations: The Coast Guard Historian's Office (CGHO)* and the U.S. Government Printing Office (USGPO)** are both located in Washington, D.C. The U.S. Naval Institute (USNI)*** is in Annapolis, Maryland. Selected documents pertaining to the Russian merchant vessel **Kapitan Man** were acquired by the author from the Commander, Thirteenth Coast Guard District, under a Freedom of Information Act Request (FOIA), 28 January 2001.****

A Bill. S.2337. In the United States Senate. To Create the Coast Guard by Combining the Life Saving Service and Revenue Cutter Service (May 26, 1913)." CGHO.* Updated: March 2000.

"Academics." U.S. Coast Guard Academy Homepage, August 25, 2002. Updated: July 2001.

"Academy History and General Information." U.S. Coast Guard Homepage, July 18, 2001. Updated: July 1998.

"Admiral James M. Loy: Saying Goodbye." **Coast Guard,** July 2002, 7-9.

"Admiral Thomas H. Collins, Commandant, U.S. Coast Guard." Coast Guard Historians Office. Updated: Friday June 14, 2002.

"Admissions." U.S. Coast Guard Academy Homepage, August 25, 2002.

"African Americans in the United States Coast Guard." CGHO. Updated: January 1999, 1-8.

"Alexander Hamilton's Letter of Instructions to the Commanding Officers of the Revenue Cutters." Treasury Dept., June 4th, 1791. CGHO. Updated: April, 1999.

Baker, A.D. III, Editor. "Combat Fleets." **Proceedings,** U.S. Naval Institute,*** September, 2001, 3-4.

"Breaking The Ice." Associated Press, St. **Paul Pioneer Press,** January 2, 2001.

Browning, Christopher (QM1, USCG). "Coming Together." **Coast Guard,** USGPO, October 2001, 15-17.

Burns, PA3 Anastasia (USCG). "Building International Friendships." **Coast Guard,** July 2002, 13-14.

Burns, Jim. "Key Congressional Chairman 'Skeptical' of Haitian Promises." CNSNEWS.COM. December 29, 2000.

Cameron, Layne. "Standing Watch." **American Legion Magazine,** July 2000.

Canney, Donald L. "Rum War: The U.S. Coast Guard and Prohibition." CGHO. Updated: June 2000.

Canney, Donald. "The Coast Guard and the Environment." CGHO. Updated: October, 2000, 1-8.

Cannon, Ensign Wallace L. (USNR). "Coast Guard Needs Enlisted Intel Specialists." **Proceedings,** February 2002, 70-71.

Carr, PA1 Scoff (USCG) and Cpl. Zachary Crawford (USMC). "Partners in Protection." **Coast Guard,** July 2002, 16-22.

Casey, PA2 Megan (USCG). "Safety on the Rocks." **Coast Guard,** February 2002, 19-23.

Cecil, Andrea. "Deep Freeze Locks Up Great Lakes." Associated Press. **Post Bulletin,** Rochester, Mn., January 6, p. 3A

"Celebrities Who Served In the Coast Guard." CGHO. Created- January 1998. Updated: June 2000.

Chachere, Vicki. "Cops: Teen Pilot Supported bin Laden." Associated Press, January 6, 2002.

"Chiefs of the Revenue Marine Bureau and Commandants of the Coast Guard." CGHO. Updated: August 2000.

CNN.com/U.S. News. "Two Dead, One Missing in Georgia Helicopter Crashes." March 9, 2002.

CNS News, "Bush To Ask for $11 Billion for Border Security." January 25, 2002.

"Coast Guard Academy History and General Information." CGHO. Updated: July 1998.

"Coast Guard Aids Humanitarian Efforts in NYC; Ensures Port Security as New York Harbor Reopens." **Coast Guard News,** USCG Atlantic Area Public Affairs, 13 September, 2001.

"Coast Guard Alerts All U.S. Ports To Possible Attack By Terrorists." **The Oakland Tribune,** June 10, 2002.

"Coast Guard: Attack from Divers, Swimmers Possible." **USA Today,** June 10, 2002, 7A.

"Coast Guard Auxiliary More than Equal to the Task." **Coast Guard,** December 2001/January 2002, 7.

Weaver, Mark. "Coast Guard Band History." U.S. Coast Guard Website, January 4, 2001.

"Coast Guard Establishment Dates." FAQs from the Historian's Office. CGHO. Created: 1998.

"Coast Guard Chief Moves to Air-Safety Post." **USA Today,** May 31, 2002, 8A.

"Coast Guard Korean War Chronology." Office of Coast Guard Historian. Updated: December 2000.

"Coast Guard Looks at Deaths of 3 in Lifeboat." **The New York Times,** February 16, 1997.

"Coast Guard Medevacs Navy Crewman." USCG Atlantic Area Public Affairs, Portsmouth, VA., April 25, 2002.

"Coast Guard Stations Deteriorating." **Milwaukee Journal Sentinel,** October 1, 2001.

"Coast Guard Praised for Cocaine Busts." Associated Press, **Post Bulletin,** Rochester, Mn., 29 September 2000.

"Coast Guard to Honor WWI Vessel and Crew 1999.

" **Naval History,** September/October,

"Coast Guard Warns of Sea Attack." **Washington Post,** AP, June 10, 2002.

Collins, Admiral Thomas H. (Commandant, USCG). "Charting A New Course For The 21st Century- Commandant's Direction 2002." **Sea Power,** August 2002, 9-10.

Conway, Joe (Captain, USCG, Retired). "Coast Guard Answers 9/11 Call." **Proceedings,** U.S. Naval Institute, November 2001, 39-40.

Craft, Harry (PA1, USCG). "Last Surviving Cutter Hosts Tribute." **Coast Guard,** February 2002, 7.

"Crew Is Rescued After Fire on a Navy Sub." **The New York Times,** May 23, 2002, A-1 8.

Curl, Joseph. "Bush will seek $11 billion to secure U.S. borders, The

Washington Times, January 26, 2002.

D'Agnostino, Joseph A. "No Plan to Deport Deported Aliens." **Human Events,** Week of October 22, 2001, 5.

Dao, James and Steven Lee Myers. "Pentagon Activates First Wave of Guardsmen and Reservists." **The New York Times,** September 17, 2001.

_____. "Pentagon Is Seeking New Anti-Terror Command." **The New York Times,** February 6, 2002, A11.

Davey, Kenneth C. "Sailors Dressed Like Soldiers." **Naval History,** September/October, 1999, 44-48.

Dechant, Lt. Cmdr. Rick (USCG) and Lt. Paul Fawcett (USCG). "D9 Steps Up Great Lakes Security Presence." **Coast Guard,** December 2001 /January 2002, 13.

DeMarino, PA2 Danielle (USCG). "A Little Office Rivalry." **Coast Guard,** May 2002, 10-15.

"Department of Humanities." U.S. Coast Guard Academy Homepage, October 3, 2002. Updated: 12 October 2000.

Dettmer, Jamie. "Tighter Security in Store for Seaports." **Insight,** February 25, 2002, 22-23.

"Dog Rescued After 19 Days On Abandoned Ship." Associated Press, **Post Bulletin,** April 22, 2002.

"During an Average Day." USCG Atlantic Area and Ninth Coast Guard District Home Page. Updated: June 11, 2002.

"During World War Two." Vols. I and !!, 1946. File 34/514. Unpublished papers of the United States Coast Guard donated to The South Carolina Historical Society, 100 Meeting Street, Charleston, South Carolina, 29401-2299.

Drudge Report, "Still No Sign of Missing Crop Spraying Plane." October 4, 2001.

"Edmund Fitzgerald Accident Report." National Transportation Safety

Board Marine Accident Report (Adopted 4 May 1978), based in part on the U.S. Coast Guard
Marine Board of Investigation which convened at Cleveland, Ohio, 18 November 1975. Office of Coast Guard Historian, June 1999.

"Enlisted Career Guide," Jobs That Matter. United States Coast Guard, 2001.

"Environmental Protection." Coast Guard Historian's Office, 12 December 2000.

"FAQS From the Historians Office.- Commandants of the Coast Guard." Updated, August 2000.

"FAQS: What Celebrities Once Served in the Coast Guard?" Updated, June 2000, Coast Guard Historian's Office, 1.

Fanning, Timothy 0. "Unanswered Questions." **Sea Power,** August 2002, 5.

Farrell, Captain Louis (USCGR). "A View from the Inside." **Coast Guard,** December 2001/January 2002, 36.

Farris, Joan (PA3, USCG). "Parade Marks Exhibit Opening." **Coast Guard,** February 2002, 6.

"Fleet Week" and "Amid Festivity, A Moment of Solemnity." **The New York Times,** May 23, 2002, A-1, A-27.

Flynn, Stephen E. (Cmdr, USCG). "Homeland Security Is a Coast Guard Mission." **Proceedings,** U.S. Naval Institute, October 2001, 72-75.

Fournier, Ron. "Series of Attacks Rattles New York, Washington, Nation." **Post Bulletin** (Rochester, Mn), 11 September, 2001, p. 3A.

Fow, Robert E. "Enlist the U.S. Coast Guard." **USA Today,** Friday, December 28, 2001, 13A.

"Frank Albert Drew, Keeper of Green Island Light Station (1909-1929)." Obtained from "Welcome Aboard" brochure of the USCGC Frank Drew WLM 557), commissioned on June 17, 1999, and docked in Green Bay, Wisconsin in the Summer of 1999.

****Freedom of Information Act Request from author dated 28 January 2002, related to the Soviet vessel **Kapitan Man** incident (1997). The FOIA request was sent to the 13th Coast Guard District Legal Office. The legal review was completed March 20, 2002. The FOIA documents were received by the author with a post date of 04 April 2002 with a letter of explanation from Rear Admiral Erroll Brown, Commander, Thirteenth Coast Guard District in which he stated the following:
"In response to your request, I am releasing 4 sets of documents in their entirety, consisting of 40 pages. I am also withholding 36 documents consisting of 112 pages of potentially responsive material which are exempt from release under FOIA subsections of 5 USC 552." (See Appendix F)

Friedman, Norman. "Fighting Far from the Sea." **Proceedings,** U.S. Naval Institute, December 2001, 4-6.

Fuss, Charles M. "Lobster War at Flamingo Cay." **Naval History,** June 2002, 46-49.

"Galapagos Spill Moves Toward Center of Archipelago." **The New York Times** (AP), January 23, 2000, A1, A8.

Gault, Owen. "Destiny Rode The Wind. " **Sea Classics,** Challenge Publications, Inc., May 2002, 8-13.

Gertz, Bill. "Russian Ship Not Searched Thoroughly in Laser Incident." **The Washington Times,** June 27, 1997, A3.

Goure, Daniel. "After 11 September: The War at Home." **Sea Power,** Navy League of the United States, Arlington, Va. February, 2002, 46-49.

Grant, Mary Lee. "Coast Guard Elite Swim Into Eyes of Hurricanes." Associated Press. **Post Bulletin,** Rochester, Mn., July 3, 2000.

Grisafe, Chris (PA3, USCG). "Back in Blue." **Coast Guard,** December 2001 /January 2002, 27.

Grover, Gretchen G. (Captain, USNR). "The Coast Guard's Pacific Colonizers." **Naval History,** August 2002, 43-47.

"Heroes: The World's Best Coast Guard: Catherine Moore, U.S. Lighthouse Service and Coast Guard." **Coast Guard,** (inside front cover)

March 2002.

"Heroes: The World's Best Coast Guard: Coast Guard Air Station New Orleans." **Coast Guard,** (inside front cover) June 2002.

"Heroes: The World's Best Coast Guard: Coast Guard Station Cape Charles, Va." **Coast Guard** (inside front cover), July 2002.

Hessman, James D. and Gordon I. Peterson. "MARAD Confronts New Maritime Security Challenges." **Sea Power,** May 2002, 11-12.

————. "A Performance Based System of Systems." **Sea Power,** August 2002, 12-16.

————. "Precision, Expertise, and Professionalism." **Sea Power,** April 2002, 9-12.

Hessman, James D. (Editor in Chief). "A Constellation of High Honors for Loy; Challenges and Opportunities for Collins." **Sea Power,** July 2002, 1.

————. "Former Commandant Loy Receives Navy League's 2001 Admiral Burke Leadership Award." **Sea Power,** August 2002, 1.

————. "The Maritime Dimension." **Sea Power,** April 2002, 26-27.

Hoback, Thomas S. "Deepwater or Deep Trouble." **Proceedings,** U.S. Naval Institute, August 2001, 73-74.

Holland, Rear Adm. W. J. (USN, Ret.)., Editor-in-Chief, **The Navy.** Personal correspondence between the author of this text, Thomas P. Ostrom, and Adm. Holland, dated 11 January 2002, re: comments on the book **The Navy,** Navy Historical Foundation, 2000.

Horodysky, Daniel. "How the U.S. Merchant Marine Fared During WWII." **Insight,** January 3, 2000, 46-47.

Howe, Cmdr. Jim (USCG). "The Need for Big Speed." **Proceedings,** U.S. Naval Institute, December 2001, 58-60.

"Images of Curtis Bay." **U.S. Coast Guard Yard at Curtis Bay,** The Brooklyn-Curtis Bay Historical Committee, 1976 (updated June 02,

2001; edited b Duane E. Tressler and transcribed by John Green-street).

"Inch by Inch, Step By Step." **Insight,** October 4, 1999, 35.

"Interview." **Sea Power,** March 2002, 16.

Ilsemann, Fred. "Upgraded ESM for Coast Guard Cutters." **Proceedings,** September 2002, 77-78.

"James M. Loy." USCG Commandant, 1998----. CGHO. Compiled: March 2000.

Janofsky, Michael. "Extra Law Enforcement Officers Are On Patrol." **The New York Times,** October 8, 2001.

Johnson, Tim. "Security Tightened at U.S. Seaports." St. **Paul Pioneer Press,** November 3, 2001, 11A.

Johnson, Jeff. "INS Moves to Restructure: Some in Congress Want Agency Replaced." CNS News, January 01, 2002.

"Jobs That Matter." **Enlisted Career Guide,** United States Coast Guard, 2002, 1-17.

Jones, Susan. "Will Environmentalists Cost the U.S. a Key Coast Guard Base?" CNS News, February 01, 2002.

"Just Minutes Away." **Post Bulletin,** Rochester, Mn., October 29, 1999.

Kampschror, Beth. "Bosnia Peacekeepers to Step Up Hunt For Former Bosnian Serb Leaders." CNSNews.com, December 14, 2001.

Keith, Leon Drouin. "FBI Says West Coast Bridges Target." Associated Press, November 1, 9:55 PM, ET.

Kelley, Commander Michael R. (USCG). "The Shoal Waters of Homeland Security." **Proceedings,** May 2002, 65-70.

Kelly, Captain James F., Jr. (USN, Ret.). "Broaden Armed Forces' Roles At Home and Abroad." **Proceedings,** October 2002, 2.

Kiley, Kathy. "Homeland Security Could Join Cabinet." **USA Today,** 3 May 2002, 4A.

Kirk, Lt. Cmdr. Mark Steven (USNR, and U.S. Representative). "The Best Defense Is a Devastating Offense." **Sea Power,** June 2002, 11-19.

"Kudirka Comes Home." **The Baltic Times,** Riga, Latvia, published on Global Lithuanian Net, September, 23, 2001.

Kolb, Richard K. "In Peril Upon the Seas: Surf Soldiers Make the Ultimate Sacrifice." VFW, August 2000, 26-30.

Kraushaar, Petty Officer Leslie. "Coast Guard Efforts." Letter to the Editor, **USA Today,** January 15, 2002, 12A.

Lentz, Rebecca. "U.S. Coast Guard Saxophonist Comes Home to Perform." **Post Bulletin,** Rochester, Mn., July 27, 1994, 4B.

Lewan, Todd. "There's No Glory Being a Fish Cop on the Bering." Associated Press. **Post Bulletin,** Rochester, Mn., Saturday May 8, 1999, 9A.

Loy, J.M. (Admiral, Commandant of the USCG). "An Open Letter to Team Coast Guard." **Coast Guard,** December 2001/January 2002, 3.

Maier, Timothy. "Aviation Legend." **Insight,** February 28, 2000, 10-13.

"Master Chief Petty Officer of the Coast Guard To Carry Olympic Torch Through Washington Streets." **U.S. Coast Guard News,** USCG Headquarters, Washington, D.C., 13 December 2001, 1-3.

McConnaughey, Janet. "Gulf Discovery May Revise History." Associated Press, **Post Bulletin,** Rochester, Mn., June 9, 2001.

"Military Academies Closed to the Public." **Post Bulletin,** Rochester, Mn., September 13, 2002, 4A.

"Missions of the United States Coast Guard." USCG, July, 1997.

"Navy SEALS Inspecting Radioactive Ship Off New Jersey." Fox News, September 12, 2002.

"Net Results." **U.S. News and World Report,** August 11, 1997, 15-16.

"New Coast Guard Cutter on Duty on San Francisco Bay." (Associated Press, **The Sacramento Bee,** December 19, 2001, 14.

"New Coast Guard SWAT Unit." **The Washington Times,** National Weekly Edition, September 23-29, 2002, 1.

"New Layer of Bureaucracy Won't Scare Off Terrorists." Editorial, **USA Today,** October 9, 2001, 14A.

"Ninth Coast Guard District: The Admiral's Corner." USCG Historian's Office and Home Page. Updated: January 9, 2001 and June 11, 2001.

Noble, Dr. Dennis L. (SCMST, USCG, Ret.) "Unless There Was Death." **Proceedings,** U.S. Naval Institute, December 2001, 64-69.

Novack, Robert. "Possible Escalation of War." **Conservative Chronicle,** May 26, 1999.

"Officer Candidate School Celebrates 60 Years." February 12, 2002, Academy Public Affairs Office. U.S. Coast Guard Academy Website, August 25, 2002.

"Oil Spill Moves To Center of Galapagos Ecosystem." **New York Times,** January 23, pp. 1 and A8.

Olsen, Rear Admiral Robert C. (USCG). "Superintendent's Welcome." U.S. Coast Guard Academy Homepage, August 25, 2002.

"On Patrol." **Coast Guard,** April 2002, 4.

Ostrom, Thomas P. "Peacetime Culture of Vietnam Tied to Military Roots." Column in the **Post Bulletin,** Rochester, Mn., December 2, 1998.

_____. "The U.S. Navy Performed Valiantly in the Vietnam War." Column in the **Post Bulletin,** Rochester, Mn., December 15, 1998.

_____. "Coast Guard Officer's Book Recalls Drama, Duty at Sea."

Column in the **Post Bulletin,** Rochester, Mn., June 29, 1999.

_____. "Coast Guard Goes To Depths." Column in the **Post Bulletin,** Rochester, Mn., March 4, 1997.

_____. Personal papers, U.S. Coast Guard training memorabilia.

_____. "Kapitan Man Incident." Personal correspondence with Thirteenth Coast Guard District Officials, letter 5290 dated 22 January 2002; telephone conversation with Lt. Melanie Bell, 13th Coast Guard District, Seattle, Wash., 1-28-02. Freedom of Information Act documents released and sent to author with the approval of Rear Admiral Erroll Brown, Commander Thirteenth Coast Guard District. For documents, exceptions and letter of explanation from Adm. Brown, see Appendix G.

Pear, Robert and Judith Miller. "Entire Nation on High Alert As Security Is Stepped Up." **New York Times,** October 8, 2001, B1.

Peterson, Gordon I. "A Two-Front War: Defense and Homeland Security Top Budget Priorities." **Sea Power,** Navy League of the United States, Arlington, Va., February 2002, 16-17,

"Pioneers Want Women in Combat Role." Associated Press. **Post Bulletin,** Rochester, Mn., November, 1992.

"Policy Changes and Major Events & Their Influence on the Missions & Capabilities of the U.S. Coast Guard and its Predecessor Services. " CGHO. Updated: April 1999.

Powers, Paul (GWR1, USCG). "Mergers of the Millennium." **Coast Guard,** USGPO, October 2001, 11-17.

Price, Scott T. "The Forgotten Service in the Forgotten War: The U.S. Coast Guard's Role in the Korean Conflict." Office of Coast Guard Historian, 1-7. Updated: August, 2001.

"Pull Over, Sailor." **The Wall Street Journal,** August 9, 2002, W1, W4.

"Resort Closing Threatens Refueling Base." **Post Bulletin,** Rochester, Mn., February 1, 2002, 4A.

Ritter, John. "In San Francisco, Sea Marshals Scrutinize Arriving Ships, Crews." **USA Today,** October 9, 2001, 4A.

Robinson, Ericka, (BM3, USCGR). "We Always Must Be Vigilant." **Proceedings,** February 2002, 28-29.

Roden, Commander Paul J. (USCG) "The Shoal Waters of Homeland Security." **Proceedings,** July 2002, 14-16.

Rodriguez, Paul M. "Perfect Gray Suit May Be One of Many." **Insight,** May 6, 2002, 16-17.

Russell, Richard A. "Project Hula: Secret Soviet-American Cooperation in the War Against Japan." No.4. The U.S. Navy in the Modern World Series. Naval Historical Center, Dept. of the Navy, Washington, 1997, 1-44.

Sanial, Lt. Cmdr. Gregory J. (USCG). "National Security Depends on Deepwater." **Proceedings,** November 2001, 76-79.

Sahbandar, Oubai. "TSA Chief Steps Down." CNSNews.com, July 18, 2002.

Schafer, Susanne M. "Bush to Activate Reserves." Associated Press, 14 September 2001.

Scheina, Robert. "Coast Guard Aviation." CGHO. Updated: January 1999.

Schmid, Randolph E. "Ice Breaks Away From Antarctica." Associated Press, **Washington Post,** May 21, 2002.

Schuler, Kropf. "Civil War-Era Sub Recovered Off South Carolina." Reuters, August 8, 2000.

Schwartz, Jerry. "Death Toll Expected to be in the Thousands in the Terror From the Sky." Associated Press, **Post Bulletin** (Rochester, Mn), 11 September, 1A.

"Search and Rescue." Coast Guard Historian's Office. Updated: January 1999.

Seper, Jerry. "Oil Sites, Power Plants to be Guarded as Ashcroft Increases

Security Alert." **The Washington Times,** October 15-21 (National Weekly Edition) 2001, 8.

Shaw, Lt. Danny G., (USCG). "Catching Up With Migrant Smugglers." **Proceedings,** July 2002, 43-45.

Spellman, PA3 Ron (USCG). "Astonishing Sea Stories." **Coast Guard,** March 2002, back cover.

Sperduto, Tom (PA2, USCG). "Ground Zero." **Coast Guard,** December 2001/January 2002, 45-49.

"Station Makes Year's Largest Bust." **Coast Guard,** March 2000, 2.

"Station New London." Office of Coast Guard Historian, April 30, 2002.

Stubbs, Captain Bruce (USCG, Ret.). "We Are Lifesavers, Guardians, and Warriors." **Proceedings,** April 2002, 50-53.

_____. "We Salute All Reservists." **Sea Power,** February 2002, 39-42.

_____. "It's the Right Thing To Do. "Proceedings, July 2002, 35-36.

Strobridge, Truman. "The U.S. Revenue Marine, Its Cutters and Semper Paratus." **The United States Coast Guard and the Civil War** (Office of the Coast Guard Historian) pp. 1-9.

Summers, Col. Harry G., Jr., Col., United States Army, (ret.) "A Quarter Century in the Writing, the Official Armed Forces Histories of the War Are Finally Nearing Completion." **Vietnam,** April, 1999, 6, 50, 55+.

Swanson, Stevenson. "Lake Ice Freezes Factories' Plans." **Chicago Tribune,** Sunday March 27, 1994, Sec. 7, p. 3.

"The Coast Guard's Role in the Search for Amelia Earhart." CGHO. Created: 1998.

"The Industrial Base." **Sea Power,** August 2002, 31.

"The United States Coast Guard in the Northland." Marine Safety Office, Duluth, Mn. Updated: 7/19/99.

Tilley, John A. "A History of Women in the Coast Guard." CGHO. Added: January 1999, 1-8.

Thomas, PA3 Amy (USCG). "Pedal Pushers." **Coast Guard,** July 2002, 28-31.

Thomson, Robin J. "The Coast Guard & the Women's Reserve in World War ll." CGHO. Updated.- January 1999.

Thompson, Ginger. "Cuba Felt the Sept. 11 Shock Waves With a More Genial Castro Offering Help." **The New York Times,** February 7, 2002, A9.

Thorsen, Vice Adm. Howard (USCG, Ret.). "Jump Starting Coast Guard History." **Proceedings,** August 2002, 48-49.

_____. "Annual Reviews: The U.S. Coast Guard." **Proceedings,** May 2002, 98-99.

Toppo, Greg. "Coast Guard Praised for Cocaine Busts."
Associated Press. **Post Bulletin,** Rochester, Mn. September 29, 2000.
"Tybee Lighthouse." Photo by Ben Padgett of the Historic Tybee Island Light Station in Savannah Harbor, Georgia. Personal collection of author, Thomas P. Ostrom.

"U.S. Coast Guard: A Historical Overview." CGHO. Updated: January 1999, 1.

"U.S. Coast Guard Clashes With Russian Fishermen." Reuters, August 7, 1999.

"U.S. Coast Guard Museum." USCG Home Page, July 18, 2001. Created: November 25, 1996. Updated: November 1997.

"U.S. Coast Guard Office of Law Enforcement." CGHO. Updated-10/02/2000.

"U.S. Coast Guard Station, Bayfield, Wisconsin." Created: February

8, 1996.

"U.S. Coast Guard: Units and Locations." Coast Guard Historian's Office, Updated: 11 June 2002.

"U.S., Columbia Make Huge Cocaine Bust on High Seas." Reuters, September 11, 2000.

"U.S. Government Anti-Terrorism Agencies, Sept. 11, 2001. **The American Spectator,** November/December, 2001, 55.

"Vessel Designation.- LV 34." Office of Coast Guard Historian, 5/15/02, pp. 1-2. Photo in author's (Thomas P. Ostrom) collection of Charleston Lightship 34 taken in 1916, #145103, Leib Image Archives, York, Pennsylvania.

Walsh, Don. "Seaport Security: The Impossible Dream? **Proceedings,** February 2002, 89).

"Wars in which the Coast Guard Served, and Casualties." CGHO. Created: January 1998.

Webster, Capt. W. Russell (USCG). "Too Tired to Tell?" **Proceedings,** U.S. Naval Institute, December 2001, 61-63.

_____. "The Next Disaster: Ready to Respond?" **Proceedings,** U.S. Naval Institute, September, 2001, 48-51.

Wells, Master Chief W. R. (USCG, Ret.) "Crisis at Cedar Keys." **Naval History,** U.S. Naval Institute, April 2002, 41-45.

_____. "History Is Part of Semper Paratus." **Proceedings,** U.S. Naval Institute, August 2002, 46-48.

"When Did the Coast Guard Adopt the Slash for Cutters, Boats and Aircraft?" CGHO. Created: January 1998.

Wilder, Kimberly (PA2, USCG). "in the Wake of Terror- The U.S. Coast Guard Responds to Terrorist Attacks Against America." **Coast Guard,** USGPO,** November 2001, 8-11.

Williams, Jack. "There's Heat and Life beneath frigid Arctic Ocean."

USA Today, December 10, 200 1, 11 D.

Williams, Michelle. "At Sea, A Grim Search For Lost Marines."
Associated Press. **Post Bulletin,** Rochester, Mn., December 10, 1999.

Winfield, Nicole. "Exiles Set Sail for Cuba with U.S. as Escort." Associated Press,
Post Bulletin, Rochester, Mn., March 2, 1996.

Wolter, Lt. Cmdr. William J. (USCG). "Building Coast Guard Leaders."
Proceedings, U.S. Naval Institute, December 2001, 85-87.

"Women Reach New Heights in Military Service."
USAA Magazine, August/September 2002, 16.

Worthington, Captain George R. (USN, Ret.).
"We Have the Craft for Littoral Warfare." **Proceedings,** October 2002, 128.

Wyman, Robert (CW02, USCG). "Deep Trouble." **Coast Guard,** US-GPO, November 2001, 13-16.

Yost, Adm., Paul A. (USCG, Retired). "Toss The Coast Guard A Life Ring." **Proceedings,** U.S. Naval Institute, September, 2001.

LaVergne, TN USA
22 October 2009
161685LV00003B/76/A